# POLICY FOR A CHANGE

## Local labour market analysis and gender equality

Edited by Sue Yeandle

This edition published in Great Britain in 2009 by

The Policy Press
University of Bristol
Fourth Floor
Beacon House
Queen's Road
Bristol BS8 1QU
UK

Tel +44 (0)117 331 4054
Fax +44 (0)117 331 4093
e-mail tpp-info@bristol.ac.uk
www.policypress.org.uk

North American office:
The Policy Press
c/o International Specialized Books Services (ISBS)
920 NE 58th Avenue, Suite 300
Portland, OR 97213-3786, USA
Tel +1 503 287 3093
Fax +1 503 280 8832
e-mail info@isbs.com

British Library Cataloguing in Publication Data
A catalogue record for this book is available from the British Library.

Library of Congress Cataloging-in-Publication Data
A catalog record for this book has been requested.

ISBN 978 1 84742 054 1 hardcover

Cover design by Qube Design Associates, Bristol
Printed and bound in Great Britain by MPG Books, Bodmin.

# Contents

# List of figures and tables

## Figures

## Tables

# Preface and acknowledgements

While all the contributions in this book have been written by members of the Gender and Employment in Local Labour Markets (GELLM) research team, the studies undertaken as part of the GELLM research programme could not have been completed without the support of our research sponsors and partners, the other members of the GELLM team, or our colleagues, friends and families.

I would like to record my sincere thanks to the following organisations and individuals who variously provided the encouragement, inspiration, advice, support, suggestions and resources without which the GELLM research programme could not have been successfully completed.

## Organisations providing sponsorship and support

The European Social Fund (main sponsor); the Equal Opportunities Commission; the Trade Union Congress (TUC); the local authorities in Birmingham, Camden, East Staffordshire, Leicester, Newcastle, Sandwell, Somerset, Southwark, Thurrock, Trafford, Wakefield and West Sussex; and our universities, Sheffield Hallam University and the University of Leeds.

## Local authority partners

The following gave support to the team in their respective local authorities, often contributing well beyond their brief to ensure successful engagement and communication and to support project delivery: Mashuq Ally, Sue Bearder, Lisa-Marie Bowles, Melanie Chan, Ann Copsey, Vera Markos, Paul McGloin;, Harish Mehra, Christine Paley, Surinder Punn, Paul Redfern, Sue Reed, Celia Sweeney, Claire Tunley and Guy Wisbey.

## GELLM Research Team

In addition to the contributors to this volume, members of the GELLM team, based at Sheffield Hallam University between 2003 and 2006, included: Ian Chesters (GELLM administrator), Pamela Fisher, Lorna Hewish, Gerard Poole, Christopher Price, Lucy Shipton, Bernadette Stiell and Anu Suokas (GELLM researchers) and Tim Strickland (financial adviser). Sincere thanks also to our external academic advisers for the Programme: Ed Fieldhouse, Damian Grimshaw and Irene Hardill.

## Individuals

Many individuals helped, in many different ways, with ideas, encouragement and support. Thanks to: Rose Ardron, Kevin Bonnett, Christine Booth, Sue Botcherby,

Marion Canavon, Sheila Coates, David Coats, Anna Coss, David Darton, Lee Egglestone, Mary Evans, Felicity Everiss, Richard Exell, Chris Gardner (who died in 2006), Rebecca Gill, Tony Gore, Carole Hassan, Sylvia Johnson, Helga Krüger (who died in 2008), Jo Morris, David Perfect, Ryan Powell, Samm Wharam, Rebecca Wilding and Sylvia Yates. We also wish to thank almost 1,200 people who took part in the 22 GELLM workshops and seminars, held in different parts of the country, to debate the policy significance of the research findings, which were initially disseminated in 52 separate GELLM reports, produced by the different members of the GELLM research team. The perspectives and ideas debated at these events also influenced our thinking and approach, and helped ground our analysis in the everyday lives and realities of women living in local communities.

## Research participants

Over 600 people took part in the GELLM research programme by giving research interviews or participating in focus groups and workshops; several thousand more completed GELLM surveys and questionnaires; we are indebted to them all, and thank them for their time and for allowing us to enquire into different aspects of their lives. It has been our aim to draw attention to their views, experiences and circumstances, and to base the analysis presented in this book on women's real lives, in the context of shifting public policy agendas and changing local labour market contexts.

Finally, my personal thanks to all the contributors to this book – and to their partners and families, who have helped sustain their commitment over five years – for their engagement with the GELLM research programme, and for their support in reaching together, as a team, for the wider goal of producing policy-engaged evidence about women's lives and work.

*Sue Yeandle*
*University of Leeds*
*June 2008*

# Notes on contributors

**Cinnamon Bennett** is a Senior Research Fellow in the Centre for International Research on Care, Labour and Equalities (CIRCLE) in the School of Sociology and Social Policy, University of Leeds. Her research interests are in the areas of equality and diversity policy and practice in organisations, European equality policy, and women's labour market participation. She gained a practitioner's perspective on implementing equality policy whilst working as the Gender Manager of the Objective 1 Programme in South Yorkshire (2001–04).

**Lisa Buckner** is a Senior Research Fellow in the Centre for International Research on Care, Labour and Equalities (CIRCLE) in the School of Sociology and Social Policy, University of Leeds. She is a Fellow of the Royal Statistical Society and during the 1990s worked at the Office for National Statistics on the development of the 2001 Census. Specialising in demographic and quantitative methods, her areas of research interest are in gender, employment, caring and equality at the local level.

**Karen Escott** is a Principal Lecturer in Planning and Urban Policy at Sheffield Hallam University (SHU). A trained planner, her research interests over the last three decades have centred on the interrelated themes of public policy, social and economic analysis and equal opportunities. She has worked on a wide range of applied research projects at SHU and in previous posts at the Centre for Public Services and Sheffield City Council. Her most recent research focus has been on local labour markets, gender and regeneration.

**Linda Grant** is a Senior Lecturer in Social Policy at Sheffield Hallam University. Her research has focused on women's employment, particularly part-time employment, women's economic disadvantage within local labour markets, and the impact of social policy on women's lives and economic circumstances.

**Ning Tang** is a Senior Research Fellow in the Centre for Education and Inclusion Research at Sheffield Hallam University, with research interests in transnational education; gender and employment; and women's and men's working time and employment patterns. Her PhD, based on a sociological study of work and motherhood in different country contexts, was awarded by the University of Aberdeen.

**Sue Yeandle** is Professor of Sociology at the University of Leeds, where she is Co-Director of the Centre for International Research on Care, Labour and Equalities (CIRCLE). Sue directed the Gender and Employment in Local Labour Markets Research Programme between 2003 and 2006, and has published widely on the relationship between work, care and family life and on gender and the labour market. Her first book, *Women's working lives: patterns and strategies*, was published by Tavistock in 1984, and she co-edited *Changing places: women's lives in the city* in 1996 (Paul Chapman Publications). In 2007, with Clare Ungerson, she edited *Cash for care in developed welfare states* (Palgrave Macmillan) and (with colleagues) published the *Carers, employment and services report series* (Carers UK).

# About the GELLM research programme

The GELLM research programme was funded through a core European Social Fund grant supplemented with 'match funding' from the Equal Opportunities Commission, the TUC and 12 English local authorities. It was conceived in 2002, and developed in close cooperation with the project partners, who provided advice, research access and information throughout, and organised and participated in a range of specially arranged events and activities at which the GELLM local research findings were presented. These events were designed to raise local awareness of gender and local labour market issues, to advise practitioners, policy makers and other interested parties on local issues and their significance for local priorities, and to consider how the research findings could be fed into local policies and developments.

The GELLM research programme produced a substantial body of evidence about women's and men's positions in the labour market in England, drawing on extensive analysis of official statistics and other documentation, and evidence collected in six new research studies. In addition to 12 Gender Profiles of local labour markets (Buckner et al, 2004a–i, 2005a, 2005b, 2006), the GELLM policy-focused output comprised six new Local Research Studies (LRS) focused on:

- Women's part-time employment (LRS1 *Working below potential: women and part-time work*, Grant et al, 2005, 2006g–l, carried out in six local authorities); based on 333 women who provided personal information (89 of whom were also interviewed face-to-face), interviews with 22 senior managers, and discussion meetings with 29 trade union representatives from nine different unions, plus additional statistical analysis.
- The difficulty some women face in accessing paid work (LRS2 *Connecting women with the labour market*, Grant et al, 2006a–f, carried out in five local authorities); this study involved further statistical work, mainly using the 2001 Census, face-to-face discussions with 101 local women, and interviews with 51 representatives of local organisations.
- The experiences of women from different ethnic groups in accessing the labour market and progressing within it (LRS3 *Ethnic minority women and access to the labour market*, Stiell and Tang, 2006a–e; Yeandle et al, 2006j, carried out in six local authorities); based on extensive statistical work at the local level, workshop-based research with 93 local women in the areas studied, and secondary analysis of local documentation.
- The factors affecting qualified women's career development in public sector jobs (LRS4 *Career development for women in local authorities*, Bennett et al, 2006a–e; Bennett and Yeandle, 2006, carried out in four local authorities); based on

1,871 survey responses, discussion meetings with 106 women, and interviews with 11 local authority managers.
- The impact of urban regeneration interventions and policies on women living in poor neighbourhoods (LRS5 *Addressing women's poverty: local labour market initiatives*, Escott et al, 2006a–f, carried out in six local authorities); additional statistical research, 14 focus groups involving 133 local women who were either 'outside' work or in low-paid jobs, and 81 interviews with local stakeholders.
- The supply and demand issues affecting employment in domiciliary care (LRS6 *Local challenges in meeting demand for domiciliary care*, Yeandle et al, 2006c–i, carried out in six local authorities), based on additional statistical analysis and a new survey of 88 independent sector providers of domiciliary care.

In each case, the GELLM local research studies produced 'locality reports' that presented the findings of that study in each of the participating local authority districts, with recommendations for policy makers and local practitioners, and a 'synthesis' report, drawing together the findings of all the investigations on that topic and offering a comparative analysis of the results. While it is impossible to summarise all the results of these GELLM research programme studies here, we can briefly note that among their key findings, we were able to:

- develop the concept of 'working below potential', demonstrating that it affected 54% of women in low-paid part-time employment, and is mainly caused by the way that jobs are structured;
- show that 1.4 million women in England were outside paid employment but wanted to work – refuting the view that most women not working for pay are content to be outside paid work;
- confirm that among the 2.1 million ethnic minority women of working age, many are exposed to persistent labour market disadvantage, struggling to access work at all, or securing employment only in less attractive labour market segments, or at levels below those for which they are qualified;
- show that, even in large public sector organisations, many well-qualified women who aspire to have a successful career are hampered in achieving their occupational goals because of the accelerating pace of work, a lack of senior jobs available on a part-time or flexible basis, and a male-oriented organisational culture;
- demonstrate that local regeneration schemes had not targeted women (even where they were highly visible in the statistics of inequality), showing that most local regeneration projects had not helped poor women to access jobs, and that many disadvantaged women felt they were not listened to in their encounters with service providers;
- highlight the way local labour market conditions were affecting the recruitment of domiciliary care workers, including in some areas where many women were seeking to enter paid work, noting that in some places, initiatives to create

career structures and opportunities for progression and to widen the pool of recruits had met with a degree of success.

In addition to exploring local-level labour market statistics and undertaking new research, the GELLM research programme also aimed to raise awareness about gendered inequality in the local labour market in each locality, through publications, consultations and an active dissemination strategy. During the three years of the programme, the team held 22 local 'public' events, attended by well over a thousand people in key local roles: officials in a wide range of local public sector agencies; employers and trade unions; local councillors; and representatives of local voluntary sector agencies. The events provided an opportunity for policy makers, practitioners and representatives of many local/regional agencies to debate the research findings, consider their implications and (often in separate, later meetings) to devise strategies to address the issues raised. The team also held meetings with senior managers in most of the partner local authorities, in some cases securing their support in making 'gender mainstreaming' a priority feature of future local developments.

# Abbreviations and acronyms

| | |
|---|---|
| CAM | Controlled Access Microdata |
| DCLG | Department for Communities and Local Government |
| DfES | Department for Education and Skills |
| DoE | Department of the Environment |
| DWP | Department for Work and Pensions |
| E | East (region of England) |
| EC | European Commission |
| EM | East Midlands (region of England) |
| EOC | Equal Opportunities Commission |
| ESF | European Social Fund |
| ESRC | Economic and Social Research Council |
| EU | European Union |
| GELLM | Gender and Employment in Local Labour Markets |
| GOYH | Government Office for Yorkshire and the Humber |
| HESA | Higher Education Statistics Agency |
| IDeA | Improvement and Development Agency |
| IFS | Institute for Fiscal Studies |
| LB | London Borough |
| LEGI | Local Enterprise Growth Initiative |
| LGAR | Local Government Analysis and Research |
| LGMA | Local Government Modernisation Agenda |
| LLTI | Limiting long-term illness |
| LRS | Local Research Study |
| LSC | Learning and Skills Council |
| LSPs | Local Strategic Partnership |
| MAs | Modern Apprenticeships |
| NAPE | National Action Plans for Employment |
| NDC | New Deal for Communities |
| NDLP | New Deal for Lone Parents |
| NDPU | New Deal for Partners of the Unemployed |
| NE | North East (region of England) |
| NJC | National Joint Council |
| NMW | National Minimum Wage |
| NRU | Neighbourhood Renewal Unit |
| NW | North West (region of England) |
| ODPM | Office of the Deputy Prime Minister |
| ONS | Office for National Statistics |
| RDAs | Regional Development Agencies |
| SAMs | Small Area Microdata |
| SARs | Sample of Anonymised Records |
| SDA | Sex Discrimination Act |

| | |
|---|---|
| SE | South East (region of England) |
| SEU | Social Exclusion Unit |
| SRB | Single Regeneration Budget |
| SSDA | Sector Skills Development Agency |
| SW | South West (region of England) |
| TECs | Training and Enterprise Councils |
| TfW | Training for Work |
| TUC | Trade Union Congress |
| UN | United Nations |
| WBG | Women's Budget Group |
| WM | West Midlands (region of England) |
| Y&H | Yorkshire and the Humber (region of England) |
| YMCA | Young Men's Christian Association |
| YTS | Youth Training Scheme |

# ONE

# Introduction

*Sue Yeandle*

This book, *Policy for a change: local labour market analysis and gender equality*, is about the position of women in the labour market; as such, it forms part of a now large body of literature on this important topic. As readers will find, however, it makes a very distinctive contribution, and fills an important gap, because it addresses two critically important but frequently neglected dimensions of women's labour market situation. First, it contextualises women's position – in relation to accessing employment, developing a career or work record and fitting work into 'the rest of life' – in the broader public policy context that shapes their experiences; and second, it explores evidence about women in all their diversity at the local level, considering how, in 12 different parts of England, the structure of local labour market opportunities, as well as the practices of employers and managers and the available local infrastructure, shapes women's working lives.

As will become clear, this approach highlights a range of problems that analyses focused on a narrower definition of policy relevant to employment and the labour market do not address. It also firmly underscores some of the dangers of relying on statistical analysis at national or regional level, which can hide more than it reveals, and may give rise to inappropriate policy responses. The book also differs from most other edited collections in that it draws on both a substantial body of statistical work and on a set of new, multi-method and multi-disciplinary studies. These fully integrated investigations, conceptualised from the outset as a coherent programme of research, were developed and carried out by the research team to which all authors of the contributions included in this book belonged. The individual results of these investigations are available as a series of gender profiles, synthesis reports and locality reports (outlined in the 'About the GELLM research programme' section in the book), made available in 2004–06 to the programme's partner agencies in the 12 English local authorities that co-funded the GELLM research programme. They have already been used by those agencies to inform and guide local-level policy developments and to raise awareness of specific local issues affecting women.

This opening chapter sets the scene for the later contributions to the book, which is divided into two main parts. In the first (comprising Chapters Two and Three), we consider a wide range of concepts and debates about women and employment, seeking to 'make the connections' between different policy fields relevant to women's labour market situation, and to take into account the most important structural features shaping the way labour markets are changing and developing. Chapter Three then sets out some of the 'myths, puzzles and problems' that need to be explored and examined if progress is to be made in tackling some of the most resistant barriers to gender equality in labour force participation. It also asks whether women will have the chance to exercise genuine choices about how, across the life course, they engage with paid work and achieve their own career and employment goals.

In the second part of the book (comprising Chapters Four to Eight), different members of the GELLM research team contribute five chapters, again all specially written contributions, that focus on the GELLM research evidence in new ways, each designed to explore the issues outlined in Chapter Three. Here the first three chapters focus on what local-level analysis reveals about segregation and clustering in the labour market among women (Buckner); on how different groups of ethnic minority women fare in different parts of the country (Yeandle and Buckner); and on why it is so difficult for some women, particularly those from disadvantaged neighbourhoods, to access paid employment (Escott). Chapter Seven (Grant) examines the way that job design and working hours – and in particular the growing number of part-time jobs in the economy – create disadvantage for women, trapping them in mid-career in jobs that do not use their full potential, and which waste their skills and talents. Chapter Eight looks at why, for so many qualified women who aspire to be successful in their jobs and careers, it continues to be 'tough at the top' (Bennett and Tang). In these five contributions, the authors draw on data relating to the localities studied in the GELLM research programme, and on the studies undertaken as part of it. In exploring the themes and issues outlined in Chapters Two and Three, however, the chapters in the present volume offer an analysis rather different from the policy-oriented accounts and recommendations included in the original study reports, which were designed to meet the needs of our project partners. Those reports also contained discussion of the public policy context (at both national and local level) for the topic investigated, provided an outline of relevant literature, legislation and policy, and supplied full methodological details. To gain a complete view of the policy-engaged approach taken by the team in putting the research programme into operation in the selected local labour markets, interested readers may therefore wish also to consult these reports (outlined in the preface at the start of the book, with bibliographic details included in the References at the end of the volume).

We conclude *Policy for a change* with a final chapter that summarises the most important issues raised in the earlier chapters and in the output of the overall GELLM research programme, focusing on why it is so important to understand the local context for women's employment and labour market situation if policy makers, employers and others are to find effective solutions to the deep-seated, and seemingly intractable problems outlined earlier in the book. In the book's appendices, readers will also find a set of concise profiles of each of the local labour markets studied, a data table providing key statistical information about each of the localities, and a short summary of each of the GELLM studies, with brief methodological information. Some readers may wish to consult these appendices before reading Chapters Four to Eight, as they provide additional contextual details relating to the topics discussed within them.

## Women and labour market disadvantage

It may be thought that the broad parameters of women's disadvantage in engaging with the formal labour market, across the life course, are now well documented and understood. Overall, women's distribution across the full range of occupations and industries is rather different from that of men, and their work tends to be lower paid. Although for most groups of women labour force participation has increased, bringing women's employment rates close to those of men, far more women than men hold part-time jobs, which continue to be mostly lower-graded positions offering limited pay and prospects, despite (by 2001) representing almost a third of all jobs in the economy.

Combining the kind of work they can obtain with the caring responsibilities that have historically been part of women's family role (looking after both dependent children and family members who are sick, frail or disabled) is often challenging and difficult, making this a further issue of particular significance for women. The costs of alternative care can act as a disincentive to take up paid employment, and suitable services, especially in relation to the care of adults and disabled children, are often not available (Yeandle and Buckner, 2007). Although the concept of 'work–life balance' has now entered popular discourse and (in recent years) has been explicitly addressed in legislation and public policy, within most organisations paid work, especially at higher grades and in well-rewarded positions, continues to be organised in the traditional ways originally designed to fit the working lives of male breadwinners, and the attitudes and behaviours of managers and supervisors often draw on stereotypes and beliefs about women's orientations to work that no longer fit the reality of their lives. These issues are strongly emphasised in the contributions to this volume by Grant and by Bennett and Tang.

One of the most perplexing elements of this situation is that women's much-improved access to education, including higher education, and their achievements at school, which now considerably outstrip those of boys when measured across all subjects, have not translated into better outcomes for them in the workplace. Sex differences in the 'human capital' of the workforce have declined significantly since the 1970s, and no longer provide very much of an explanation for the enduring 'gender pay gap' (Grimshaw and Rubery, 2007). Yet even among those graduating at the same time, with the same kinds of degrees, pay differences favouring men emerge within a short time, before the impact of motherhood and family-building behaviour is seen (Purcell and Elias, 2004). This has caused some to conclude that it is perhaps in women's aspirations and in their attitudes to their jobs and careers – and for some women their preference for prioritising family responsibilities and household management – that the explanation for their continuing disadvantage in the labour market can be found (Hakim, 2002), a position debated in various chapters in this volume.

What we are able to show in *Policy for a change*, drawing on our new investigations, is that some of the key problems creating labour market disadvantage for women are to be found in the design of jobs, in the operation of organisational cultures, and in the attitudes not so much of women workers as of the senior men (and some women) responsible for managing the organisations in which they work. In some of the later chapters in this book we consider the role of attitudes, values and practices in disadvantaging women in the labour market. We note a widespread failure to modernise organisational practices; a reluctance to recognise the value of the skills, attributes and qualities that women bring to jobs in the traditionally 'female' segments of the labour market; a failure to adjust ways of working to fit 21st-century patterns of family life; and the very uneven recognition of what contemporary (and now widely shared) values relating to equality and diversity mean for working life and practices.

The situations of two specific groups of women – those who live in disadvantaged neighbourhoods and ethnic minority women – are particularly worrying. In this book (Escott), and elsewhere in the GELLM research reports, we offer clear evidence that many women living in England's poorest neighbourhoods are unable, as opposed to unwilling, to enter the labour market. These women include a disproportionate number of women with health problems, of lone parents and of carers, many of whom have missed out on educational opportunities and gained very limited work experience. Often they face acute problems in accessing paid employment, in part because the quality of job opportunities near to where they live is so poor. As discussed in detail later in the book, their difficulties also relate to inadequate local infrastructure (information, advice and guidance services relating to education and employment; public transport; childcare; care services, and so on), to the operation of the benefits system, and to the way the social exclusion they so often experience affects their confidence and self-esteem. Many of these women feel they are not listened to, understood or taken seriously; the GELLM research programme found strong evidence that public policy interventions, especially those designed to 'regenerate' local areas, had failed to prioritise their needs and had not delivered positive labour market outcomes for them.

In most localities and in some cultural contexts, women in ethnic minority groups continue to experience acute labour market disadvantage too, as we have shown elsewhere (Buckner, et al 2007) and demonstrate in some detail in Chapters Four and Five. Here, among the elements of this situation that should be of particular concern to policy makers are: the much higher unemployment rates found among economically active women in certain ethnic minority groups; the fact that many of these women have embraced educational opportunities with considerable commitment, yet continue to find themselves stuck in lower labour market positions; and the evidence that those ethnic minority women who have experienced racial harassment or prejudice report its very long-term effects on their confidence in accessing paid employment. The evidence about ethnic minority women's labour market situation is thus, as discussed later in the book, strongly suggestive of continuing discrimination, both intentional and unintentional, as well as disadvantage, with gender and ethnicity intersecting in ways that prevent many of these women from obtaining access to high-quality jobs and careers.

## Local economies and the UK labour market

We made a very deliberate choice in developing the GELLM research programme to focus on gender equality in *local* labour markets (Yeandle, 2006c). As indicated in Chapter Two, this decision was informed by previous experience of working with local agencies, and by the perception that for women, labour market opportunities really were affected, in very important ways, by the places in which they lived. We wanted to gain a deeper understanding of the factors shaping the labour market 'choices' women were making, and to capture, at the most opportune moment, the value of the evidence available from the 2001 Census, with its unique capacity to provide data across a range of important variables at local authority district level, with scope also to undertake some analysis at ward level or at even more detailed geographical scales.

Only quite a small proportion of people in employment – 16% of men and just 9% of women, according to the 2001 Census – travel more than 20 kilometres between their homes and their regular place of work. As shown in the GELLM gender profiles, especially among those aged over 25, women are also more likely than men to work very locally, to travel to work on foot, and to use local public transport in accessing their paid jobs. This means that the nature, range and quality of the work opportunities available in the localities where they live are absolutely crucial for women, who – in part because of their family and caring responsibilities, but also related to other factors, including their lower average hourly pay – are more likely than men to actively seek employment close to where they live.

There is no perfect definition of a 'local labour market', as the geographical range within which people look for work, either when seeking to enter the labour market or when looking for a new position within it, perhaps to advance their career or improve their pay, is highly dependent on other factors. Very well-qualified people, or those with scarce skills or who can command high pay, may, at particular life stages, be prepared to travel long distances to work or to relocate. Some, as others have shown, are prepared to adopt a weekly commuting pattern, living away from home during the working week and returning to their main place of residence only at weekends. But these people are still rather exceptional, and they often possess substantial 'human capital', in return for which they can command high pay and other benefits in the labour market. For most labour force participants, especially those who live with or near a partner, children or other relatives, the range of jobs available within easy daily travelling distance from their home forms their de facto local labour market. Many, and especially those who can command only modest hourly rates of pay, will also make decisions about employment that are influenced by the cost of daily travel to work, or the availability of convenient public transport. Those who have responsibility for children or for others who rely on them for daily care or support will also need to consider how they can fit travelling to schools, nurseries or other care facilities into their daily schedule, which may also limit the opportunities they can consider. Some will be able to cast their net more widely if they can find work in a labour market segment where flexible working is possible, but as we will show later in the book, there is often a penalty to pay for this choice, which may restrict their access to promotion and better pay, a problem that is particularly acute if they decide to work on a part-time or reduced hours basis.

Bearing in mind these factors, we decided in the GELLM research programme to use local authority districts as a reasonable proxy for a functional local labour market encompassing the employment behaviour of most local residents, especially women. In making this choice we were aware that in some places – for example in our two London boroughs – many residents cross local authority district boundaries in travelling to work. We were able to accommodate this factor by including in our statistical analyses, for most of the variables investigated in preparing the gender profiles, data at the regional level too. In many local authorities, however, the experience of most residents, especially women, was that they lived and worked within the boundary of the same local authority.

All local labour markets, and indeed all the organisations operating within them, are subject to factors that cause them to change over time. Firms and businesses are set up, grow, decline or close. Decisions taken at national or international level frequently affect the prospects of any that are part of larger organisations. Patterns of demand for goods and services change over time and call for the growth or contraction of particular types of jobs. In Chapter Two we discuss, in broad outline, some of these factors, highlighting the well-known fact that employment in the traditional manufacturing sector has been declining in almost all parts of the English economy, while jobs in some parts of the service sector have been growing. Over the course of any individual's working life, some processes of technological change inevitably make certain jobs or skills obsolete, or reduce demand for them, while others open up new opportunities, creating job roles that did not exist at all for previous generations. It is nevertheless widely recognised that, in any given region or district, historical patterns of employment exert an important influence. This affects local attitudes to education, training and skills acquisition, shapes expectations about the kinds of jobs available and who (in terms of age, sex and ethnicity) is likely to hold them, and creates a labour market environment in which the local economy is perceived in a particular way. Thus in the period of the GELLM research programme, some local economies had major employment sectors thought to be under threat (for example where there were large-scale closures affecting a whole industry undergoing restructuring), while others were relatively stable (perhaps where many jobs were held in segments of the public sector, such as education and health, where the total number of jobs had changed little in recent years); or had sectors that were experiencing a period of sustained job growth (for example in the retail, leisure or commercial services sector).

The localities studied (with the regions within which they were located shown here in brackets) included: three large English cities – Birmingham (WM), Leicester (EM) and Newcastle (NE); two London boroughs, Camden and Southwark (LBs); two large county councils (within which five and seven local authority districts, respectively, were located), Somerset (SW) and West Sussex (SE); and five smaller towns and districts: East Staffordshire (WM), Sandwell (WM), Thurrock (E), Trafford (NW) and Wakefield (Y&H). This set of local authorities provided a very wide range of labour market situations, and enabled the study to include at least one district in each of the nine English regions. By including authorities across a broad spectrum – in terms of their socio-economic deprivation indicators (Sandwell to West Sussex), their 'rurality' or focus on urban agglomerations, their diversity (from Somerset's tiny ethnic minority population to the very diverse populations found in Leicester, Sandwell and the two London boroughs), and their situation as regards population growth/decline – we were able to examine women's situation in a wide range of labour market settings.

As discussed in some of the chapters that follow, some of the localities had experienced or were facing considerable, locally specific, labour market pressures from contracting sectors (notably in the decline of manufacturing sector employment in Leicester, Birmingham, Wakefield and Newcastle). Almost all were experiencing changes associated with the expansion of part-time employment in the service sector, with the way information technology was affecting local jobs, and with employment shortages in employment segments heavily dependent on public expenditure, such as employment in social care.

## The evidence base

The GELLM research programme was designed with analysis of the 2001 Census (with the 2001 Standard Tables from it newly released as the research began, and commissioned tables and special data sets becoming available during the period of our research) at its core. The Census enabled us to explore gender, locality and ethnicity in labour market behaviour at the local level and as such was our prime statistical source. We analysed data from both the 2001 and the 1991 Censuses, using the Census standard output, specially commissioned tables, the 2001 Census Sample of Anonymised Records (SARs), the 2001 Census Small Area Microdata (SAMs) and drawing on data at both district and ward level. We also used the following, all of which, like the Census, provided gender-disaggregated data: the Labour Force Survey, the New Earnings Survey (subsequently replaced by the Annual Survey of Hours and Earnings), and the Census of Employment (later the Annual Business Inquiry/Annual Employment Survey). In addition, we used other statistical data made available (sometimes on special request) by various government departments and agencies: the Department for Education and Skills

(DfES), the Department for Work and Pensions (DWP), Connexions (via its Annual Activity Survey), the Higher Education Statistics Agency (HESA), and Ofsted.

Secondary analysis of these sources enabled us to produce the 12 GELLM gender profiles, which subsequently became important reference documents for the set of new, multi-method studies specially developed within the programme. These enabled us to widen our evidence base considerably, producing an extensive body of qualitative data as well as additional survey material. Across the whole programme, we ran three specially devised surveys: two surveys of women workers (LRS1, distributed in 22 workplaces, and LRS4, distributed in four workplaces) and one survey of employers in the social care sector (LRS6, in six localities). We conducted focus group research in three of our studies (LRS2, LRS4, LRS5) and ran arts-based workshops as a means of engaging with ethnic minority women in LRS3. Individual face-to-face interviews were conducted with women workers and managers in LRS1 and LRS4, and with representatives of local statutory and voluntary organisations in LRS2 and LRS5. We also undertook a substantial amount of documentary analysis in several of the GELLM studies, notably LRS3, LRS5 and LRS6.

Achieving the volume of research activity involved in the above was only possible because of the partnership arrangements put in place with the local authorities providing co-funding for the research. In some cases, we were also able to develop valuable relationships, including opportunities to negotiate additional research access, with local voluntary sector agencies, and with other bodies, such as local employer forums, regional development agencies and learning and skills councils. All of these contacts were also valuable as ways of informing our understanding of local circumstances, local decision-making processes and of the way that central government priorities and objectives were being pursued at the local level. The access these arrangements gave us to individual contacts, to local documentation and to already existing local groups and partnerships was important in informing the team's understanding of local problems, local issues and local achievements; it assisted us in setting up our local studies and came fully to fruition in the final stages of the research programme, when the GELLM team's activities were focused on dissemination, gender mainstreaming, consultation with senior staff and action planning with relevant agencies.

## Working in partnership to envision change: fairness, diversity and choice

The GELLM research programme gave the research team the opportunity, through its partnership arrangements, to go beyond the more traditional academic approach of documenting, analysing and theorising evidence about its core topic – in our case the factors that cause women to experience disadvantage in their local labour markets – and to engage directly with policy makers and practitioners, enabling them to use our research findings to raise local awareness of women's circumstances and to see how, across a wide range of policy fields, existing policies and arrangements could be changed to create better opportunities for achieving gender equality in relation to employment and the labour market.

Within the team, which drew together subject expertise in sociology, social policy, urban and regional studies, statistics, geography and community studies, there emerged a shared research ethic, involving a commitment to produce accessible evidence that could be used at the local level to improve local policy and outcomes for women, and a desire to create a genuine partnership involving mutual exchange of expertise and knowledge. Underpinning this approach was a shared aspiration to identify, where possible, ways forward that could be of benefit to local women, especially the most disadvantaged. Our aim was to contribute, through our research, to policy developments in which, within local labour markets, women could envision the personal possibility of entering paid employment on equal terms, being treated with fairness in their attempts to engage with and progress within the labour market, and in ways that were respectful of the diversity and differences among them. In this way we aspired, through the research, to make a small contribution to enabling women to exercise freer and more informed choices about how they themselves wished to fit paid employment into their lives. In this book, therefore, we aim not only to highlight the disadvantage that women face within their local labour markets, but also to show how policy, in a range of different spheres, contributes to and deepens that disadvantage, and to draw attention to some of the ways in which that situation could be changed.

# Part One
## Making connections: concepts and debates

# TWO

# Local labour markets in public policy context

*Sue Yeandle, Cinnamon Bennett, Lisa Buckner, Karen Escott and Linda Grant*

## Introduction

This chapter presents a broad outline of the public policy context in which the topic of gender and local labour markets addressed in this book needs to be understood. It lays out our claim that while public policy has engaged very actively with the labour market in recent decades, it has not done so in ways that offer most women – especially poor or disadvantaged women – opportunities for change, achievement of their potential, or equal access to the best rewarded and most influential labour market positions.

In the opening sections of the chapter we outline some of the major structural factors affecting local labour markets in England, noting major demographic shifts and key issues of labour supply and demand, with particular reference to developments in the localities included in the GELLM study. Here our concerns are with population and workforce ageing and with changing family lives and rising demand for care, as well as with industrial restructuring and changing patterns of employment. In the second part of the chapter we give our attention to the different arenas in which policy makers have addressed local labour market issues, often with the explicit aim of influencing and shaping local economies. Here we consider policy emphases and developments relating to labour market activation, to urban regeneration and neighbourhood renewal, to skills and productivity, and to (in)equality and diversity.

Although in recent decades local labour market problems have been addressed in at least some of these ways in all the localities studied, our review emphasises that, overwhelmingly, the actions taken have used 'gender-blind' approaches. Without objectives specifically addressing the labour market needs or circumstances of women, local agencies have often missed key opportunities to support disadvantaged local residents in entering or progressing in the labour market, and have struggled to work together to address local problems. Usually the key focus at local level has been on tackling high rates of recorded unemployment (frequently with a focus on local youth unemployment or problems of initial labour market entry, devoting most energy to the situation of young men), or on responding to the collapse of local jobs (often in one major industry where there has been a significant loss of jobs by local men). Meanwhile, throughout the Labour administrations since 1997, the focus at national level has been on 'welfare to work', with activation policy high on the agenda, targeting mostly men among the 'inactive' young and the over 50s, disabled people, and ex-offenders in 'New Deal' programmes. Lone parents have been a key focus of New Deal provision, too, and are mostly women, but in the special situation of being sole breadwinners with dependants, and frequently benefit claimants.

Understanding of how local labour markets operate depends on knowledge about three key issues: the demand for (paid) labour in the locality, and how it is structured and changing; the local supply of (paid) labour and its characteristics (the skills, qualifications, age, health, experience and other characteristics of available employees and their access to paid work through local transport systems and other socio-economic infrastructure); and information about the other demands on the local workforce, such as their (unpaid) caring or family responsibilities, that may cause them to deploy their labour in particular ways. The extent to which a locality can draw on a supply of labour from elsewhere through migration (international or otherwise), local transport systems, or by raising local economic activity or employment rates (through labour market activation policy, or designing jobs in different ways) is also relevant.

The structure of local labour market demand is discussed in considerable detail in our other GELLM publications, with key issues summarised in Chapter Five of the present volume. In the English economy as a whole there was a net increase of over 3.5 million jobs between 1991 and 2002, divided between almost 1.5 million additional full-time and over 2.1 million additional part-time positions (Yeandle et al, 2006c, pp 18–22). Two points need to be made in relation to this: first, the distribution of jobs between different local economies has been very uneven. This has led to concerns about 'overheating' of the economy in some areas (for example, parts of the South East), while other localities have seen significant job losses and continue to experience relatively high levels of unemployment. Second, men's and women's engagement with the additional full and part-time jobs created has been very different. Overall, 58% of the extra part-time jobs, but only 44% of the extra full-time jobs, were taken by women. The rise in part-time employment among men has been concentrated among those at labour market entry and exit points – while for women part-time employment typically occurs mid-career, is strongly associated with family formation and with the acquisition of unpaid caring responsibilities, and (underpinned by legislation affecting parents and carers since 2002[1]) is reported to be the preference of many mid-career women (see also Grant, this volume).

## Structural issues

Among the various structural issues affecting the supply of labour in local labour markets we can highlight three that are currently of considerable importance: demographic change (patterns of age and family situation), migration (movements between localities or between countries) and the response of local residents to shifts in the types of jobs available near where they live. Demographic shifts, which can be summed up as 'longer and more complex lives', call for changes in when, how and for how long paid work and employment fit into men's and women's life courses. Migration, which involves moving from one place to another, either within or beyond local areas, can be primarily 'economic' in nature (undertaken as part of a search for paid work, or for more desirable paid work) but may have other underlying causes. In theory, it can displace local labour, although economic migrants have historically almost always been attracted to localities where there are shortages of either labour or skill. Changes in demand for labour – through economic restructuring, resulting in job or workplace creation, decline or (re)location – arise from a multiplicity of factors, with a range of impacts on local residents' propensity to seek (and find) employment.

## Demographic shifts

The most important features of contemporary demographic change are: population and workforce ageing (and consequent changes in the 'age-dependency ratio'); changes in family structure, family formation and in the labour force participation of mothers; the increased (unpaid) care demands on people of working age; and raised levels of illness and disability. As is well known, a decline in the birth rate over several decades, together with improved life expectancy, mean that the overall population in England is ageing, bringing about a change in the ratio between people of 'working age' and those who have reached state pension age. Thus while in England the post-war 'baby boom' kept the number of people aged over 65 equal to about 24% of the total working age population for a quarter of a century from the early 1980s, this figure is set to rise in the years to 2021 to about 31%.[2]

Linked to this, the average (median) age of the whole population increased from 34.1 years in 1971 to 38.8 years in 2005 (ESRC, 2007a). Indeed, at the start of the 21st century, for the first time ever, England had more people aged over 60 than under 16 (2001 Census; ESRC, 2007a). The workforce was ageing too; by 2021 its median age is expected to reach 41.3 years (Shaw, 2006), and official projections suggest that by 2021 for every person over state pension age the number of people of working age will have fallen (from 4.6 in 1971) to 3.2.[3]

The declining number and proportion of young people is particularly important in labour market analysis. By 2021 there will be almost 250,000 fewer young people in the UK than in 2004. Thus, while as recently as 1971, young people (aged 16–24, most of them yet to become parents and without dependants) made up over a fifth (22%) of the working age population, by 2005 this figure had fallen to 18% and was still declining. As the young population shrinks (and remains in full-time education for longer) a higher proportion of jobs in the economy will need to be filled by people aged over 24.

The number of people aged 25–44 years is declining too. By 2021 there will be almost 20,000 fewer people in this age group than in 2004, a development that, given the growth in demand for part-time workers, and the fact that many women enter part-time work after becoming mothers, is of considerable importance.

By contrast, the mature workforce of people aged 45–65 has been rapidly expanding. By 2021 it is predicted that there will be 2.2 million more people of this age in the working age population than in 2004. Needing to work longer to fund the pensions they will require in their extended later lives, people in this age group are the most likely to be caring for a sick, disabled or frail relative (Buckner and Yeandle, 2005; Turner, 2005) alongside their paid job. As discussed elsewhere, in the future there will be more older people, many of them needing the support of friends, relatives or formal services (Yeandle et al, 2006c), and this will mean more men and women will need to combine paid work with an unpaid caring role, perhaps making part-time employment even more attractive (Yeandle and Buckner, 2007).

The ageing of the working population has been accompanied by important changes in family structure and formation too. Far more people now live alone (up from 3 million in 1971 to 7 million in 2005), there are fewer 'traditional' family households (comprising two parents and their dependent children) and there is a higher incidence of family breakdown and re-formation. In 2005, 24% of dependent children lived in lone parent families, compared with just 7% in 1971. For most women, childbearing has been occurring later, with mothers' average age at the birth of their first child rising from 23.7 in 1971 to 27.3 in 2005 – and more women have been remaining childless, whether by choice or otherwise; 18% of women born in 1960 had no children at age 45, compared with 11% of women born in 1940.

The labour market behaviour of mothers has changed rapidly in the decades we are reviewing. In 1979 only 24% of women had returned to paid work 11 months after the birth of their first child, whereas by 1996 this figure had risen to a striking 67% (Gatrell, 2004). As widely noted in the literature, a range of factors lie behind this development, but significant increases in the cost of housing, evident in all the localities studied (Buckner et al, 2004a–i, 2005a, 2005b, 2006), as well as changes in access to mortgages have both contributed to changes in women's labour market behaviour.

The 'feminisation' of the total workforce over the second half of the 20th century has been widely commented upon, and has been visible in overall labour force data for England since the 1950s. This trend is related to many different developments, but it is worth noting that, deprived of part of their traditional recruitment pool (school leavers) and seeking to expand their workforces or to fill new positions, employers in many (not all) occupations have been actively recruiting women for some decades. As noted by others, women's economic activity rates have been rising steadily since the early 1950s, increasing their total share of all employees from about one third at that time, to around one half in the mid-1990s (Walby, 1997).

## Migration

Migration, both between localities within England and the rest of the UK (Coleman and Rowthorn, 2004; Hatton and Tani, 2005; Parikh et al, 2007) and into and out of the UK, has also been an important component of population change in recent years, with significant implications for local labour markets. Data on 'within UK' migration show reductions in population for some localities and regions, but gains for others. Some places lose and others gain population of working age. England as a whole saw its working age population increase by 1.24 million people between 1991 and 2002, yet our GELLM study included some localities (such as Birmingham, Newcastle and Sandwell) that had net losses of working age population between these dates, while others (for example, Somerset, West Sussex and Thurrock) experienced large net increases (Yeandle et al, 2006c, p 19).

Net migration patterns into/out of the UK have been the subject of considerable public and political discussion, with a recent detailed analysis showing rising employment rates for most non-UK born residents between 1995 and 2005 (Sriskandarajah et al, 2007). Between 1982 and 1992, migration into the UK is estimated to have accounted for 17% of total population growth, rising to 65% in 2005 (analysis based on Office for National Statistics (ONS) mid-year population estimates, births and deaths 1982–2005).

An important consequence of both historical and recent patterns of migration and settlement is that while some parts of England are now very much more ethnically diverse than at any previous time (including London, Leicester and Birmingham, all included in the GELLM study), other areas retain populations that are still overwhelmingly White and UK-born in composition. These uneven population shifts are factors of considerable importance in local labour analysis, with the gender composition of minority populations, and gender differences in settlement and community formation particularly important (topics explored further in Chapter Five).

In the 2001 Census, 91% of the population in England defined themselves as White (variously the British, Irish and Other White groups), with 9% (4.5 million people) assigning themselves to the different non-White ethnic groups (an increase from 2.9 million to 4.5 million between 1991 and 2001). In 2001 about half the non-White population identified as Asian, about a quarter as Black, and about 14% as of 'Mixed' ethnic origin. Since international migrants are on average younger than the already resident population, and because most minority ethnic groups have higher net birth rates (Robson and Berthoud, 2003), the UK's ethnic minority population is considerably younger than the White population. In 2004, the median age for White people was 40 years, compared with 27 years for ethnic minorities. Consequently, the ethnic minority share of the working age population is relatively large – 3.26 million (9.3% of people of working age) in 2004 (ESRC, 2007b). In most ethnic minority groups, including the Indian, Pakistani and Bangladeshi groups, women form between 48% and 52% (both

UK-born and non-UK born) of residents; in the Black Caribbean group, women are 55% of UK-born and 53% of non-UK born residents (ONS, 2006c).

Across England, the geographical distribution of the population has also undergone significant change. Between 1982 and 2002, two regions (the North East and the North West) lost population through falling birth rates and people moving away. Every other English region saw population growth, with London and the South East gaining most (Figure 2.1), and London (and in the GELLM study the boroughs of Camden and Southwark) particularly noteworthy since male population growth considerably exceeded female. As shown in additional detail elsewhere (Buckner et al, 2004a–i, 2005a, 2005b, 2006), at the local level these changes are particularly marked. These structural issues form a challenging context for the development of local labour market policy designed to support women, but as we now go on to show, they also need to be considered in relation to factors affecting women's labour supply.

**Figure 2.1: Population change in England, selected regions and districts, estimates for 1982–2002, by sex**

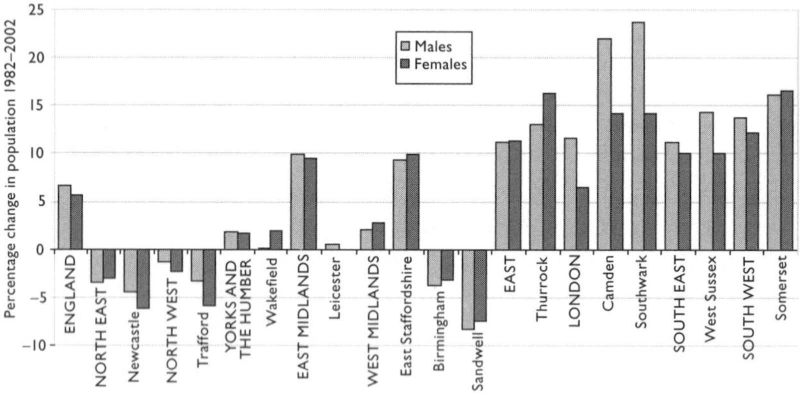

*Source:* Mid-year population estimates 1982–2002, ONS

## Labour supply as a response to demand

The labour market context for the population changes described above is one of significant job growth. As already indicated, there was marked job growth in the 1990s; however, between 2004 and 2014 the number of jobs in the UK economy is expected to rise again, by a further 1.3 million, to 31.6 million (Dickerson et al, 2006). It is thought that these new jobs will be taken up by men and women in roughly equal numbers, and that about half the new jobs taken up by men – and three fifths of those taken up by women – will be part-time positions.

Between 1999 and 2004, working age economic activity rates changed little, averaging about 61% overall. Behind this stable picture lay considerable volatility, however; a marked rise in the female participation rate, offset by a fall in the male participation rate. Indeed, the share of jobs held by women has increased more or less steadily for 30 years, with women representing 45% of all people in employment in 2001, compared with just 37% in 1971 (1971–2001 Censuses). Throughout this period, notable changes have included the decline of employment in manufacturing as the economy has become more service based (Grant et al, 2006g) and the increased importance of part-time jobs. Forecasters expect the proportion of jobs held by women to remain fairly constant between 2004 and 2014, and that part-time employment will continue to grow (Wilson et al, 2006).

Often thought to have affected mainly male, full-time employees, manufacturing job losses in recent decades in fact hit both sexes hard. Across England, men lost 350,000 manufacturing jobs between 1991 and 2002, albeit gaining some 12,000 part-time positions in the sector. Women in manufacturing lost a large number of both full-time (238,000) and part-time jobs (58,000). Analysis at local level shows that these developments were felt very unevenly across the country (Figure 2.2).

In the 12 GELLM gender profiles of local labour markets (Buckner et al, 2004a–i, 2005a, 2005b, 2006) we highlighted the major changes in labour demand seen in each of the localities studied by both industrial sector and occupation. As shown elsewhere (Yeandle et al, 2006c, p 19), a rather varied local picture emerged where other employment sectors were concerned. Thus whereas Thurrock saw a 6% increase in the share of local jobs (held by women) in distribution, hotels and

**Figure 2.2: Percentage change in manufacturing jobs, by employment status and gender**

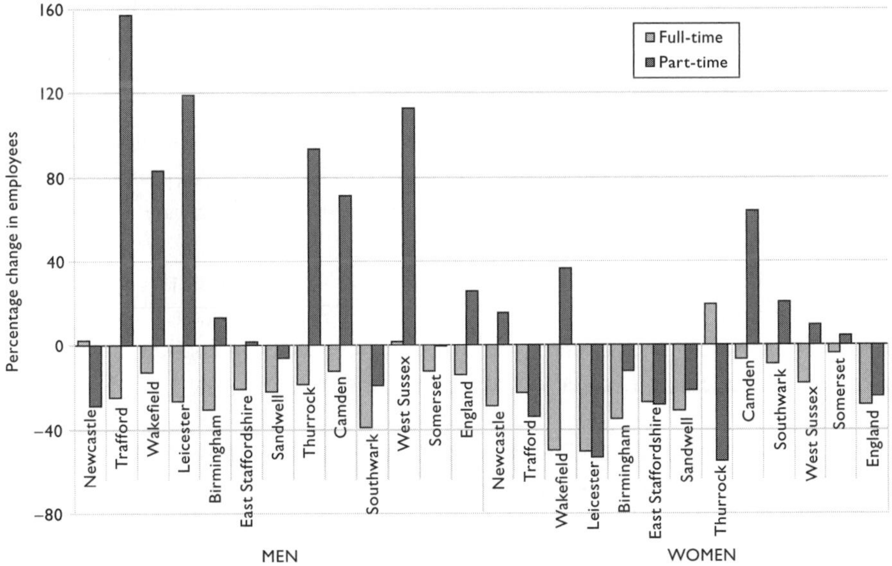

*Source:* Census of Employment AES 1991, ABI 2002, Crown copyright.

restaurants, in Sandwell the share of all female jobs in this sector barely changed at all (+0.1%). Birmingham and West Sussex both saw an increase in the share of female jobs held in banking, finance and insurance, but in Somerset and Thurrock the share of women's employment in this sector fell. In Sandwell, there was a 6.8% increase in the share of female jobs in the public administration, education and health sector, and rises in other areas too, yet in Birmingham and Thurrock these figures were negative. These examples indicate considerable complexity and variability in local labour market demand, which can be affected by decisions made by national and international organisations to close, relocate, grow or contract their operations, as well as by the health of small local businesses and the scale of entrepreneurial activity specific to a local economy. As we show in later chapters, because women, with their more limited travel-to-work patterns, are even more strongly affected by developments in their local labour markets than men, these local variations in demand for labour are especially important for them.

We turn now to policy developments relevant to labour force participation at the local level, the second topic of this chapter, presenting a brief summary of policy developments in four distinct but overlapping fields. Readers will also find further information about policy developments relevant to the six GELLM local studies, in each of the GELLM synthesis reports.

## Policy relevant to women's participation in the labour market

Most analysts would characterise policy on the labour market in England in the past 30 years as neo-liberal. Influenced by, and in turn affecting, EU employment policy, in England the labour market has been the focus of a range of activation policies (alongside some important new employment legislation, including the introduction of a national minimum wage and new employment rights for employees), with work seen as the key to solving problems of welfare and social security. As others have pointed out, an 'adult worker' model (Lewis and Giulliari, 2005) has at the start of the 21st century effectively replaced the previously dominant 'male breadwinner' model of employment, and flexibility and work–life issues have come to the fore in policy debates. At the same time, government has committed itself to substantial 'deregulation' of the labour market (even listing 'regulatory reform' in the title of one of its own departments).

In this second part of the chapter we have chosen to focus on policy fields that have been prominent in public policy, but where issues of women's welfare, and their labour force participation and progress in the labour market have, in our view, been inadequately understood and addressed. These policy fields are:

- labour market activation and reform of the social security system;
- regeneration and social inclusion;
- skills and productivity;
- equality and diversity.

In this section we stress the way these different policy fields have had an impact on and affected women, emphasising the broader consequences of the lack of 'joined-up' policy making.

## Labour market activation and reform of the social security system

Welfare reform has been a major focus of public policy, with implications for the operation of the labour market and people's engagement with it. Involving a range of 'activation' policies and designed to reshape the relationship between benefit claimants and the labour market, the reforms have been associated with rising employment rates and declining unemployment rates and have sought to rebuild the welfare system around paid work. Here we set out some of the implications of policy in this area for women seeking work in their local labour market.

In many respects, the Labour government's approach to welfare reform in recent years has proved successful (Millar, 2000). The period has been marked by rising employment rates (especially among lone parents), and together the New Deal programme, tax credits, the national minimum wage and the National Childcare Strategy have provided incentives for claimants to enter paid work. Building on policies introduced in the Thatcher period, the Labour administration added new incentives to enter paid work and has been more successful than previous governments in reducing unemployment and tackling economic inactivity.

Despite this, informed assessment of the New Labour programme indicates that some intractable labour market issues hinder progress (Hirsch with Millar, 2004; McKnight, 2005). Widespread low pay means getting a job does not necessarily lift labour market entrants out of poverty, and welfare reform has not assisted claimants to access good quality jobs or achieve progress at work. Policy has been less successful in helping those furthest from the labour market, with some groups faring particularly poorly. Young people aged 16–17 still experience disadvantage and exploitation in the labour market; unemployment rates among 18–24-year-olds remain high; there is high long-term unemployment among 25–49-year-olds (McKnight, 2005); and poverty is widespread among benefit claimants. In all these aspects there are specific outcomes for women and for different groups of women.

A key feature is that official approaches no longer rely on the 'male breadwinner model' that informed the Beveridgean post-war welfare state. Each man and woman is now deemed to have a responsibility to engage in paid work, implying a new interpretation of the responsibilities of women claimants, especially mothers, in relation to the labour market: 'individual citizens themselves ... need to meet the responsibility to take the necessary steps to re-enter the labour market when they have a level of capacity and capability that makes this possible' (DWP, 2006, p 2).

In the GELLM study we considered a range of issues relating to how welfare policy affects women who are seeking work in their local labour market, including how far policy is sensitive to (and is successful in overcoming) women's economic disadvantage in the labour market. Men and women engage with the labour market in different ways, with women much more concentrated in lower-paid, lower-skilled and part-time work. Many women take breaks from paid work to take on caring roles, often experiencing downward occupational mobility when they return to work, especially if it is part-time (Francesconi and Gosling, 2005). Thus there are strong reasons for expecting that the movement from welfare to work will have a different significance and different outcomes for men and women.

In addition, the GELLM study revealed a large group of women who are disconnected from the labour market and want to work, but who are not engaged with the welfare system (Escott and Buckner, 2006; Grant and Buckner, 2006). Here the absence of clear policies to assist this group (discussed in Chapter Six) is of critical importance. There are also important differences between women, both in relation to their distance from the labour market, and in terms of their social characteristics, especially age and ethnicity (Yeandle et al, 2006j). In later chapters in this book we discuss the limits of policy with respect to these. Our analysis has also confirmed that, while engagement with the labour market tends to take place at the local level for both men and women, this is particularly important for women, who more often seek work close to home and to their children's schools, making it salient to ask: how far can a national programme of welfare reform overcome local labour market barriers to work?

The welfare-to-work approach has been built on previous changes to the welfare system in the UK, but also reflects changes and developments in social security systems in the US and Europe. The current process of UK reform began in the 1980s, when a strict benefit regime, a reduction in the value of some benefits, and new tests and conditions for job seekers were introduced (Finn, 2003). During this period, the reduction in the value of some benefits made it much harder for many claimants to make ends meet and operated as an indirect work incentive (Oppenheim and Lister, 1996). Benefit changes were associated with a growing inequality between waged workers and claimants and deepening poverty and debt amongst claimants (Walker and Walker, 1987). The Conservative government expressed its desire not to 'featherbed' the unsuccessful (Lister, 1989) and pursued a strategy of inequality (Walker, 1990). Key legacies of this period have been the maintenance of a strict benefit regime and the continuing low value of benefits, with a particularly negative impact on households with children: in 2002–03, 74% of (working age) adults in workless households with children were living in poverty (McKnight, 2005, p 44).

Welfare reform developments beyond the UK are also important because some policy ideas have transferred here, and experiences abroad provide lessons for the analysis of the UK system. In particular, the highly gendered nature of developments in the US – focused on lone mothers – informed UK thinking about this group. US developments were based on new conceptualisations of claimants, emanating from neo-conservative and neo-liberal thinking, which saw them as 'welfare dependent' and as an 'underclass', cut off from mainstream society and not sharing its values and aspirations (Murray, 1984; Deacon, 2002).

The post-war view that claimants were victims of changing socio-economic circumstances was replaced with arguments more reminiscent of the 19th century, informed by notions of 'undeserving poor' and 'less eligibility' – thinking that also resonated in the UK. As we discuss in Chapter Six, the GELLM study showed some women claimants in England experiencing the disapproval (and contempt) of others, and feeling both stigmatised and socially excluded.

In the US the discourse about benefit claimants took on a gendered and racialised tone, reflecting new thinking that lone mother claimants, particularly Black mothers, were actively choosing a life on benefits and thus should be compelled to work. Resultant changes to the system had major impacts on women with children, introducing stricter eligibility criteria, time limits for the receipt of benefits and mandatory work requirements (Grant, 2000). Yet analysis of these policy developments in the US demonstrated that: 'women barred from welfare aid [will] compete in a segment of the labor market that is already saturated with job seekers, with the result that low wages will be driven lower' (Piven, quoted in Grant, 2000, p 366). Furthermore, as noted in relation to the UK: 'Incentives and help for people in non-working households to move into work have not been matched by incentives and help for people to progress within work or to get better quality jobs' (Hirsch with Millar, 2004, p 1).

While welfare reform in the UK has affected both men and women, the GELLM study has revealed the harsh reality of the labour market for women claimants returning to work, with those part-time jobs available on the open labour market often low paid and lacking in progression opportunities (Grant et al, 2006g), and women living in deprived neighbourhoods faced with very poor-quality job opportunities (Escott and Buckner, 2006; Grant and Buckner, 2006).

Examples of active labour market policy and a new emphasis on conditionality in benefit systems are evident across countries in the European Union (EU) (Yeandle, 2003). This has been bolstered by the wider EU Social Policy Agenda (which aims to raise EU employment rates to 70% by 2010 and 60% for women) and, following the Lisbon summit in 2000, by new EU employment guidelines that emphasise the importance of reforming benefit and tax systems to 'provide incentives for unemployed or inactive people to seek and take up work' (Yeandle, 2003, p 49).

In the UK a range of new policies have been introduced since 1997, transforming the welfare system using a 'work first' approach (DSS, 1998; HM Treasury/DWP, 2001), with New Labour arguing that the welfare system must operate in a way that contributes to economic growth and supports the UK's competitiveness in a globalised economy (HM Treasury, 2003; Taylor-Gooby et al, 2004). The old, Beveridgean welfare system is characterised as 'passive', detrimental to economic growth and too heavily influenced by conceptions of the rights of claimants – and is replaced with a new contract between the state and the citizen, based on claimants' responsibilities to work/seek work (DWP, 2006; Page, 2007). Changes to the system have been focused on reinforcing work incentives to reduce 'welfare dependency' amongst benefit claimants and create 'employment opportunity for all', to be achieved not only through active labour market policies but also through the creation of 'flexible labour markets', unconstrained by unnecessary regulation (HM Treasury, 2003; McKnight, 2005).

Critical to reform in the UK has been the New Deal programme, initially focused on young people and the long-term unemployed, and later extended to lone parents, disabled people, older unemployed people and the partners of unemployed people. With a range of 'carrots' and 'sticks' aimed at re-engaging people with the labour market, the New Deals provide 'work-focused interviews' and assign claimants to a personal adviser. In a change designed to place paid work at the heart of the welfare system, they have brought together social security and statutory job search services, and improved employment rates, with the personal adviser a key aspect of success, although performance in the role has been variable (Millar, 2000). New Deal participants have emphasised the value of this practical help and advice that, as revealed in the GELLM study, is not always available (see Chapter Six).

Alongside the New Deals, New Labour has introduced both a national minimum wage and a system of tax credits to supplement the wages of specified groups of people on a means-tested basis, aiming to 'make work pay'. Other new measures have included the National Childcare Strategy, a Child Tax Credit and a Childcare Tax Credit. While tax credits have undoubtedly been an incentive for some people to enter paid work, some participants in the GELLM study felt they were not generous enough to warrant moving from welfare to work. Other issues include the risk that tax credits may encourage low pay, and a concern that, in the long term, they may not be affordable as a means of income redistribution (Bennett and Hirsch, 2001).

Over time, the scope of these reforms has widened, with the UK government arguing that the Lisbon targets can only be met by addressing both unemployment and inactivity (HM Treasury, 2003), and setting an 80% employment rate. Thus the focus on unemployed claimants has been widened to a range of working age people who are not in paid employment but who are claiming benefits (Kemp, 2005) and the focus on lone parents, claimants of incapacity benefit and older workers (DWP, 2006) has been sharpened. This nevertheless leaves some groups of economically inactive women, including young women aged 16–17 and non-claimant women who want to work, lacking policy support (see Chapter Six).

As the net of activation policy has spread, a localised dimension with a growing focus on benefit claimants living in deprived neighbourhoods has also been introduced. Despite a history of urban regeneration and neighbourhood renewal investment (see below), pockets of worklessness persist in particular localities, and closing the gap between average employment rates and those in deprived neighbourhoods has become a key government objective (HM Treasury, 2004c). Here the main focus has been on low employment rates among young people and some groups of black and minority ethnic people, with economically inactive women a less prominent target group. In proposals outlined in 2006, each local area was asked to develop a consortium of local partners, including employers, to raise local employment rates, improve the local economy and contribute to the (national) 80% employment rate (DWP, 2006). However, as noted by others (Hirsch with Millar, 2004) and confirmed by the GELLM findings, local differences in employment opportunities are an important factor affecting the success of welfare reform. Throughout this book we discuss what this means for women.

As we have seen, successive governments have failed systematically to outline how reform might affect or engage men and women differently. Through development of the New Deal for Lone Parents – implicitly a policy measure focused on lone mothers since the vast majority of lone parents are women – the government has signalled that lone mothers are viewed as having the same responsibility to work as other targeted benefit claimants (DWP, 2006), reflecting the official view that welfare reform is essential to address a range of new risks associated with the late 20th and early 21st centuries. These include high divorce rates and the rise of lone parent households (Taylor-Gooby et al, 2004), as well as wider aspects of demographic, family and structural change. There is also evidence of some new thinking about women's relationship with the welfare state and with the labour market; but as we will show in this book, it has not yet translated into effective policies supporting women's full or equal engagement with either the employment system as a whole, or with opportunities in their local labour markets.

## Regeneration and social inclusion

Urban policies, including 'regeneration' policy, have been informing local approaches to tackling labour market disadvantage for over 30 years. Addressing problems in the most deprived urban areas, they represent responses to industrial restructuring and are rooted in the concerns of successive governments about the physical and social decline of many communities. In many localities, economic investment has been achieved through these policies, and much discussion about cities has emphasised the importance of local labour markets (Gordon and Turok, 2005), but arresting the decline in labour market participation among those living in deprived areas has proved difficult, raising questions about whether neighbourhood policies can be effective in regenerating local labour markets (Lupton, 2003) and providing a focus for our own work on women's poverty and labour market disadvantage (Escott and Buckner, 2006; Grant and Buckner, 2006). Here we discuss regeneration policy in the context of measures to address labour market inequality and the focus on 'neighbourhoods', and reflect on whether gender and equality have been adequately addressed in local programmes.

Originating in post-war policy on rebuilding cities and addressing regional inequality, urban policy has been characterised by a large range of initiatives and experiments (Cochrane, 1999). The impact of economic change on local communities emerged as a concern for policy makers in the 1960s, when community development projects, the urban programme and educational priority areas were introduced. These area-based initiatives resulted in a new

---

focus on deprived communities. Although designed to support social and welfare policies, it soon emerged that inequality was linked to wider structural changes in the economy. Unstable local economies, with declining industries and rising unemployment, often centred on the decline of full-time male manual jobs.

The economic dimension was emphasised a decade later in *Policy for the inner cities* (DoE, 1977), which introduced a stronger focus on economic development, including the Industrial Improvement Areas initiative. In the 1980s the assumption that run-down areas would benefit from relaxing planning powers and state support to the private sector was manifested in the Urban Development Corporations and Enterprise Zones; Inner City Task Forces, established in 22 areas in 1986, sought to boost 'economic opportunities through industrial development, business support and training' (Lupton, 2003, p 10). These policies adopted a limited view of economic development and did not explore labour market issues at a local level or consider the wider impact of industrial restructuring on local jobs.

The 1990s saw the emergence of flagship projects such as City Challenge and the Single Regeneration Budget (SRB) programme, designed to promote social and economic regeneration and respond to community needs. These initiatives relied on local partnerships and their targets included skills development and employment creation; yet once again they were insensitive to diversity, despite the fact that women and ethnic minority groups were over-represented in the localities concerned (Brownhill and Darke, 1998).

From 1997 onwards New Labour continued to support SRB, broadening the remit of its urban renewal approach to address challenges highlighted through the work of the Social Exclusion Unit (SEU, 1998) and the Urban Task Force (1999). A new Neighbourhood Renewal Strategy sought to improve the quality of life in the most deprived areas, focusing on five priorities – work and enterprise, crime, education and skills, health, and housing and the physical environment (SEU, 2001). The employment target aimed to reduce the difference between the employment rates of disadvantaged groups and the national rate, and to increase employment rates for lone parents, ethnic minorities, people aged 50 and over, those with the lowest qualifications and those living in local authority wards with the poorest labour market position (ODPM, 2005). The almost complete absence of gendered analysis in the SEU's national strategy for urban renewal (YWCA, 2001) and the highly targeted, area-based New Deal for Communities (NDC) programme yet again signalled a lack of recognition in public policy that women experience disadvantage differently from men.

These area-based initiatives have sought to achieve multiple objectives in response to complex processes of change. Underpinned by national developments (such as the Neighbourhood Renewal Fund and the urban regeneration companies), but locally focused, they were given little guidance on tackling complex employment problems, and did not address equality issues. Regional Development Agencies tasked with reducing deprivation by 10% in the poorest wards – an aim also promoted through the Sustainable Communities Plans for the English regions (ODPM, 2005) – sought to tackle disadvantage by balancing economic success with social justice. Although they included a focus on new jobs and economic growth, and on strategic approaches to skills, transport and infrastructure, gender equality is a dimension of labour market policy and regional competitiveness that has been almost completely overlooked in regional and sub-regional strategies (Escott, 2007). Indeed, this has been the case even across New Labour's more recent regeneration agenda, in which 'neighbourhood'-based approaches include emphasis on both performance management and community engagement (ODPM, 2004), and programmes to foster partnerships between public, private and voluntary bodies (Hill, 2000).

Ironically, under New Labour, these policies were promoted alongside strategies to empower communities: to increase citizens' voices and involvement; to encourage harmonious social relations between groups; and to counter discrimination and exclusion – all areas where women tend to be particularly active. Organisational and political tensions between the needs and priorities of meeting national targets while simultaneously addressing local needs are dimensions of the potential contradictions evident in delivering regeneration policy at the neighbourhood level (Diamond and Liddle, 2005). Yet gender issues rarely emerge at either level, with policies failing to address differences between men and women in relation to local education or transport services, care provision, planning or economic development (Oxfam, 2005, 2007).

The specific problems of low employment rates and persistent disengagement with the labour market became much more explicit during New Labour's third term. Low levels of economic activity and poorly performing services were identified as key factors that drive an area into decline, and the revitalisation of local economies and improved services seen as the key to regeneration (Cabinet Office, 2005). It was argued that weak local economies perpetuate low skill levels and a lack of incentives for residents of deprived areas to take paid work, as well as discouraging employers from investing in these areas. The policy response has been to establish Local Enterprise Growth Initiatives (LEGIs) to develop enterprise and investment in the context of sustainable growth (NRU, 2006). Service coordination, social enterprise and private sector involvement are recurring themes in the first round of LEGIs (NRU, 2006), but it seems that once again women's disconnection from the labour market has been overlooked (Grant et al, 2007).

Within the GELLM research programme, one study focused on women's poverty in six local authorities, finding that gendered analysis was missing across all regeneration and labour market activation initiatives (Escott and Buckner, 2006). Regeneration investments had been made in each of the study localities in the past decade, and these local schemes included initiatives designed to assist local residents in gaining training, skills and support in accessing employment, with the central aim of assisting local residents to take full advantage of the new opportunities linked to the wider regeneration of the area; yet here too all the initiatives studied had failed to consider gender differences in employment (Escott and Buckner, 2006).

Continuing concerns about the nature and effectiveness of policy in this area are highlighted by the government's own statement that regeneration programmes and area-based initiatives have failed to support deprived areas effectively (Cabinet Office, 2005; HM Treasury, 2007). The third Labour administration moved away from the area-based emphasis to a concern with mainstreaming improvements through public services, and improved neighbourhood management. Associated with the emphasis on local services, policies to promote economic investment and address labour market inequality are increasingly viewed as central to an integrated, joined-up policy approach that incorporates a range of services and expenditure. In addition to the pressure to 'mainstream' neighbourhood renewal in public services, the government's State of English Cities (Parkinson et al, 2006) and Sustainable Communities Plan (ODPM, 2003) recognised that life chances in deprived neighbourhoods are heavily influenced by the quality of public services (such as health care and education), yet even then did not consider the complexity of accessing training and employment for different groups of women.

Many local economic measures (from employment and training programmes to business start-up schemes) are now managed through Local Strategic Partnerships (LSPs), established to provide strategic direction for local regeneration initiatives. The reorientation of welfare policy to the neighbourhood level is reflected in recent moves to develop a City Strategy, with 15 areas across Britain being funded to tackle worklessness (from the government's Deprived Areas Fund) after devising their own plans and targets to support people into work. The intention is that through the Working Neighbourhoods Fund local agencies will shape the delivery of the government's welfare and regeneration agenda to help people move off incapacity benefit, and will have access to improved data-sharing, and a greater ability to influence the provision of training opportunities and employment programmes at a local level (DCLG/DWP, 2007). Lack of gendered analysis in the policy framework determining the new arrangements is likely to limit the effectiveness of this fund in supporting some of those groups on the margins of the labour market.

While policy makers now promote equality across public services, the specific application of equality, and more particularly gender equality, is much less tangible even where there have been attempts to address labour market disadvantage through regeneration investment. The GELLM programme found that while regeneration policy aims and objectives had been geared to addressing local neighbourhood problems, they were generally weak on the economic and labour market strategies required to tackle the unemployment, low pay and financial hardship faced by many women (Escott and Buckner, 2006). Baseline data, and the monitoring and evaluation systems used in assessing the impact of regeneration schemes, were not gender sensitive, and the practical delivery of regeneration and labour market initiatives, including those administered through local authorities, Job Centre Plus and the Learning and Skills Council, did not ensure that differences between men and women's position were reflected in local projects. Gender was not a condition of regeneration funding, monitoring or outcomes.

The policies did not take into account the particular experiences women had of their neighbourhood or of how they viewed issues of job opportunity, access and services in relation to engaging with the local labour market. Thus two key areas of weakness in regeneration policy have been the lack of a gender analysis and targets and inadequate links between welfare policy and regeneration policy (Grant et al, 2007).

Urban policy in the UK emerged during the 1960s from the issues of poverty and exclusion discovered in cities seeking to adjust to economic and social restructuring. The more recently termed 'regeneration' policy is concerned with a range of factors and themes associated with labour markets and the local dimension of labour market change. Regeneration programmes have typically emphasised skills needed to acquire employment, but have not clearly identified local labour market characteristics. Greater understanding of the complexity and diversity of local neighbourhoods and the role that men and women play in the labour market has been identified as a missing part of policy making aimed at meeting employment targets and improving labour market opportunities in the most deprived areas of the UK. There is, as yet, no systematic analysis and recognition of the gendered and localised nature of women's employment in this field of policy. This omission has been particularly important in the area of women's employment and may, in part, explain the limited impact of government policy on labour market activity in deprived areas.

## Skills and productivity

At the national level, government and policy makers in the UK have placed increasing emphasis on the skills of the workforce in recent years, arguing that UK skills 'remain fundamentally weak by international standards' and are 'holding back productivity, growth and social justice' (Skills for Business, n.d.; Leitch, 2006). In the past 40 years government has put different strategies in place to address weaknesses in workforce skills, increase the qualifications level of the adult population and address issues of labour supply and demand. The context throughout has been major economic restructuring, significant demographic change, increasing international competition, accelerating technological progress and the challenges of globalisation.

Consistently missing from this agenda, however, has been any serious assessment of how far the largely 'gender-blind' employment and skills policies adopted in the UK have constituted missed opportunities to tackle key issues. Problems of labour supply and concerns about returns on investments in qualifications and skills have only rarely been tackled by consideration of whether gendered labour force participation and behaviour might be a crucial element in the UK's skills and productivity problems. This section briefly considers the skills and training policy context that lies behind the experiences of the women of working age who are the focus of this book.

For governments, much of the debate about skills and productivity has been about how responsibilities should be distributed between the state, employers and individuals. In the 1960s (and until the 1980s), the problem was tackled through a system of industrial training boards, funded through compulsory levies on employers, who acquired statutory training responsibilities under the 1964 Industrial Training Act. During this period, state education was extended and improved, the school leaving age raised to 16 in 1972, a comprehensive system of secondary education introduced (in the 1970s and 1980s) and higher education expanded following the Robbins Report (1963). Key reforms were introduced in the qualifications system and, underpinned by the 1975 Sex Discrimination Act (SDA), girls' and women's experiences of school and the wider education system improved significantly from the mid-1960s onwards.

During the 1970s and 1980s, many more girls and young women achieved qualifications, stayed on at school beyond the minimum leaving age and entered higher education. Girls nevertheless continued to specialise in highly 'feminised' subjects at school, to enter female-dominated occupations when they began paid work, and to select training courses and degree programmes that would equip them mainly for 'female' job roles – as nurses, teachers, health professionals and secretaries (Crompton and Sanderson, 1990, pp 54–8; Lewis, 1992, p 87).

In the 1970s and 1980s, public policy on skills and training was dominated by the economic crises and unemployment that followed the 'oil shock' of 1973. Skills policy became focused on the employment rate and on managing unemployment, with most attention and funding commitments directed at the problem of 'youth unemployment'. The key objective in this period was reducing unemployment, especially among the young and among men. Thus despite the SDA, only limited attention was given to enabling girls and women to access a wider range of skills and jobs in this period. Small programmes with modest funding operated from time to time, sometimes with significant local impact or with life-changing consequences for individual women (Rees, 1992), but never on a scale capable of transforming girls' and women's opportunities to contribute to the economy at the national level.

In 1989, 72 Training and Enterprise Councils (TECs) were established, tasked with unifying the enterprise and skills agenda and putting employers in charge of the skills system. TECs focused mainly on government employment and training programmes – the Youth Training Scheme (YTS), Training for Work (TfW) and the system of Modern Apprenticeships (MAs). Lasting barely a decade, they were replaced in 2001 by the Learning and Skills Council (LSC), responsible for supporting a 'lifelong learning' agenda. Operating through local offices throughout England, the LSC also had responsibility for the further education system. In the same year, a new Skills for Business network of 25 Sector Skills Councils and a national Sector Skills Development Agency (SSDA) were set up, to 'engage employers in the design of qualifications and training as well as working to tackle skills shortages and gaps' (Leitch, 2006, p 48). Regional Development Agencies (RDAs) were also established, required to develop regional skills and economic strategies, and to form regional skills partnerships with LSCs, with joint responsibility for equality and diversity issues.

The 2006 Leitch Review of Skills heralded further significant changes in skills and training policy, recommending 'stretching objectives' for skills at all levels and across all sectors and setting up a new Commission on Employment and Skills (in 2008). Yet, like its predecessors, the Leitch analysis paid scant attention to gender issues, taking little note of the significance of men's and women's unequal access to employment, skills, training and jobs – or of the need for up-skilling and retraining among women 'returners' to the labour market, or the waste of women's talents (Grant et al, 2005, 2006g–l; Connolly and Gregory, 2007), which had been clearly demonstrated in a series of reports commissioned by government: the *Kingsmill review of women's pay and employment* for the DTI (2001), the DTI report on women's work and productivity (Walby, 2002) and the Women and Work Commission report (2006).

As we show in later chapters of this book, the under-use of women's skills and qualifications is a major problem in the labour market, damaging their own careers and prospects, but also holding back organisational performance and feeding into economic deprivation at local levels. We comment further on this theme in the concluding chapter of the book, where we highlight what our analysis means for policy making. This topic also needs to be addressed in relation to wider policy on equality and diversity, another key theme running throughout this book, with which we now conclude the present chapter.

## Equality and diversity

Historically, campaigning and policy on equality between women and men has often been focused on labour market issues and on topics connected with the labour market: the right to fair treatment in applying for jobs and accessing employment; the right to equal pay; access to education and training, the right to qualifications and to enter the professions; maternity rights and protection for women at work; and policy on childcare, flexible employment and work–life balance. In this field, the policy developments of the late 20th century and beyond have their origins in the campaigning and achievements of both first- and second-wave feminism, and in the way conceptualisations of equality developed in the 20th century, taking into account divisions and differences relating not only to gender but also to race and ethnicity, to dis/ability, to religion and faith, to age, to sexual orientation and to differences of culture, language and values.

Central to equality and diversity policy over the past 30 years has been the landmark legislation enacted in Britain in the 1970s: the 1970 Equal Pay Act (effective from 1975); the 1975 Sex Discrimination Act (which covered both education and employment); and the 1975 Employment Protection Act (which accorded many employed women their first substantial maternity rights). Together with other legislation at around the same time on 'race relations', sexual and family matters such as male homosexuality, divorce and abortion, and with later legislation on disability rights, these Acts of Parliament laid the foundation for a modern, 'progressive' approach and paved the way for subsequent developments in the field.

As argued elsewhere, in the field of equalities, legislation has the function of setting standards, as well as establishing the basis for investigations, compliance, enforcement and prosecutions (Yeandle, 2005). Without complementary policies, however, equalities legislation can have only limited impact, as it needs to operate in conjunction with both 'positive action initiatives' and equalities 'mainstreaming policies' to make it effective (Yeandle et al, 1998; Bennett and Booth, 2002). Positive action, which involves targeted investments to rectify past disadvantage, the establishment of enhancement and support programmes, and specific responses to the lobbying and interests of active groups, can open up channels of opportunity for both individuals and groups who have faced discrimination or exclusion on the basis of gender or other characteristics. Mainstreaming establishes baselines to define the relative situation of women (or other groups); allows judgements about choice, fairness and equity to be made; creates opportunities to plan actions, strategic activities and detailed policy; and involves assessment of the impact of how policies affect different groups, engaging all through consultation and decision-making.

In the English labour market, positive action initiatives have often been led by (or called for) by the equality commissions (operating separately, from their inception until 2007 when their combination into the Equality and Human Rights Commission began[4]). Much positive action activity has involved opportunistic, ad hoc or voluntaristic campaigns and projects, often arising from powerful lobbying on the part of those groups – across the diversity spectrum – that have succeeded in becoming well organised. As seen above in relation to skills and training, positive action schemes have been developed by a variety of agencies, including central and local government, and have often been led by voluntary and third sector bodies, to promote women's access to a wider range of better opportunities in the labour market. However, these schemes have usually been small scale, have often operated only over short timeframes, and have consequently had limited general impact, however valuable they may have been in advancing the situation of individual women.

Much investment in this type of activity has come through the EU Structural Funds, linked to regions or groups identified as facing particular disadvantage in engaging with the labour market. Here EU policy on the 'reconciliation of work and family life' (arising from the principle of equal treatment of men and women, enshrined in all EC Treaties since 1957) was the initial impetus for these developments, playing an important role in setting the terms of the debate about gender equality in the UK. Subsequently, equal opportunities, with particular reference to gender, became a specific feature of the European Employment Strategy (which implemented the Lisbon Agreement from 2000) and thereafter, until 2004, each EU member state's National Action Plan for Employment (NAPE) contained a specific section describing how progress towards gender equality in the labour market was being tackled and monitored. When the NAPEs were replaced in 2005 with new national reform programmes for each member state, however, the EU guidelines were revised and the focus shifted away from gender equality. It could be argued that gender has subsequently re-emerged in the new focus, from 2007, on 'flexicurity' (otherwise known as 'working life from a new perspective'). The flexicurity approach includes 'pathways' designed to 'tackle skills and opportunity gaps among the workforce' and to 'improve opportunities for benefit recipients and informally employed workers', stating that: 'Flexicurity should support gender equality by promoting equal access to quality employment for women and men, and by offering possibilities to reconcile work and family life' (EC, 2007, p 20). However, the explicit focus on equality of opportunity between women and men, which was a key feature of the NAPE, does appear to have been substantially diluted as these changes have occurred.

It needs nevertheless to be acknowledged that, supported with resources from EU Structural Funds, EU policy on equality of opportunity between women and men provided an important stimulus to those (limited) policy developments in England that addressed gender equality in the labour market. In particular, the European Social Fund (ESF) provided resources for a wide range of labour market interventions, with ESF funding specifically supporting interventions designed to promote women's access to employment, their progress within organisations and their recruitment into occupations and industries traditionally dominated by men. In 2002 new ESF funds were made available for research in England into ways of tackling gender discrimination in employment (under EU Objective 3, Policy Field 5, Measure 2), and it was with a core grant made available through these arrangements that the GELLM research programme was developed and implemented in 2003–06 (Bennett, 2008).

The concept of gender mainstreaming (an approach first developed by the UN and later by the EU as a key strategy for achieving gender equality) was fundamental to EU-led equalities developments from the 1980s onwards (Hoskyns, 1986; Yeandle et al, 1998). Essentially simple and all-embracing, and potentially powerful, gender mainstreaming became a funding requirement in EU Objective 1 programmes after 2000 and consequently had an impact in relevant UK regions. In South Yorkshire, for example, the 2000–06 Objective 1 programme made tackling gender inequality in the labour market a feature of its activities, appointing both a gender manager and a gender champion, and allocating £10 million to a strand of work designed to tackle occupational segregation, promote women's achievement in the labour market and public life, develop new ways of facilitating work–life balance and address male disadvantage, especially among those with no qualifications (GOYH, 2004).

Because gender mainstreaming involves getting the facts about the circumstances of different groups, establishing how far differences arise from free choice, and to what extent they are the product of indefensible unfairness or discrimination, it offered an appropriate model for developing a research programme. That it also meant involving all relevant parties to engage with and consider strategies for achieving fairer outcomes and changing practice made it additionally attractive. In the concluding chapter of this book we consider some of the wider impact of the GELLM research programme, arguing that it succeeded in opening up new debates and in deepening understanding of women's circumstances in relation to the local labour markets studied. The GELLM programme was regarded by partner agencies as novel and innovative, reflecting the fact that policy-engaged research of this type had not been undertaken before, and that at local level it provided many new insights into women's situation and labour market circumstances, even where the data being explored were official statistics relating to the locality, and theoretically available to anyone investigating the local labour market situation. In some localities it was also welcomed as a particularly timely development, coinciding as it did with a number of significant milestones in equality and diversity policy developments at national level. These included the report of the Women and Work Commission (2006) and two official equality reviews (set up by the Prime Minister, and reported in 2006). There was also new legislation, notably in the form of the 2006 Equality Act, which set up the Commission for Equality and Human Rights and placed a new duty on public bodies to promote gender equality (from 2007), and the 2006 Work and Families Act, which introduced new rights for some working parents.

In this chapter we have set out our view that, in localities throughout England (the focus of our programme of research), women's interests have often been ignored and poorly understood by policy makers, with the result that most interventions designed to create a more effective labour market, accessible to all and offering progression opportunities for everyone able to benefit from them, have not worked well for most women. In the next chapter we focus on a set of policy-relevant issues, conceptualised as 'myths, puzzles and problems' in policy and theoretical analysis of women's labour market position, before going on in the later chapters in the book to explore each of these in more depth and detail, drawing on the findings of the GELLM research programme.

## Notes

[1] Parents of children under age 6 and parents of a disabled child under 18 gained the right to request flexible working arrangements under the 2002 Employment Act. This right was extended to most carers of sick, disabled or frail adults in the 2006 Work and Families Act.

[2] This is calculated as the ratio of people aged over 65 to the rest of the adult population (those aged 16–64).

[3] Mid-year estimates 1971–2005; and 2004-based projections 2011–21 from ONS, Government Actuary's Department, General Register Office for Scotland, Northern Ireland Statistics and Research Agency.

[4] In 2007 the Equal Opportunities Commission, the Disability Rights Commission and the Commission for Racial Equality were combined to form the Equality and Human Rights Commission.

# THREE

# Women's labour market situation: myths, puzzles and problems

*Sue Yeandle, Cinnamon Bennett, Lisa Buckner, Karen Escott and Linda Grant*

## Introduction

This chapter outlines a set of difficulties – conceptualised here as 'myths, puzzles and problems' – that need to be addressed if women's position in their local labour markets is to be understood, explained and addressed in public policy. It draws on a reading of the now extensive literature on women and the labour market, and considers some of the 'received wisdom' about women and employment. The chapter identifies a number of themes to which we return in later chapters of the book. In it, we highlight some aspects of women's employment and labour market situation that remain poorly understood, and consider topics where evidence, theories and 'knowledge' have been produced – and where (in some cases) policy actions have been developed – but where interpretations and theories are contested, misleading or incorrect, or where apparently intractable problems remain.

The critical backdrop to this discussion is a question often posed (and one initially addressed to us by some policy makers and practitioners, both at national level and in some of the localities studied in the GELLM research programme). With both jobs held by women and labour market opportunities on an upward trajectory, and with improving educational outcomes and qualification levels among young women (often exceeding the achievements of young men), what is the difficulty for women in participating in and progressing in the labour market? Surely at the start of the 21st century women have better jobs, more opportunities in the labour market and more choices and options than at any previous time? The chapter challenges the assumptions behind this perspective, paving the way for our presentation (in later chapters of this book) of evidence from the GELLM studies.

The new evidence produced in the GELLM research programme between 2003 and 2006 – an extensive and detailed body of evidence about women's situation in 12 local labour markets – provides a wealth of local-level, gender-focused data about women's experiences of paid work and access to employment. As we move through the chapter, we highlight a range of topics, arguing that in each case there are three types of concern to which our evidence can be applied: myths about women in employment that have wide currency and have influenced policy; puzzles where there are competing theoretical positions or gaps in understanding; and problems that have been tackled at the practical or theoretical level (or both), but which have not gone away. Using this approach to understanding women's position in the labour market, the chapter explores questions relating to: educational attainment; how work is valued and paid; part-time work; low pay and poverty; disconnection from the labour market and access to paid work; and workplace cultures and structures of opportunity. As readers will find, each of these topics is a recurring theme in later chapters of the book.

## Educational attainment

Over the last 30 years, differences in the outcomes of education for boys and girls have been the subject of considerable study and debate (Younger et al, 2005). When gender differences in pupil attainment first became the focus of systematic social research, boys were the main beneficiaries of the educational system, measured by their performance during compulsory schooling and beyond (Deem, 1978, 1980; Griffin, 1985; Arnot et al, 1999). Indeed right from the beginnings of publicly funded education and well into the 1970s the odds in terms of formal qualifications and success at school seemed firmly stacked against girls, who were denied equality of educational opportunity, offered programmes of study considered 'suitable for their sex' and prevented from entering certain occupations and professions.

In 1975 the Sex Discrimination Act was passed, promising girls protection from discrimination and fair access to education, and building on earlier policies designed to deliver more socially egalitarian educational outcomes (Delamont, 1989; Halsey et al, 1980; Rees, 1992). For more than a decade after this, up until 1988, at the all-important end of compulsory schooling both sexes showed very similar overall educational attainment. Had parity of educational outcome for boys and girls been achieved? As they entered the labour force, would young women's access to better jobs and well-rewarded employment improve? Things certainly looked more promising for young women; indeed, after 1988, a 'reversed' gender gap emerged, with girls attaining better results than boys – a gap now familiar to most, and the subject of much public debate. This new gender gap, which showed girls out-performing boys, has remained in place ever since: thus by 2006–07, 66.4% of girls, compared with just 57.7% of boys, achieved five GCSE grades A*–C (DfES, 2007b).

Some analysts claim that this reversed gender gap is something of an artefact, and primarily a product of the national curriculum (introduced in 1988); others emphasise the impact of changes in the examination system (Machin and McNally, 2006). Some argue that generalisations about either sex are unhelpful (Younger et al, 2005). Nevertheless, when the GELLM research programme began in 2003 the 'underperformance' of boys had become the focus of considerable public discussion, policy intervention and debate, and girls in general were widely thought to be doing well at school. Consequently, limited attention was being given to variations in their performance at local level, as national and local education authorities turned much of their attention to concerns about the underachievement of certain groups of boys.

The GELLM gender profiles published in 2004 (Buckner et al, 2004a–i, 2005a, 2005b, 2006) and other GELLM research nevertheless showed that:

- While girls' attainment in tests and examinations at school was above that of boys in most forms of assessment in almost all localities, very significant variation in their attainment was still visible between localities. Indeed in a few places, in some GCSE subjects, girls' level of attainment still fell below that of boys.
- Pupils of both sexes were continuing to make gendered choices at the A-level stage (although the most popular topics of study varied from one place to another). Furthermore, there were marked gender differences in the proportion of pupils gaining 'good' A-level passes. On this measure, in some localities, girls did not out-perform boys.
- The relatively small number of pupils who left school at 16 still followed gendered paths as they entered paid employment, reinforcing existing occupational segregation (Connexions, 2004). In 2004, 43% of young male school leavers entered skilled trades, while it was commonplace for young women school leavers to enter personal services occupations (39%), jobs in sales and customer services (16%) or administrative and secretarial posts (13%). In addition, 22% of young male school leavers and 15% of young women went into low-paid, low-skilled, elementary occupations (Buckner et al, 2006).
- Those who stayed in education in 2003–04 after completing GCSEs made distinctly gendered choices too. Young men favoured mathematics, English, physics and history, while many young women chose English, psychology, social studies and biology. In making their selections, girls are influenced not only by teachers, parents and peers but also by media images of working life and by a powerful culture of gendered expectations (Madden, 2004). Girls' attainment continued to outstrip that of boys at this stage; the proportion of young women gaining two or more A levels (or equivalent) increased from 20% in 1990/91 to 45% in 2004/05, compared with 18% to 35% for young men (ONS, 2006b).

In higher education, the past 40 years have seen a huge opening up of opportunity, from the Robbins reforms of the mid-1960s through to the New Labour target for 50% of all those under 30 to participate in higher education. There has been a very large increase in women's participation; between 1970/71 and 2004/05; while the numbers of young men in higher education more than doubled (from 416,000 to 1,068,000), among young women they rose seven-fold (from 205,000 to 1,426,000), and by the mid-1990s more young women were recorded studying for first degrees than young men for the first time.

Yet the focus and experience of students in higher education remains highly gendered; in 2004/05 the three most popular subjects studied by women were 'subjects allied to medicine' (19% compared with 5% of men), 'education' (11% compared with 5%), and 'business and administrative studies' (11% compared with 15%), suggesting that many female graduates, like their many non–graduate predecessors in previous decades, are still destined to enter nursing, teaching and office work, which do not attract the highest pay. Among male undergraduates, the most popular subjects were 'business and administrative studies', 'engineering and technology' (12% of men, less than 2% of women) and computer science (10% of men, 2% of women) (ONS, 2007). As for attainment in higher education, in 2004/05, of those obtaining their first degrees, about 11% achieved a first-class degree (similar proportions of men and women), while 46% of women and 39% of men were awarded an upper second. Thus, a higher proportion of women than men achieved a 'good' degree (ONS, 2007).

At the other end of the spectrum, among people of working age the proportion of women who lacked any formal qualifications was (in England in 2001) smaller than for men in all age groups, by 3–4 percentage points. And while the percentage of men who held a university degree or higher-level qualification was fractionally above that for women among those aged over 25 (less than 1 percentage point), among 16–24 year-olds, 12.5% of women, compared with 10.7% of men, were already graduates (Buckner et al, 2004a). Ethnic minority women gained qualifications especially rapidly between 1991 and 2001, so that by the latter date, women aged 25–44 in the Indian (37%), Black Caribbean (28%) and Black African (28%) groups were more likely to have a degree than White women of the same age (25%) (Yeandle et al, 2006j, p 17).

Meanwhile, in a separate major study, it emerged that young women's superior attainments in formal qualifications were not being mirrored in their achievements in the labour market, particularly in relation to pay. Thus while women had indeed 'closed the gap' in higher education, a marked 'graduate gender pay gap' still persisted, with men going into the same occupation with the same class of degree commanding a higher salary than equivalent women (Purcell, 2002).

## The gender pay gap

Despite women's significantly improved qualifications, for those at work the 'gender pay gap' – which has persisted despite over 30 years of legislation on equal pay – remains significant, at 83% in 2005 (compared with 74% in 1985 (ONS, 2006b). Yet, confirmed in our GELLM local labour market investigations, there is a common perception that women in the 21st century have equitable access to jobs and pay, and that the pay systems and structures put in place by employers operate without reference to the sex of the employee. In this section we briefly summarise some of the factors that lie behind women's lower pay, which (as shown in the chapters on the gender pay gap in each of the GELLM gender profiles) was evident in all of the local labour markets we studied.

---

Among full-time employees in 2003, we found the gap between men's and women's average weekly earnings ranged from almost £76 per week in Sandwell, to significantly higher figures in Trafford (£119), Wakefield (£120) and Somerset (£127) (all close to the English average, £123). The largest weekly gender pay gaps among full-timers were seen in London (£163), Thurrock (£189) and West Sussex (£161). Among women working part-time, hourly pay rates in England as a whole were much lower than for other groups; in 2003, they reached just 60% of the average hourly pay of male full-time workers, 73% of the average hourly pay of full-time women workers, and 87% of the average hourly pay of male part-timers. Again there was considerable variation from place to place. In Sandwell, which had generally low rates of pay, women part-timers earned 75% of the hourly pay of men in full-time work; and 84% of the average pay of women working full-time. However, in West Sussex, where average pay was much higher, the pay gap was also larger: here women in part-time work earned just 57% of the hourly pay of male full-timers, and 77% of the hourly pay of women in full-time jobs.

Most commentators regard the overall gender pay gap as a product, at least in part, of occupational and industrial segregation by sex – both in the industries and occupations in which men and women work, and in the levels at which they are employed (Anderson et al, 2001; Kingsmill, 2001; Rake, 2001; Grimshaw and Rubery, 2001, 2007). It is also claimed: that some kinds of pay system tend to work to the detriment of women (Morrell et al, 2001); that women's attitudes to work, family and career, and the behaviours associated with these attitudes, are relevant factors (Hakim, 2002); that women are lower paid as a result of their lesser accumulated 'human capital' (Becker, 1985, 1993); that in the job changes they make ('job shopping') men tend to improve their pay levels, whereas women, for a range of reasons, are less successful at achieving this (Manning, 2003); and that gender differences in psychological attitudes, notably self-esteem in relation to work, are also relevant. As Manning and Swaffield (2005) show, however, these last explanations do not, when tested using British panel data, explain much of the quite large gender pay gap that emerges in the 10 years after labour market entry. The latter authors posit various types of discrimination and gender differences in labour market 'ambition' as other possible explanations still to be explored, while in a review for the EOC in 2007, Grimshaw and Rubery make the case for new initiatives to address pay inequality, operating at four levels: the labour market, the occupation, the organisation and the workplace/job level (2007, p 132).

The difficulty of securing pay equity between men and women has long troubled UK policy makers and trade unions, usually on grounds of social justice. Campaigns for equal pay go back more than a century, and a pay gap has been officially recognised and measured since the introduction of the 1970 Equal Pay Act. The culmination of campaigning over many years, this legislation focused on 'equal pay for equal work' (Hoskyns, 1986). It was amended (during 1982–84) in response to a 1981 decision of the European Court of Justice (Pillinger, 1992;

Booth and Yeandle, 1999), and since that time has provided a statutory right to equal pay for 'work of equal value'.

While pay has been a key focus of collective bargaining in unionised segments of the labour market, and the historical role of the trade unions in campaigning for higher wages is widely acknowledged, the most notable successes of the trade union movement in this arena were mainly in the male-dominated trades, often leaving women workers out or, in some cases, letting them down (Boston, 1980; Walby, 1986). Indeed, it was because of their continued strong concentration in low-paid jobs that the introduction in 1997 of a national minimum wage (an early, contested, move of the incoming Labour government) had a disproportionately beneficial effect on women workers, who represent about 70% of beneficiaries (Low Pay Commission, 2003).

Action on low pay alone, however, cannot close the pay gap, which is also affected by pay at the upper end of the pay spectrum (Yeandle, 2006b). Here, pay is more often individually negotiated, and even if women are qualified for and secure senior level jobs, they may not know what other senior staff are paid, or be awarded the highest salaries. Recent calls for 'top pay' restraint have not been supported by any new policy measures and, although it is clear that here men are the main beneficiaries, there are no controls at the upper end of the pay spectrum (although equal pay legislation applies and can be invoked on a case-by-case basis). And while the pay gap varies significantly by educational level, as Purcell has shown, based on a major survey of graduates, it remains important even among the best-qualified labour market entrants:

> The earnings of women graduates lie mainly in the range of £15,000 to £24,000 per annum. Male graduates have a wider dispersion of earnings at the upper end of the distribution, with significantly more men than women earning £30,000 or more per annum some four years after gaining their first degree. (Purcell et al, 2005, p 93)

This is particularly important since, as Manning and Swaffield put it in relation to a wider group of labour market entrants, 'women never make up the ground lost in the first 10 years after labour market entry' (2005, p 13).

Renewed action to address the gender pay gap was called for following both the report of the Equal Pay Task Force, set up by the Equal Opportunities Commission in 1999, and the consultations undertaken by the Women and Work Commission (EOC, 2001; Women and Work Commission, 2006). In reporting their findings, the Equal Pay Task Force and some members of the Women and Work Commission called for employers to be required by law to conduct equal pay reviews that could check for and address discriminatory outcomes and uncover any unintentional discrimination in their pay structures and systems. Although the government has rejected this approach, some organisations have voluntarily undertaken equal pay reviews. However these have often been rather limited in both scope and outcomes (Neathey et al, 2003, 2005; Shafer et al, 2005). Most trade unions and many academic commentators now believe a voluntary approach to pay reviews cannot be effective in tackling unequal pay, but government in the UK has remained opposed to this step, particularly in view of opposition to it from among employer bodies.

Later in this book we see how the way women experience the labour market in different parts of England affects labour force participation, employment prospects, and career options. While pay is certainly not the only factor motivating women's labour market behaviour, it has many significant effects for them, including not only their financial well-being across the life course, but also the importance they and others attach to their employment, and the way they feel about it. In the next section we look at how work is valued, focusing on why so much of women's work is low paid.

## How work is valued

Why have women remained concentrated in low-paid work? And why are the jobs women do so often poorly rewarded? In this section we consider some of the background to women's continuing concentration at the bottom of job hierarchies; and raise some questions about why the gap between women's and men's pay has remained so stubbornly persistent. We also give further consideration to the enduring puzzle about women's labour market situation, touched on above: why, when women and men have (in theory) access to the same skills, qualifications and labour market opportunities, does occupational segregation persist? And why have campaigns to draw women into 'non-traditional jobs' had such modest impact? This is important because the clustering of women in some jobs, employment sectors and occupations – a topic explored in more detail in Chapter Five – in part explains their lack of pay parity in the labour market. We conclude this section by highlighting one of the really critical problems about women and work, which underscores the importance of the broader agenda addressed both in the GELLM research programme and in this book, which is that inequality and unfairness in pay distorts labour market participation, has undesirable consequences for employers and employees alike, and – for individuals and their families – carries a life-long impact on women and their dependants that is unjust and indefensible.

Historically, paying women lower rates than men has, throughout Western Europe, been an almost universal practice, albeit one rendered relatively invisible in some industries and occupations by sharp divisions between the work done by men and women (Bradley, 1989; Hufton, 1995). Well into the 20th century, women's hourly rates of pay, salaries and piece rates were significantly lower than those of men, a practice also seen back in the mid-18th century, when employing whole families was common in some of the early textile mills and factories under the patriarchal 'family system' (Baines, 1970; Pinchbeck, 1981). Throughout this time, the commonest form of labour outside the family – employment in domestic service – was also almost totally segregated into separate roles for men and women, and the wages of women and girls employed in domestic service, as in agriculture where they also often laboured, were always among the very lowest paid for any form of work.

Historians of women's work have shown that, as paid work for women outside the home emerged in workshops, in factories, in agriculture and in the early service industries, even where trade unions emerged and began to negotiate rates of pay, women's work was almost universally paid at rates below those set for men. This was often justified (if at all) on the basis of women's lesser strength, stamina, skill or need for wages (Alexander, 1976; Davidoff, 1986; Walby, 1986; Hufton, 1995). The emergence, in the later 19th century, of an ideology of the 'male breadwinner' entitled to earn a 'family wage' found strong support in some parts of the trade union movement. This set of values, which became embedded in the minds of employers, fellow workers and women employees, created a vicious circle of expectation that women's wages would be small and did not need to be sufficient to support a whole family (Lewis, 1992; Crompton, 1999). This view was also associated – especially in those parts of the economy where men had secured relatively high rates of pay – with the concept of 'pin money' and with the view of women as secondary earners, whose rates of pay and job security were less important than those of male workers. As we shall see (in Chapter Seven), these concepts still resonate today in contemporary wage-setting practices, particularly in relation to part-time work.

Legislation giving women workers special protection from some of the dangers of the workplace in the 19th century (alongside similar protection for workers who were children) also contributed to the view that women's labour was not equal in worth to that of men; even though (as mechanisation and technological developments reduced the need for physical strength and the structure of the labour market changed with the creation of office work, new technical and professional roles and jobs in the public sector) this justification lost much of its relevance (Esping-Andersen, 1993). Increasingly what mattered was education (especially some degree of numeracy and literacy), technical skills, intellectual abilities and (especially in the later 20th century) interpersonal skills. Furthermore, as wartime experience had shown, it became evident that women could perform a wide range of jobs, including those requiring skill, strength and training in dangerous and difficult environments (Boston, 1980; Braybon, 1981). Throughout the late 19th and early 20th centuries a succession of female pioneers – mostly emerging from the middle and upper classes where the limited opportunities for women to contribute to life outside the home were a source of enormous frustration for talented women – breached the boundaries of virtually all the professional and technical positions from which they had previously been disbarred, either through the rules of professional bodies, or through their exclusion from education and qualifications (Spender, 1987).

In an important article, published in 1980, Phillips and Taylor showed how women's paid work had been systematically undervalued when the skill level of jobs was assessed. With women's skills and expertise unacknowledged or denied, low pay and poor prospects inevitably followed. This analysis showed that, even in those roles where women were commonly employed, gendered judgements were made about the skill, training and expertise required in manual jobs, so that the epithet 'unskilled' or 'semi-skilled' was routinely applied to women's job roles. Men's work, on the other hand, was much more likely to be evaluated as 'skilled' and deserving of higher pay. This article highlighted not only inequality in employers' practices, but also complicity in parts of the trade union movement. Later, government and officials endorsed these judgements in the way official employment statistics were collected, effectively sustaining a dual system in which women's work could only very exceptionally attract a pay rate comparable to that of men.

Added to this, access to a career was extremely difficult for women well into the middle of the 20th century, as virtually all women were expected to give up their positions on marriage. During this period, 'careers' were for single women too 'unfortunate' to secure a husband; and marriage and motherhood seemed incompatible with economic independence or professional achievement. As the roles of mother, wife and homemaker became blurred and linked to ideologies of progress and domestic harmony, especially during the 1940s and 1950s, women – except the poorest of them who had no choice but to take what work they could get – found themselves 'confined' to the home and encouraged to prioritise care and domestic management over any desire to earn a living or develop a career. The 'feminine' work to which women were thought 'best suited' – cleaning, shopping, cooking, laundry, caring for children and those who were sick, old or frail, and managing household accounts (all essential tasks crucial to the maintenance of everyday life) – became ever more strongly associated with them as women. It also became increasingly devalued, for, unlike other forms of work, their labour was unwaged, did not generate social esteem, and was completely disconnected from the formal career and pay systems emerging in waged labour and the formal labour market.

This historical background is important in understanding the contemporary situation of women in employment. Although rapid social change in the later 20th century, including the influence of 'second-wave' feminism, was to lead to the landmark legislation offering the prospect of equality between men and women (notably in the 1970 Equal Pay Act and the 1975 Sex Discrimination Act, but also in other legislation and policy relating to the family, education and the labour market), these three crucial historical features continue to affect women's position and prospects in the labour market in the 21st century. We can summarise them as: an assumption that pay is 'not so important for women'; a belief that for women family roles take precedence and reduce their commitment to their careers; and an assessment that women's labour is less skilled, less important and of lesser value than that of men. This, as we shall see in Chapter Seven, is why part-time pay remains so low, the 'Cinderella segment' of the contemporary labour market. It explains why the 'glass ceiling' still limits women's ambitions and achievements in management and professional careers (as we discuss further in Chapter Eight), often holding them back unless they (can) choose to delegate aspects of their caring and domestic roles. It is why much of the work women do for pay, by drawing them into jobs which require skills in health, care, education and the public sector, or in catering, hotels, leisure and retail, reinforces those structures of occupational segregation (considered in more detail in Chapter Five) that underpin the gender pay gap. As others also argue, describing the 'undervaluation' of women's work as a 'thread which links together the three causes of the gender pay gap: occupational segregation, discrimination and women's unequal share of family responsibilities', this feature of women's labour market situation continues to be 'overlooked' in virtually all areas of employment policy (Grimshaw and Rubery, 2007, p v).

Nevertheless, it is an historical background that is subject to strong and continuing pressures for change. The equalities legislation of the last 30 years, signalling as it does deeper shifts in social and economic structures and in cultural values and beliefs, now not only outlaws discrimination on the grounds of sex (and of race, disability, and other sources of difference (Squires, 2003)), but also calls for the 'promotion' of gender equality in the 2006 Equality Act. Thus the (considerably amended) legislation on equal pay is now reinforced by pay equality schemes (however unevenly implemented), equal opportunities policies and high-profile legal actions, and has the formal commitment of trade unions and employers alike. In the workplace, the rights of parents and carers to combine their family roles with paid employment have been given more support; more employers take the 'work–life balance' agenda seriously, and they now have a 'duty to consider' the reasonable requests of these employees to work flexibly (Hayward et al, 2007). Across Europe, the broader demographic and labour market context calls for higher employment rates and for labour market activation and worker retention policies that can enable those currently disconnected from the labour market to join it, and those at risk of dropping out of employment to be supported to hold on to their jobs and careers (EC, 2005). Within families, decades of rising average standards of living and well-established expectations about home ownership call for more households with multiple earners. And as society, employers and families look for a yield on the considerable investments they have made in education, skills and vocational training, it makes less and less sense to deny women the opportunity to achieve their full potential in the labour market.

## Part-time work

Part-time employment, often referred to as an explanatory factor in relation to the gender pay gap, emerges as one of the most difficult puzzles in UK labour market studies. On the one hand, many women voluntarily choose to work part time, and studies report that the majority are content to do this (Burchell et al, 1997). On the other hand, part-time jobs are associated with a range of negative consequences for women workers, such as low pay and poor labour market status and opportunity (Grimshaw and Rubery, 2001; Manning and Petrongolo, 2004; Francesconi and Gosling, 2005; Grant et al, 2005, 2006g–l). This puzzle has generated an important body of work that touches on many critical issues in the study of women's employment. It is important because, if women workers are in fact content with low pay and poor job opportunities, the equality agenda and policies to improve women's pay and circumstances at work lose most of their significance.

Part-time employment has been a major feature of the British labour market over the past 30 years and remains an important pattern of employment for women, for whom there is a strong association between the presence of children and part-time working (Burchell et al, 1997). Since 1981, approximately 37% of women in employment (and 40% of women employees) have been employed in part-time jobs, a percentage that has remained more or less constant throughout the period. However, the number of women in part-time employment has grown by nearly 650,000 since 1981 (1981, 1991, 2001 Censuses), accounting for 32% of the growth in women's employment, and part-time employment has been especially favoured by employers in some industrial sectors and for certain occupations. On the face of it, this suggests a well-functioning labour market, with a ready supply of part-time jobs meeting the desires and needs of the growing numbers of women (and men) seeking part-time employment, and with employers offering part-time jobs in response to demand in the labour market. On this view, the recent expansion of part-time employment appears to offer a 'win–win' situation for women and employers alike.

Yet, despite this rather rosy perspective, part-time employment and part-time jobs have been subjected to a critical appraisal by feminist scholars and other academics, trade unions and women themselves over the past 30 years. In much of this work, the surface picture of women 'freely' choosing the part-time jobs they occupy has been challenged, yet it maintains a strong hold on the popular imagination and thus retains its potential to inform the thinking of policy makers.

That most part-time jobs are of poor quality is well supported by the evidence. One key factor here is the segregation of part-time jobs into a small range of industries and occupations. In England in 2001, 59% of part-time women workers were employed in just three industrial sectors: health and social work; education; and wholesale and retail (Grant et al, 2006g, p 6). This segregation is also evident in terms of occupation, with 78% of part-time women workers found in just four occupational categories: elementary occupations; sales and customer services; personal services; and administrative and secretarial work (Grant et al, 2006g, p 11). These are industries and occupations dominated by women workers and characterised by low pay. As we have indicated, part-time working is itself associated with low pay, and maintaining an independent financial existence on part-time wages alone is extremely difficult (Harkness, 2002).

The large pay gap between full-time and part-time working (the 'part-time pay penalty') is associated with the industrial and occupational segregation of part-time jobs, and it has long been known that, for women, moving into part-time work is associated with downward wage and occupational mobility (Martin and Roberts, 1984; Blackwell, 2001; Manning and Petrongolo, 2004; Francesconi and Gosling, 2005). Once in a part-time job, most women find their career paths blocked; there are few promotion opportunities for part-time workers, and access to training is often restricted (Grant et al, 2006g). These factors, which tend to distinguish part-time from full-time jobs, raise important questions about why women 'choose' to occupy such jobs.

There is little dispute that some women voluntarily choose to work part-time hours, usually at particular points in their lives. Hakim interpreted this evidence of choosing part-time hours in new ways; her thesis – that women who seek part-time jobs are part of a distinct group of women workers with particular preferences in the labour market – has been controversial; they are 'grateful slaves' who lack a career-focused orientation to work (Hakim, 1991, 1995, 1996, 2000). Hakim implies that many part-time women workers are content with the inferior quality of their jobs. Her argument (discussed in Chapter Eight of this book) has engendered wide debate, questioning both the notion that women exercise 'free choice' in the labour market and the feasibility of distinguishing between different types of women in the way suggested.

Focusing on 'choice', Fagan (2001) has highlighted the constraints affecting women's relationship to the labour market, noting a range of factors and processes, in the policy sphere, in the household, in the labour market and within workplaces. There has also been much critical discussion of the contention that part-time workers form a group with specific orientations to work that distinguish them from full-time workers (Crompton and Harris, 1998; Fagan and O'Reilly, 1998; Procter and Padfield, 1999). However, this categorisation of female workers has been challenged as little more than a myth because women's orientations to work tend to shift and change over time. Indeed, some have argued that the very distinction between part time and full time is unhelpful in the study of women's employment, given the diversity among women, the wide range of employment contexts in which they engage with the labour market and the variation in what is meant by part-time working (Warren and Walters, 1998; Walsh, 1999).

Unravelling the puzzle of women's part-time employment and challenging some of the myths that surround it is made even more difficult when we consider the extent to which women in part-time jobs are 'working below their potential'; that is, not using their skills, education and labour market experience when they take up part-time jobs. The GELLM survey of 333 women employed in low-paid part-time jobs in 22 workplaces across England found that 54% were 'working below their potential' defined in these terms (Grant et al, 2005, 2006g–l). In 2004, a follow-up survey to test these findings found that 51% of part-time workers were working below their potential, with an estimated 2.8 million women workers in Britain working below the potential they had already demonstrated in previous jobs (Darton and Hurrell, 2005).

Are women really choosing to squander their skills in jobs that offer so little opportunity for advancement? Research to date suggests that a wide range of factors must be taken into account, including: gender divisions in the home, the cultures within different workplaces, the scope and quality of services for women workers and children, the lingering effect of state policies on dominant thinking and values with respect to the gender division of labour, and the actions and policies of employers and trade unions. To unravel the part-time puzzle and explore the myths about part-time working among women, we need to consider this range of factors and processes, and we explore these issues more fully in Chapter Seven.

## Women, low pay and poverty

Women's poverty is not, and has never been, a specific focus of public policy in the UK. Although since 1997 reducing child poverty has been a key government target, with low pay recognised as a major cause of in-work poverty, a gendered analysis of poverty and low income has been overlooked in labour market and welfare policy (Palmer et al, 2006). The post-1997 Labour government, as we saw in Chapter Two, has targeted particular groups in employment and welfare policy, including those who are unemployed, lone parents, the young and those with disabilities, but men and women have not been considered separately.

A number of ideas underlie policies designed to promote employment, contributing to the myth that 'work pays' for all, including women. When considered together, the following assumptions represent a major failing in understanding how to address poverty. These assumptions are: that 'worklessness' is largely a problem for men, that many women are not dependent on their (own) low income, that low pay does not really matter for women who have a partner in work, and that child poverty can be addressed by supporting parents into work and by welfare reform.

In general, debate about improving employment rates and addressing household and child poverty has taken place without clear reference to the labour market disadvantages that many women face. Thus, while tackling low income is a central feature of anti-poverty strategy, the importance of work-focused policies, including welfare-to-work initiatives and childcare provision, is claimed without reference to the complex needs of different groups of women (Minoff, 2006). The argument offered – that paid work and support through welfare policy are the solutions – is particularly problematic in relation to women, whose labour market disadvantage, combined with the poor value attached to their work, often affects their earnings throughout their lives. Here we discuss different dimensions of the problem of income poverty for women.

Women are more likely to live in poverty than men, and to have experienced poverty at some time in their lives (Payne and Pantazis, 1997). Women are also known to suffer recurrent and longer spells of poverty more often than men (EOC, 2003; DWP, 2004). Because most official poverty statistics present data at the household (rather than the individual) level,[1] most income and pay data is not disaggregated by gender, and lifetime impacts are not often shown. This means that women's greater susceptibility to poverty can remain hidden. Recent research exploring the scale of women's poverty links much of the problem to low income (Yeandle et al, 2003). Thus studies have shown that 40% of women (compared with less than 20% of men) had individual incomes of under £100 a week (Rosenblatt and Rake, 2003) and that 22% of women (compared with 14% of men) had persistently low incomes (Bradshaw et al, 2003). Furthermore, after housing costs, women were 16% more likely than men to live in households with incomes below 60% of the average (calculated from Kemp et al, 2004), and 30% of women had incomes predominantly made up of tax credits and benefits (Women and Equality Unit, 2003).

Women in some groups have been identified as particularly disadvantaged. Thus lone parents (91% of whom are women) and retired women who live alone are especially at risk, reflecting the lower average incomes of women (Bryson et al, 1997; Bradshaw et al, 2003). Women in some ethnic minority groups also face high exposure to poverty, as they are both more likely to be outside employment and to be in low-paid work than White women (Buckner et al, 2007; and Chapter Five of this volume). Women are also known to be the main managers of family poverty, often dealing with high levels of debt within the household and associated difficulties, including stress, low morale and mental health problems (Pahl, 1989; WBG, 2005).

There is a relationship between 'economic inactivity' and poverty, but employment does not necessarily provide an escape from poverty for women. In spite of changes to the tax and benefit system designed to 'make work pay', problems associated with low wages persist. Poverty among women living in couples and lone mothers is often caused by employment on low earnings (Millar and Ridge, 2001; WBG, 2005). Part-time work, low-status work and the pay gap between women's and men's wages all contribute to women's poverty, while insecure work, occupational segregation and lesser access to promotion ensure that many women have very limited options to increase their own earned income (Bradshaw et al, 2003). Low-wage employment is a particularly high risk for low-income households already in receipt of benefits, especially if women do not fall within one of the welfare policy target groups.

As we emphasise in later chapters, the problem of making work 'pay' is particularly important for women living in deprived communities, who often feel economically isolated. The introduction of the national minimum wage in 1998 and tax credits in 2003 have been beneficial for many low-paid women workers, but in deprived neighbourhoods the impact of these measures remains limited (Escott and Buckner, 2006). In addition, new patterns of employment and new employment sectors have created particular challenges for women without up-to-date skills, qualifications or work experience; many are disconnected from the labour market because they cannot afford to live on the low wages on offer to those whose skills do not readily match those required in the better jobs available locally (Toynbee, 2003; Escott and Buckner, 2006).

While it is well known that unemployment heightens the risk of poverty (Gallie et al, 2003), the puzzle of explaining why women's poverty persists and why work does not pay highlights the inadequacy of conventional approaches in employment policy. Unless the specific situation of women is understood, a focus on unemployment or on the gap between job supply and job demand cannot be enough. For, as we have seen, although there are more women in the labour market – both mothers and women without children – and although since 1997 a series of policy measures have sought to boost income and tackle barriers to work, the problem of women's income poverty appears to be getting worse. How can this be explained?

First, the incidence of low pay has increased in recent decades, reducing the efficacy of work as a route out of poverty (Kemp et al, 2004). In 2006, 19% of working age adults lived in households below the poverty line, half of them in households where someone was in paid work. While tax credits helped more than a million children in working households out of poverty, the numbers needing such help rose sharply and half the children in poverty were in families already doing paid work (Palmer et al, 2006). Furthermore, three quarters of extra income created over the last decade went to households with above-average incomes. This further increased income inequality, which in 2006/07 reached the highest level since 2001/02, a development attributed to weak growth in incomes at the bottom of the income distribution (Brewer et al, 2007).

Contradicting other policy developments (see Chapter Two), tax credits can create disincentives for a second earner in a couple household with children, encouraging a single breadwinner model (Brewer and Shephard, 2004). And as means tested in-work support may reduce the incentives in households where one low-paid member is joined by another also on low pay, making 'more' work pay has become an increasingly uncertain strategy (Bennett and Millar, 2005).

The myth that women are 'doing better' in the labour market is also challenged by evidence that inequality among women appears to have increased. While many mothers who gained employment in the past 30 years already had a working partner and lived in households that benefited from employment growth, the situation of women without a working partner hardly improved at all between 1974 and 2003 (Berthoud, 2007). Those in low-paid employment also find it difficult to benefit from policies designed to support working parents. Working Families Tax Credit may have helped secure the material needs of low-income working families, but low-paid employment remains precarious, and the insecurity experienced by low-income working families may increase unless their transition into employment is supported more strongly (Dean and Shah, 2002).

Among low-paid women, lone mothers are the most likely to be poor. Employment among lone parents has increased, but in high unemployment areas – where more lone parents are concentrated – increases in the employment rate have been no greater than in low unemployment areas. Indeed, take-up of tax credits by lone parents has increased more in areas of low, rather than of high, unemployment (Webster, 2006) indicating that many of those women living in areas of greatest need have not benefited from these changes.

Women's poverty is thus highly problematic, and the link between low pay and income poverty remains complex. Tackling women's low income is critical to the long-term success of anti-poverty strategies, including child poverty, pensioner poverty and the high levels of deprivation experienced in poor communities across Britain. A wider range of public policy initiatives could contribute to addressing poverty among both women workers and women not currently economically active. Welfare-to-work programmes need to be linked to a gendered employment strategy, to shift the emphasis from household poverty to the experiences of individual women and men and from ensuring minimum incomes to improve women's position in the labour market (Lister, 2006). Secure, well-paid employment opportunities are required to protect them against poverty.

Strategies to alleviate child poverty would also benefit from more detailed investigation of the incomes and benefits women receive. Here the focus needs to be on women's income and pay over the life course, and on persistent poverty among women – which often commences in childhood and lasts into old age. As we show in later chapters, exploring how caring, studying and other experiences affect different groups of women is important in solving this puzzle. Targeting women in most need of support calls for a range of interventions and sustained, long-term support is often needed, with the focus shifting from entry-level, low-paid employment (which does not provide a long-term solution for women facing a lifetime of poverty) to sustainable jobs yielding a 'living wage'.

## Disconnection from the labour market and access to paid work

Unemployment and economic inactivity are central themes in labour market and welfare policy. Although official unemployment rates have fallen since the mid-1980s, the proportion of the working age population living in households where no one is in paid employment doubled from less than 7% in 1973 to nearly 14% in 2003 (Berthoud, 2007). There is a pervasive myth that, among this group, there are many women without paid work who are content with this situation, and who do not aspire to participate in the labour market. In a climate of job growth (which has benefited some women), debates about 'limited horizons' and 'cultural indifference to paid work' fuel this myth.

Although it has long been accepted that paid work is a defining feature of most men's lives and crucial to their identities, this understanding is less firmly established in relation to women, although it was raised a quarter of a century ago in studies of female redundancy that considered the social consequences of this experience for women (Coyle, 1984; Martin and Wallace, 1984). Yet, in the GELLM studies, women who wanted to work but did not have a job emphasised the importance of work for their sense of independence, self-esteem and success in life, while they and other women stressed that they also valued work for the friendships and inclusion in social life it offers (Escott and Buckner, 2006; Grant and Buckner, 2006).

One of the important messages of this book is that the key problem – why the labour market works so inadequately for this group of women, whose lives are often marked by poverty and social exclusion – has not been addressed, either in labour market theory or in policy making (this issue is considered in more detail in Chapter Six). The 'jobs gap' is well documented (Turok and Edge, 1999; SEU, 2004), yet very little research has focused on women on the margins of the labour market. And although women have higher economic inactivity rates than men, most studies of 'worklessness' have highlighted the problems of men who have become detached from the labour market (Alcock et al, 2003; Beatty and Fothergill, 1999; Faggio and Nickell, 2003). Job insecurity, another aspect of being on the margins of the labour market, is not regarded as a particular issue for women (Charles and James, 2003).

The myth that 'work pays for women' (discussed above) is central to this disconnection. For although a 'low-pay, no-pay' cycle, in which people move from unemployment into low-paid work and back again, is recognised (Kemp et al, 2004), this problem has not been analysed by gender. Nor is there adequate understanding of the diversity of this group, which (as we have seen) includes women who have been made redundant, women who have been looking for work but are unable to secure a job, women who have found work but struggled to stay in their jobs, and women who have taken a break to care for children or for older or sick dependants (Grant et al, 2007; Yeandle et al, 2007). In Chapter Six, we focus on this issue, noting also that (given the importance that women attach to work) being out of work is often experienced as depressing and demoralising. A large body of evidence has confirmed over many years that health and well-being are linked to employment opportunities, and that unemployment reduces well-being (Jahoda et al, 1972; Kelvin and Jarrett, 1985). More recently, it has been shown that those with mental health problems face particular barriers to employment (SEU, 2004), and that working for very low pay may have damaging effects on well-being (Ritchie et al, 2005).

A puzzle remains – why are women's low employment rates in poor areas persistent and, in some cases, getting worse? In the last decade policies designed to assist this group of women have been put in place, designed to improve their status in the labour market and remove barriers to employment, but they have not worked effectively for the most disadvantaged women. In this book, we show that three processes, all requiring remedial action at the local level, contribute to women's disengagement from the labour market and explain why this puzzle is difficult to solve (Grant et al, 2007).

First is the failure of welfare policy at the local level, both in terms of the services provided to women looking for work and in the kinds of jobs on offer to women who live in deprived neighbourhoods. As we saw above, the difficulty of transferring from benefits to employment is further complicated by consideration of their household finances, with many women perceiving few incentives in the tax and benefit system. Critics of policy on welfare and regulation sometimes argue that supply-side explanations of labour market disconnection are problematic. To them, key concepts used in policies for welfare reform ('welfare dependency', 'low motivation' and inadequate 'employability') (DWP, 2004, 2006) 'reorder' the unemployed from 'job ready' to 'least ready', and explain a further dimension of labour market disconnection, since what is being developed is a 'secure labour supply for insecure work' (Peck and Theodore, 2000, p 123; Webster, 2006).

Developing new ways of addressing worklessness has been a focus of government policy (as we saw in Chapter Two), but the GELLM research reveals that policy which continues to be confined to labour supply issues often fails to support workless women (Grant et al, 2007). Emphasising paid work as the best way out of poverty has assisted some women (in the Sure Start and Pathways to Work schemes, for example), but the impact has been limited (Daguerre and Taylor-Gooby, 2003). In addition to overlooking differences between women, welfare benefits, including tax credits, do not cover the full costs of childcare, and wider support is only available to those households on the very lowest incomes.

Second, regeneration and local economic development policies targeted at deprived communities have failed to address the employment problems experienced by women in these areas. Regeneration policy has been focused on local neighbourhood problems, but has been weak on the economic and labour market strategies required to tackle the unemployment, low pay and financial hardship faced by women on the margins of the labour market (Escott and Buckner, 2006). It is recognised that, for those with few skills, the local nature of the job market leads to 'spatial mismatch' in certain localities (Gilbert et al, 2003), but the gender division of labour in specific localities is rarely acknowledged in welfare or regeneration policy (Massey, 1997). Women's employment aspirations, and the barriers they face in accessing the local labour market, are also related to the 'unevenly gendered map of employment opportunities and to the gender differences in journey-to-work times and distances that create labour markets' (Hanson and Pratt, 1995, p 224). This spatial containment, often influenced by the strong relationship between home and work, is another aspect that is often ignored in debates about women's economic inactivity and unemployment. And as we show in Chapter Seven, discussion of the 'new' economy suggests that further analysis is required that recognises the gendered nature of people's social and spatial characteristics in relation to opportunities for work (Walby, 2002).

Poor quality jobs are a third factor influencing women's disengagement from their local labour market. The poor quality jobs, low pay and lack of progression opportunities in or close to the deprived neighbourhoods studied in the GELLM research programme had a major impact on workless women's ability to engage with the labour market. Others have noted that even where large numbers of unfilled vacancies exist, 'churning' (as workers move in and out of low-paid, insecure employment) tends to occur, and that labour market activation programmes mostly fail to overcome the substantial barriers to employment experienced by job seekers with limited skills and educational qualifications (Theodore and Peck, 2000).

Important policy changes are required to solve the puzzle of persistent economic inactivity among women who wish to work. These changes need to be based on a better understanding of the issues facing disadvantaged women and a proactive policy approach is necessary, addressing policy failure and building a case for more employer involvement in supporting women into sustainable employment. In later chapters, we discuss the way forward for policy in relation to the many and complex issues raised in this chapter.

## Workplace cultures

In the earlier sections of this chapter we have raised some questions about why women's improving qualifications and skills have not given them more advantage in the formal labour market, and about why so much of women's work is low paid and undervalued. We have also considered some of the specific problems that arise in relation to part-time employment, drawn attention to the relationship between low pay and poverty for women, and turned the spotlight on the particular difficulties in connecting with the labour market that face women living in disadvantaged neighbourhoods. In this section, we address some questions and concerns about what goes on within organisations and workplaces. This brings us to questions about women's careers, about their access to training and promotion, to human resources policies, to how men and women behave, informally, within the workplace, and to some of the difficulties women may encounter when they enter what can often still seem to be very much a 'man's world' (Cockburn, 1991; Halford and Savage, 1995; Lewis and Lewis, 1996). Women have entered the labour market in increasing numbers, particularly into public sector jobs, and many have penetrated those higher-level occupations (in managerial, professional and technical posts) once so difficult for women to enter. But, in spite of this, as we show in Chapter Eight, they still mostly work in organisations that, at the very top, remain dominated by men, and in which workplace attitudes, values and practices still bear the hallmark of thinking based on assumptions about workplace behaviour, relationships and beliefs based on the experience of male workers and male managers.

Drawing on our examination of relevant evidence, and on the data we ourselves generated on these topics within the GELLM research programme, in this book we challenge several widespread myths about modern workplaces, including the views that 'women are now reaching senior levels in greater numbers', and that 'sexism and racism are problems that have been overcome in organisational contexts' (especially in public sector employment). We also present evidence, particularly in Chapters Seven and Eight, that contradicts the belief that large numbers of women are not committed to their jobs, to earning money or to wielding power. We question the view that modern performance management systems offer an objective way forward, that they operate on merit or have succeeded in introducing fairness into managerial practices from which women are able to benefit.

As in the earlier sections of the chapter, we confront a number of puzzles about women's labour market situation, too. We consider why, despite increased statutory obligations and some legislative penalties on employers, women still find it so hard to 'reach the top'. We also ask why, at the workplace level, it is proving so hard to convince middle managers that better work–life support and more flexible working practices will deliver significant gains in the areas of employee retention, productivity and stress management – an area where other research has also identified slow and uneven progress (Bond et al, 2002; Yeandle et al, 2003). We also question, as others have done (Bunting, 2007), why so many middle and senior ranking employees allow their paid work to 'take over' their lives, making enormous personal sacrifices, and why, at the same time, there is an apparently widely held belief among managers that choosing to work part time or to take maternity leave or a career break shows lack of commitment to a career or senior level job (Crompton et al, 2003; Crompton, 2006).

There is ample evidence, both in the GELLM research and from other sources, that some of the factors lying behind these concerns represent deep-seated problems that remain very difficult to shift (Lewis, S., 2001; Liff and Ward, 2001; Sigala, 2005). Among the problems we identify we would highlight the many issues identified in the past decade in a burgeoning literature on 'work–life balance' and 'family-friendly employment'. With an eye to the future, these issues have contributed to debates about whether what employment policy, at either the organisational or the state level, should be seeking to achieve is to 'balance', 'reconcile', 'blend' or 'articulate' employees' lives outside work with their jobs and careers within work. This raises important issues of 'boundary maintenance', and how individuals can protect themselves from being 'taken over' by their jobs, careers and work responsibilities in the context of useful, but ever more intrusive, technologies that enable phone messages, emails and other work-based communications to invade their homes, their private moments and their family, personal and leisure time (Hochschild, 1997; Acker, 1998; Clark, 2000; Guest, 2002; Jacobs and Gerson, 2004).

We also position the debate about gender and workplace structures and practices as they relate to careers, advancement opportunities and models of achievement in enduring concerns about the unevenness of progress for women at work. This debate includes the difficulty of implementing equality and diversity policies and effective work–life policies at all levels of an organisation, and in the full range of occupations and industries (Herrington, 2004; Houston, 2005; Crompton, 2006). Why are some types of organisation, and some employment sectors, finding it so hard to address these issues? Why are some firms, professions and work teams able to provide satisfactory work contexts for women, while others continue to be dominated by male exclusionary cultures and polarisation and resentment between workers with and without caring responsibilities? What is the basis of concerns about workers who opt for flexible arrangements 'taking advantage', 'not pulling their weight', 'giving up on their careers' and putting 'unfair burdens' on other staff? And is it true that, even in organisations that embrace 'intelligent flexibility' (enabling their most highly valued employees to work flexibly/part time), ultimately these 'favoured' employees still pay a career progression penalty, cannot achieve their full potential and, because they choose to keep part of their lives separate from their careers, will never be supported and mentored for the most powerful, important and best-rewarded positions?

## Developing these themes

Above, we have set out some of the myths about women and the labour market that we believe our GELLM research findings can play a part in 'debunking'. All is not well with girls' education and training, and the education system still does not prepare girls well enough for their future lives nor secure their employment futures. The gender pay gap persists, and pay, for far too many women, is still unacceptably low, even in jobs whose social and economic value is coming to be better recognised and understood. While the introduction of the national minimum wage has improved this situation, its impact has been relatively small. Part-time employment is not a 'peripheral', unimportant aspect of the employment system, but becoming increasingly important, and may yet become an even more crucial mechanism, enabling our society to manage the pressures of work and care across the life course as it faces demographic pressures that might otherwise overwhelm it. Most women do care about their pay, and for those on low wages, there are life-long effects that will affect them in old age too. Within organisations, many women find that workplace cultures and systems, especially in relation to working hours, pay, promotion and work–life issues, do not enable them to achieve their full career potential.

The issues we have outlined present real problems that public policy has a duty not only to address, but to solve. It is of critical importance that we find ways of encouraging girls to study a wider range of subjects, and to keep their options open in relation to jobs and careers until they are able to judge not only whether they will like the content of their chosen occupation, but the rewards it brings, and how it will fit with their lives, too. It is imperative, also, that senior and well-paid posts are opened up to those who, for whatever reason, and whether in the short or longer term, want to work part time or flexibly. The alternative is the costly waste of investment in human resources, of potential and of talent. And critically, the employment system needs to generate jobs within the reach of poorer and disadvantaged women, which they can secure, which it will be financially worth their while to take, and which will offer them opportunities for personal development, to attain their own goals, and to secure a degree of financial stability for themselves and their families.

Some puzzles remain: throughout the book we highlight and address these, although inevitably not all the answers can be found in one programme of research. Prominent among these issues are the puzzles of why progress in educational achievements has not yet brought women fair rewards, and why so many young women still choose to enter jobs and careers where their employment and salary prospects are so poor. Linked to this, at a later stage in the life course, why do – literally – millions of women accept low-level jobs, low pay and the associated lower social esteem in return for the chance to work part time? Will this situation change in the future as new generations of women take maternity rights for granted, select flexible employment options and, using well-honed interpersonal skills, challenge men's often assumed 'automatic' right to occupy positions of influence, authority and control?

We now turn to more detailed consideration of all these matters in a set of specially written chapters drawing on the findings of the GELLM research programme. These chapters build on and refer to the 12 gender profiles (published in 2004–05) and six series of policy-focused research reports on the specific GELLM studies (published in 2006). The findings were debated with the 12 local authorities and other agencies who were our partners in the GELLM research programme at a range of events held in each of the localities studied in 2006, and these debates and discussions have further informed our analysis. Readers are directed to these earlier reports (available as online publications) for additional and more detailed presentations of our research findings about each locality, although brief profiles of each of the localities studied are also provided in Appendix A of this volume.

## Note
[1] In Great Britain a household is defined as being in 'income poverty' if its income is less than 60% of the contemporary median household income (Palmer et al, 2006).

# Part Two
## Gender equality and local labour markets

# FOUR

# Segregation and clustering in the labour market: men, women and local-level analysis

*Lisa Buckner*

## National policies, local people

A primary aim of the GELLM research programme was to uncover, through secondary analysis of official statistics at the local level, a truer picture of women's and men's situations in the labour market in England. Earlier work in this field showed that central government often relied on national level analysis to assess men's and women's position in the labour market and to set the level of any employment targets, despite the fact that much implementation of labour market policy falls to local and regional agencies (Bruegel, 2000; DWP, 2007). The European Union had already set an overall employment target of 60% for women by 2010 (EU, 2004), while in the UK the government had decided to strive for an 80% overall employment rate. In practice, most labour market policies have tended to be assessed and monitored using national indicators, with little attention given to local-level data unless particular problems are identified in a locality or region.

Despite this, implementation of labour market policies occurs, in reality, primarily at the local level, through the activities and interventions of local councils, local agencies and local employers. It falls to local Jobcentre Plus offices to implement national programmes such as the New Deal programmes that support people from welfare into work and, together with local employment and recruitment agencies and local employers, fill local vacancies that meet national employment targets.

In implementing labour market policy at sub-national level, agencies have frequently relied on local labour market assessments, such as those commissioned by the Training and Enterprise Councils in the early 1990s, even though this work rarely used the detailed gender-disaggregated data available, or considered its significance and implications (Escott and Buckner, 2005). A substantial body of academic work exploring employment and labour market issues at the regional level has been undertaken too, but very little of this analysis had been disaggregated by gender. The GELLM research programme was in part inspired by work for the Government Office for Yorkshire and the Humber to prepare for the 'gender mainstreaming' required by European Structural Funds regulations. This highlighted important differences in local labour market trends, industrial structure and labour force characteristics in the four metropolitan districts in South Yorkshire and found that by relying on local-level data that did not differentiate the situation and experience of men and women, major labour market issues of crucial concern to women had not been recognised (Yeandle et al, n.d.).

The decision to develop the GELLM research programme with local authority partners was informed by this earlier work. To achieve both range and depth of analysis, the GELLM partnership was formed with local authorities in each of the nine English regions. These included three major cities (Birmingham, Leicester and Newcastle), two county councils (Somerset and West Sussex), two London boroughs (Camden and Southwark) and a range of smaller districts (East Staffordshire, Sandwell, Trafford, Thurrock and Wakefield). This enabled the impact of different local labour market developments and opportunities, historical differences in industrial structure and access to transport, educational opportunities and the influence of other nearby towns, and how they affected both women and men as they sought to participate in the labour market to be analysed.

There are two key ways in which the use of labour market statistics is often inadequate and misleading as a guide for employment policy making. First, over-reliance on national and regional level analysis (each of the English regions is very large, complex and varied) often conceals and distorts the real employment situation at the local labour market level where men and women actually live, look for jobs and (mostly) find their employment. Second, ignoring heterogeneity among the workforce, and in particular the importance of gender, ethnicity and caring responsibilities, creates an inaccurate picture of how labour force participation is patterned and structured, as individual labour force participants are counted as if their sex, ethnicity and other characteristics are not important. Yet if these differences are not analysed and understood, even well-intentioned policies can have little chance of delivering results for those who perhaps need them most.

This chapter focuses on these key issues and considers different types of clustering and segregation in the labour market. Drawing on examples from the GELLM research programme and other sources to illustrate the importance of looking below the national/regional level when monitoring and analysing labour market indicators, it highlights some examples of local-level variability in:

- The type and quality of available jobs, and in the way trends in the industrial and occupational structure of employment opportunities are experienced by women and men. The configuration of local job opportunities and the scale and pace of change in particular industries and occupations both have very important gender dimensions.
- The way different groups of women and men, with different characteristics, interact with the local labour market, and how this is affected by age, family circumstances and caring responsibilities: factors that change during each

individual's life course, but which have important effects on their labour force participation.
- Local infrastructures of support for women and men seeking to access or continue in paid work, such as the availability of reliable public transport and affordable childcare.

As shown in the chapter, gender is a critically important factor in all of these, as there remains a high degree of gender segregation in both the industrial and occupational distribution of employment, and as patterns of family life and caring continue to be gendered too. These gender differences also need to be examined alongside ethnic differences in labour force participation (explored further in Chapter Five).

## Jobs

It is well established that part-time and full-time employment are not evenly distributed between women and men and that there are marked gender divisions in both the industrial and occupational distribution of employment (Walby, 1997; Miller et al, 2004; EOC, 2005b). This is readily visible at the national level: for example, men are strongly concentrated in the construction and women in the health and social care sectors; men dominate senior management positions and women dominate sales and customer service jobs; and women hold the vast majority of part-time positions.

It is also recognised that in the labour market the historical legacy, contemporary sectoral distribution of jobs and pace and direction of job change vary in each region and locality (Bradley, 1989; Walby, 1997). Yet these factors are rarely brought together so that the specific challenges in employment, welfare and equalities policy can be identified and addressed.

### The balance of full-time and part-time work

Table 4.1 shows, at selected geographical scales, the proportion of jobs held by men or women working full or part time in 1991. This date (a Census year) provides an important baseline against which subsequent change can be measured. At this point, men held 52% of all jobs, with the ratio of male full-time to part-time jobs about 9:1. Women, who held the remaining 48% of jobs, did so with a very different full-time to part-time ratio, of approximately 1:1.

There was very little regional variation in the proportion of jobs held by men, whether full time (ranging from 45% in the South East to 48% in the East Midlands) or part time (4%–5% in all regions). The regional variation was also minimal for jobs held by women, with the exception of jobs in London where, although 49% of all jobs were held by women, only 15% were held by women working part time (compared with 21% nationally). At the local level (shown here using five examples from the GELLM studies) there was a similar picture, again with only a little variation, although in Thurrock men held a rather larger share (59%) of all jobs, the vast majority of them full-time positions. The most notable exception was in the London Borough of Camden, where women held 45% of all jobs, but where only 9% of these were part-time positions; a very different ratio of full-time to part-time jobs – 4:1 compared with approximately 1:1 for women elsewhere.

When the net change in jobs between 1991 and 2002 is considered, an overall net increase in jobs (both full-time and part-time), with net increases in both full-time and part-time jobs for men and for women, is seen. This reflects the 19% increase in jobs (over 3.5 million jobs) during the period, which brought the total number of jobs in England in 2002 to over 22 million (Yeandle et al, 2006c, p 19). In the national economy this additional employment was split fairly evenly between men and women, with men gaining 48% and women 52% of the additional jobs. However, for men, these jobs were in a 1:1 ratio of full-time

**Table 4.1 Share of jobs in 1991 and share of increase 1991–2002 by full-time/part-time status and sex: England, the English regions and selected local authorities**

| Area | Share of jobs in 1991 (%) | | | | Share of increase 1991–2002 (%) | | | |
|---|---|---|---|---|---|---|---|---|
| | Men | | Women | | Men | | Women | |
| | Full-time | Part-time | Full-time | Part-time | Full-time | Part-time | Full-time | Part-time |
| England | 47 | 5 | 27 | 21 | 23 | 25 | 18 | 34 |
| *Regions* | | | | | | | | |
| North East | 48 | 4 | 25 | 24 | 3 | 40 | 15 | 42 |
| North West | 47 | 4 | 26 | 22 | 19 | 29 | 16 | 36 |
| Yorkshire and the Humber | 46 | 4 | 24 | 26 | 27 | 33 | 23 | 18 |
| East Midlands | 48 | 5 | 26 | 22 | 20 | 30 | 13 | 37 |
| West Midlands | 49 | 4 | 26 | 21 | 11 | 32 | 10 | 46 |
| East | 47 | 5 | 25 | 23 | 24 | 20 | 16 | 40 |
| London | 49 | 5 | 31 | 15 | 26 | 25 | 25 | 24 |
| South East | 45 | 5 | 27 | 23 | 31 | 18 | 20 | 31 |
| South West | 46 | 5 | 25 | 24 | 20 | 24 | 14 | 41 |
| *Selected GELLM areas* | | | | | | | | |
| Camden | 50 | 4 | 36 | 9 | 28 | 19 | 22 | 32 |
| East Staffordshire | 52 | 4 | 23 | 21 | 16 | 23 | 13 | 49 |
| Somerset | 47 | 5 | 24 | 24 | 11 | 23 | 13 | 53 |
| Thurrock | 55 | 4 | 20 | 22 | 25 | 17 | 21 | 37 |
| Trafford | 52 | 4 | 23 | 21 | 30 | 23 | 26 | 21 |

*Source:* Census of Employment/AES 1991, ABI 2002

to part-time positions; whereas for women the ratio was 1:2, with two thirds of their additional jobs being part-time positions.

At the regional level, these data show a rather more varied picture. Across the regions, at least 50% of the net increase was in jobs held by women, with the exception of London (49%) and Yorkshire and the Humber (41%); at least 50% was in part-time jobs (except in London and the South East, where 49% was in part-time work). Among men and women the majority of the net increase in jobs was in part-time employment opportunities, with the exception of London and the South East, and with a different pattern among women in Yorkshire and the Humber. Thus in the North East only 3% of the additional employment between 1991 and 2002 was among men working full time, whereas in the South East the corresponding figure was 31%. In the West Midlands, 46% of the additional employment was among women working part time, whereas in Yorkshire and the Humber the comparable figure was just 18%.

At the local level, while the majority of the net increase in jobs was again in posts held by women and available as part-time jobs (with the exception of Trafford), the ratios of male to female and part-time to full-time show much more variation. In Trafford just 21% of the net increase was in jobs held by women working part time and 30% was in male full-time positions, compared with a very different pattern (53% and 11% respectively) in Somerset.

Although all 12 of the GELLM areas experienced a net increase in the numbers of men and women employed part time between 1991 and 2002, some recorded a net decrease in the numbers of women and/or men working full time. Birmingham and Leicester saw a net decrease in full-time posts for men and women, while Newcastle and Wakefield experienced a net decrease in women's full-time posts and Sandwell in men's full-time posts. The differences in these changes arise from a range of factors, but a key aspect is the type of jobs gained and lost over the period. In the GELLM areas the greatest net job losses were seen in manufacturing (affecting both men and women), except in Camden – where the greatest net job losses were in transport and communications – and in West Sussex, where the main job losses were in the energy and water sectors. In both cases these were primarily losses in men's full-time jobs. However, there were interesting differences between the areas in the sectors where the greatest net job gains were found, namely:

- banking and finance; and distribution, hotels and restaurants in Birmingham, Camden, Trafford and West Sussex (and England);
- banking and finance; and public administration in Leicester, Newcastle and Southwark;
- distribution, hotels and restaurants; and public administration in East Staffordshire, Somerset, and Wakefield;
- distribution, hotels and restaurants; and construction in Thurrock; and
- transport and communications; and public administration in Sandwell.

In these cases, job growth in banking and finance, construction, and transport and communications tended to be in male full-time jobs, whereas jobs in public administration and in distribution, hotels and restaurants tended to benefit different groups (men and women, full-time and part-time), depending on the locality.

Job losses and gains are not just an issue of numbers in work and/or out of work, however. For example, the loss of jobs in the manufacturing sector may result in many men and women seeking new positions but lacking the skills required to access new local job opportunities, and therefore requiring additional support and retraining. The move towards more part-time employment in a local economy can also be problematic, as part-time jobs tend to be in low-skilled segments of the labour market and typically offer lower wages and reduced progression opportunities (see Chapters Seven and Nine).

## Occupational and industrial segregation

Many studies have highlighted occupational segregation by gender (Hakim, 1979; Walby, 1997; Miller et al, 2004; EOC, 2005b). Table 4.2 presents some labour market indicators for England in 2001, broken down by gender. Despite the increase in girls' attainment at school, more women going into further and higher education, and more women working at higher levels, most women still work in traditionally female occupations and industries (EOC, 2005c). Men too remain clustered in skilled trades, manufacturing and construction, and still dominate the highest-grade jobs (managers and senior officials) in almost all sectors. Although small numbers of men and women do work in non-traditional occupations and industries, such as men in the social care sector (Yeandle et al, 2006c) or women in construction (Dale et al, 2005a), many women working in male-dominated industries work in traditional occupational roles, and sectors such as manufacturing remain very segmented at the sub-sectoral level. Thus two thirds of women who work in the construction industry are employed in administrative, secretarial, personal service, sales and customer service occupations, while 72% of women working in skilled trades are in textiles and printing (2001 SARs, ONS, 2006c).

This clustering by gender in particular occupations and industries is an important factor underpinning the gender pay gap, since jobs traditionally undertaken by women tend to be less well paid than those typically held by men (Anderson et al, 2001). As others have observed, this is detrimental to both individuals and the economy as a whole (Kingsmill, 2001; EOC, 2005c). Occupational and industrial clustering is also linked to clustering in part-time employment, with women and men in some industries and occupations being much more likely to be in part-time employment than in others (see Chapter Seven).

This situation is further compounded by the fact that women are far less likely than men to work at senior levels (discussed further in Chapter Eight). Table 4.2 shows that in 2001 almost 1 in 5 men were managers or senior officials, compared with just 1 in 9 women, although this situation is improving (Burke and Vinnicombe, 2005). Compared with their male counterparts, women employed as managers and senior officials are more likely: to be younger (72% are aged under 45, compared with 63% of male managers and senior officials); to work in smaller companies (42% are employed by firms with less than 25 employees, compared with 34%); to be combining their jobs with unpaid care (12%, compared with 10%) and to live in lone parent families (9%, compared with 2%), or in families with no children (53%, compared with 43%) (2001 SARs, ONS, 2006c).

The differences in men's and women's engagement with the labour market at the national level, including the examples given in Table 4.2, are averages across all local labour markets. As discussed previously, gender and other differences at the local level can vary significantly from these figures.

To illustrate the importance of considering locality when analysing labour markets (shown in Buckner et al, 2004a–i, 2005a, 2005b, 2006), the local occupational distribution of men and women is now explored, using three of the GELLM study areas: Camden, Thurrock and Wakefield. The focus here is

**Table 4.2 National-level labour market indicators: men and women of working age, England, 2001 (%)**

| Labour market indicators | All | Men | Women |
|---|---|---|---|
| Economic activity (% working age) | | | |
| In employment | 69 | 74 | 64 |
| Unemployed | 4 | 5 | 3 |
| Student | 8 | 8 | 9 |
| Retired | 2 | 3 | 1 |
| Looking after home or family | 7 | 1 | 14 |
| Permanently sick or disabled | 5 | 6 | 5 |
| Other | 3 | 3 | 4 |
| Employment status (% working age in employment) | | | |
| Employee full-time | 68 | 78 | 57 |
| Employee part-time | 18 | 5 | 36 |
| Self-employed full-time | 10 | 15 | 4 |
| Self-employed part-time | 3 | 2 | 4 |
| Occupation (% working age in employment) | | | |
| Managers and senior officials | 15 | 19 | 11 |
| Professionals | 11 | 12 | 10 |
| Associate professional and technical occupations | 14 | 14 | 14 |
| Administrative and secretarial occupations | 13 | 5 | 23 |
| Skilled trades | 12 | 19 | 2 |
| Personal service occupations | 7 | 2 | 13 |
| Sales and customer services | 8 | 4 | 12 |
| Process plant and machine operatives | 8 | 13 | 3 |
| Elementary occupations | 12 | 12 | 12 |

**Table 4.2 National-level labour market indicators: men and women of working age, England, 2001 (%) (continued)**

| Labour market indicators | All | Men | Women |
|---|---|---|---|
| Industry (selected industries) (% working age in employment) | | | |
| Manufacture | 15 | 20 | 9 |
| Construction | 7 | 11 | 1 |
| Wholesale and retail | 17 | 16 | 18 |
| Hotels and restaurants | 5 | 4 | 6 |
| Finance and real estate | 18 | 18 | 18 |
| Public administration | 6 | 6 | 6 |
| Education | 8 | 4 | 12 |
| Health and social work | 11 | 4 | 19 |
| Travel to work – distance and method (% working age in employment who travel to work) | | | |
| < 5 km | 46 | 40 | 53 |
| 5–20 km | 39 | 41 | 37 |
| 20+ km | 15 | 19 | 10 |
| Car - Driver | 61 | 65 | 56 |
| Bus, underground, tram | 12 | 9 | 15 |
| On foot | 11 | 8 | 14 |
| Provision of unpaid care | | | |
| People of working age | 12 | 11 | 14 |
| People aged 16 to State Pension Age in employment | 12 | 10 | 14 |

*Source:* 2001 Census Standard and Commissioned Tables, Crown Copyright 2003.

on variations in the degree of occupational segregation by gender. These areas were selected as having a high, low or average proportion of women working in traditionally female occupations (administrative and secretarial, personal service, sales and customer service occupations) (see Appendix B), and because they were distinctive in other ways:

- Camden, an inner London borough, had only 30% of women and 12% of men working in these traditional female occupations. The patterns of occupational distribution among men and women were surprisingly similar, with 69% of men and 63% of women working in higher-level occupations as managers, senior officials, professionals, as associate professionals, or in technical occupations (Buckner et al, 2004e).
- By contrast Thurrock, a small but growing town in the Eastern region, had 58% of women and 13% of men in these traditionally female jobs and just 35% of men and 27% of women in higher occupations (Buckner et al, 2004g).
- Wakefield, a Yorkshire manufacturing town, with 48% of women and 10% of men in these traditionally female jobs, was close to the national profile

(48% of women and 11% of men), although there were relatively few people employed in higher-level occupations (just 35% of men and 28% of women, compared with 45% and 35% respectively in England as a whole) (Buckner et al, 2004d).

In these local areas men and women effectively operate in completely different types of labour market. Camden had very low rates of part-time employment among women residents (21%, compared with 40% in Thurrock, 44% in Wakefield and 40% in England as a whole), but relatively high rates for men (12%, compared with 4% in Thurrock, 6% in Wakefield and 7% in England as a whole) (Buckner et al, 2004d, 2004e, 2004g). Over a third of all residents in employment in Camden worked in the finance, real estate and business sector, compared with just 18% in Thurrock and 12% in Wakefield (18% in England as a whole). In Thurrock and Wakefield, a quarter of residents worked in wholesale, retail, hotels and restaurants, compared with just 16% in Camden (22% in England as a whole).

A further difference is that in Camden 62% of men and 58% of women worked outside the district (compared with 47% and 39% in Thurrock and with 36% and 23% in Wakefield). Thus the majority of working residents in Camden were not actually employed in their local area. In Camden 55% of women and 48% of men travelled to work using public transport (underground, bus and train), compared with 22% and 15% in Thurrock and just 16% and 8% in Wakefield (18% and 13% in England as a whole).

At lower geographical levels even more extreme differences in the occupational distribution of men and women are seen. In Camden's Kentish Town ward, 66% of men and 65% of women were managers, senior officials, professionals, associate professionals or in technical occupations and just 28% of women and 14% of men worked in traditionally female occupations (administrative and secretarial, personal service, sales and customer service occupations). At the other extreme, in Thurrock's Homesteads ward just 35% of men and 25% of women worked in these higher occupations, while 65% of women and 13% of men were in traditionally female occupations.

When developing labour market policy, it is crucial that different local labour market developments, opportunities and histories are taken into account, as well as access to transport and local services. The proximity of the labour market to other towns/cities or concentrations of employment, and the transport links between these, are also crucial factors. For example:

- Camden, which has good public transport links to other parts of London, allows good access to the wider London labour market which offers opportunities at all levels.
- Thurrock, with its good transport links to London is also affected by the structure of local employment opportunity, which includes one of Europe's largest out-of-town shopping complexes, and a huge building programme associated with the Thames Gateway project.

- Wakefield, which has suffered from the decline in mining and manufacturing employment, has good transport links to Leeds, Doncaster and Sheffield, yet the majority of residents work within the district.

## Women and men

In addition to 'spatial smoothing', interpretation of local labour market data is also hampered by 'gender/diversity blindness'. While much of the data collected identifies individuals by sex, gender disaggregated labour market indicators are only rarely used to monitor and compare progress towards targets, and it is even rarer to see data disaggregated by gender and/or other dimensions of diversity such as ethnicity, age or religion. This weakness in labour market analysis is remarkable given the wide range of detailed data available (for example from the Census), demonstrating that economic activity, employment and unemployment all vary very significantly by gender and by ethnicity (Lindley et al, 2004; EOC, 2006; Simpson et al, 2006; Yeandle et al, 2006j; Buckner et al, 2007).

Presenting data that are not disaggregated by gender hides differences in how men and women engage with the labour market. Thus at the national level, women are much more likely than men to look after their home or family full time, and, when in employment, to work part time, to be in administrative, secretarial, personal service, sales and customer service occupations, and in education, health and social work (Table 4.2). They are also more likely to provide unpaid care to a relative or friend who is sick, frail or disabled.

Another key difference between men and women in employment is the hours they work. While this is related to their occupation and industry (see Chapter Seven), it also varies by age, ethnicity and other dimensions of diversity, as well as life stage, family circumstances and locality. Across the GELLM areas there was a large variation in the proportion of men and women who worked part time, from 24% of women in Camden to 46% in East Staffordshire, and from just 6% of men in Thurrock to 13% in Camden. At the other extreme, 16% of women in Camden and 31% of men worked more than 48 hours a week, compared with just 4% of women in Sandwell and 18% of men in Leicester (Buckner et al, 2004a–i, 2005a, 2005b, 2006).

The variation in employment rates among men and women in different family situations is another key issue. Data in the GELLM gender profiles showed that female lone parents were much less likely to be in employment than male lone parents (48% of female lone parents were in employment in England compared with 68% of male lone parents) (Buckner et al, 2004a–i, 2005a, 2005b, 2006). Across the GELLM areas this ranged from 37% of lone mothers in Camden to 57% in Somerset, and 47% of lone fathers in Newcastle to 72% in West Sussex. Areas with relatively low employment rates for all men and women tended also to have low employment rates for lone parents.

Health also has a huge impact on labour market engagement and employment. In the GELLM areas the proportion of people who reported having a limiting long-term illness (LLTI) in 2001 ranged from 13% of women of working age in Southwark to just 8% in West Sussex, and from 18% of men in Newcastle to just 11% in West Sussex. Although areas with high employment rates tended also to have high employment rates for people with a LLTI (thus in West Sussex 47% of working age men with a LLTI and 42% of women were in employment, as were 89% of working age men without a LLTI and 77% of women), at the other end of the spectrum there was some variation. In Camden just 24% of working age men with a LLTI were in employment and in Sandwell just 26% of women. Among those without a LLTI, the lowest employment rates for men were found in Newcastle (72%) and for women in Leicester (62%).

Among people outside the labour market, a high proportion, particularly of men, are permanently sick or disabled. In Newcastle, 60% of economically inactive men (excluding students) and 28% of women were permanently sick or disabled, compared with just 37% of economically inactive men and 15% of women in West Sussex. The corresponding figures for England were 47% and 20% (2001 Census, ONS).

Women are more likely than men to provide unpaid care for a relative or friend who is sick or disabled, even if they are also in paid employment. Buckner and Yeandle (2006) showed that women and men who provide a substantial amount of unpaid care (20 or more hours per week) are much more likely than other employees to work in low-paid, low-skilled occupations, and much less likely to be managers and senior officials. This is despite the proportion of carers in these occupations being similar. Carers are also much more likely to work part time than other people in employment. At the national level, 10% of male carers and 63% of female carers providing 50 or more hours of care per week were working part time, compared with just 6% of men and 45% of women who were not carers (2001 SARs, ONS, 2006c). A high proportion of these people were in fact working less than 16 hours per week (3% of men and 27% of women providing 50 or more hours of care per week, compared with just 1% of men and 13% of women who were not carers). This may partly be explained by the requirement that to be in receipt of the Carer's Allowance carers must not earn more than £95 per week.

These differences highlight the critical need for gender disaggregated data, since not considering this factor disguises major differences between men's and women's employment and undervalues women's skills, experience and qualifications in the labour market (McDowell and Sharp, 1997). This chapter now extends the argument for analysing disaggregated data to include other characteristics that may affect men's and women's labour market engagement, such as age, ethnicity, religion, sexuality and disability. It also argues that the geographical clustering of similar groups of people, such as students, men and women from particular ethnic minority groups, and people who are outside or disconnected from the labour market, is also of critical importance.

## Multiple dimensions of diversity

Examining gender differences in isolation from other aspects of diversity produces a similar effect to the 'spatial smoothing' discussed earlier, as it disguises some of the most important differences in the way different groups of men and women engage with and progress in their local labour market. Economic activity and unemployment vary by gender and ethnicity (Lindley et al, 2004; EOC, 2006; Simpson et al, 2006; Yeandle et al, 2006j; Buckner et al, 2007) with, for example, Pakistani and Bangladeshi women far less likely than men and women in other ethnic groups to be economically active. However, women in these groups are also far more likely to be unemployed if they are economically active than women in other groups, and they also experience greater difficulty in engaging with their local labour market. In 2001, 15% of economically active Pakistani women and 17% of Bangladeshi women were unemployed, compared with just 4% of White British women (2001 Census, ONS).

There is considerable evidence too of occupational segregation among ethnic minority groups in the UK that needs to be set alongside an analysis of occupational and industrial segregation by gender (Lindley et al, 2004; Blackwell and Guinea-Martin, 2005; Simpson et al, 2006). While most of the research on ethnic minority groups and the labour market concentrates on differences at the national level, segregation at finer spatial scales is even more marked (Hanson and Pratt, 1995; Simpson et al, 2006; Yeandle et al, 2006j). For example, in 2001, 95% of all Bangladeshi men in Thurrock worked in the wholesale, retail, hotels and restaurants sector, compared with just 20% of White British men in Thurrock and with 62% of Bangladeshi men nationally. In Newcastle, 61% of Indian women in employment were in higher-level occupations, compared with 35% of White British women in Newcastle and just 17% of Indian women in Leicester (36% in England) (2001 Census, ONS; Buckner et al, 2004c, 2004f, 2004g).

In addition to this occupational and industrial segregation, there are other differences in the way men and women in different ethnic groups engage with the labour market locally (see also Chapter Five). Men and women in some groups are much more likely to work part time, or to be self-employed than White British men and women. Thus in England in 2001 less than half (48%) of Bangladeshi men who were in employment worked as full-time employees (compared with 78% of White British men and 59% of Bangladeshi women), while a third (34%) were part-time employees (compared with just 4% of White British men and 36% of Bangladeshi women). Almost a third (31%) of Chinese men in employment were self-employed (compared with only 18% of White British men and with 19% of Chinese women). Among Black Caribbean women, 73% were full-time employees, compared with only 56% of White British women.

Data for the GELLM areas revealed marked variations in employment status between men and women from different ethnic groups, both within and between areas. For example, in Newcastle, 47% of employed Pakistani women were full-time employees, compared with 76% in Camden (rates for White British women were 59% in Newcastle and 70% in Camden). Among Bangladeshi women in Newcastle, 46% were full-time employees, compared with 73% in Sandwell (and 60% of White British women in Sandwell). In Wakefield, 38% of Indian women were self-employed, compared with just 5% in Leicester (rates for White British women were 5% in both Wakefield and Leicester).

Men and women from particular ethnic minority groups were also more likely to provide unpaid care – even when they were in employment – for a relative or friend who was sick or disabled. Nationally, 16% of Pakistani women and Bangladeshi women of working age provided unpaid care, compared with just 8% of Black African women and 12% of Pakistan and Bangladeshi men. Pakistani and Bangladeshi women were also more likely to provide unpaid care if they were in employment.

## Geographic clustering and targeting resources

Effective policy making designed to support the functioning of local labour markets needs not only to target resources and monitor the impact of labour market policies, taking local labour market conditions into account, but also to consider the detailed characteristics of the local population. For example, some areas have high student populations (and consequently high economic inactivity rates), while others have high concentrations of men and women from a particular ethnic minority group, who may face specific difficulties in accessing labour market opportunities (EOC, 2007). Different areas may need different interventions based on the characteristics of their local populations (Escott and Buckner, 2006; Grant and Buckner, 2006; Yeandle et al, 2006j).

Taking high rates of unemployment among particular groups of women as an example, the kinds of policies or interventions needed and how and where they need to be implemented to tackle specific labour market problems and achieve maximum impact are now considered. In Chapter Three the common misconception that some whole groups of women do not want to work, for example women with young children or women in some ethnic minority groups, was discussed. As seen there, analysis of Annual Population Survey (ONS, 2006a) data showed, however, that 1.5 million women in England were either unemployed, or economically inactive but wanted to work (Grant and Buckner, 2006). This showed that 10% of all women of working age were not in paid employment but would like to be. However, these women outside the labour market are not evenly distributed across all local labour markets, but tend to be clustered geographically, often living in areas that have high concentrations of ethnic minority populations, or in areas of socio-economic deprivation (or both).

At the national level, the unemployment rate for women varies very considerably by ethnicity. In 2001, the unemployment rate for economically active White British women of working age was 4%, compared with 15% for Pakistani women and 17% for Bangladeshi women. These figures are quite separate from the data on economic inactivity discussed in Chapter Five. Analysis of Annual

Population Survey data (ONS, 2006a) shows that in England, a total of 37,000 Pakistani women were either unemployed or economically inactive but wanted to work, representing 15% of all Pakistani women of working age, while the corresponding figures for Bangladeshi women were 12,000 (13%) but only 9% for White British women.

Since the populations of Pakistani and Bangladeshi women are quite small, just 1.4% and 0.5% of all women of working age, a policy initiative to reduce the unemployment rates of Pakistani and Bangladeshi women to the level seen among White British women at the national level would need to place only 5,400 Pakistani women and 2,100 Bangladeshi women in jobs. A policy designed to achieve this would need to be carefully targeted geographically, however, because of the concentration of these groups in areas of high deprivation (Simpson et al, 2006; Buckner et al, 2007). In 2001, among those of working age, 75% of all Bangladeshi women in England, and 71% of all Pakistani women, lived in just 47 of the 86 Neighbourhood Renewal Areas (compared with 22% of White British women of working age) (Buckner et al, 2007). Furthermore, 76% of all unemployed Bangladeshi and 74% of all unemployed Pakistani women also lived in these 47 areas. Additional examination of local-level data shows that in 2001, 50% of all Bangladeshi women aged 16–74 lived in just six local authority districts (Tower Hamlets, Newham, Birmingham, Camden, Oldham and Luton) and that 30% of all Bangladeshi women aged 16–74 lived in just 20 wards (including 13 wards in the London Borough of Tower Hamlets and four in Birmingham).

Clearly, these high unemployment rates, of 15% or 17%, give cause for concern and suggest the need for much more effective targeting of support for Pakistani and Bangladeshi women in accessing employment. As shown elsewhere (Escott and Buckner, 2006; Grant and Buckner, 2006), and as highlighted in Chapters Two, Three and Six, there is scant evidence that, beyond a few small-scale voluntary sector projects, regeneration programmes in the most deprived areas of the country, where many of these women live, have identified them as a group in need of tailored support, or found ways of providing the advice, guidance and training they need. Yet to address the disadvantage experienced by these groups of women, policy makers need to target efforts on these districts/wards through education and training policies directed at unemployed women, through economic and regeneration policy directed at improving business investment and job creation in poorly functioning local economies, or through culturally sensitive childcare, or other means.

Not all men and women from a particular ethnic group are in a similar economic situation, as Chapter Five shows. Local data by ethnicity show that even in areas with unemployment rates close to the national average, the unemployment rates for some ethnic groups may be very different (Buckner et al, 2007). When viewed by local authority, a geographical level more appropriate for local labour market analysis and policy making, unemployment rates range from 29% to just 6% for Bangladeshi women and 25% to 4% for Pakistani women (compared with 8% to 2% for White British women). It is not appropriate to see these variations in economic activity and unemployment rates as reflecting a simple 'north–south' divide, however, as the 'highs' and 'lows' in district-level economic activity and unemployment rates do not appear in the same places (Buckner et al, 2007). Thus even in some localities where the employment rates of White British women were the same, the rates for women in other ethnic groups were highly variable, showing that although important, the structure and range of local employment opportunities did not fully explain the variations found. The different employment patterns seen among women of different ethnicity cannot be explained as simply an outcome of poor or limited job opportunities in the areas where they live if they apply to only one, or only to some, ethnic minority groups.

In the GELLM study examining women's poverty and economic disadvantage in the Byker, Monkchester and Walker wards of Newcastle (Escott et al, 2006c), clustering of women in a similar economic position, in part due to the type of housing in the area, was found. These three wards had relatively stable populations, a similar mix of ages to the rest of Newcastle, and only 4% of women of working age from ethnic minority groups (compared with 10% in Newcastle) (2001 Census, ONS). However, almost half of all dependent children in these wards lived in families with no working adult, a high proportion of women in the area were in receipt of Income Support, and two thirds of local residents rented from the council. These data revealed that although the unemployment rate for women in the area was not dissimilar to that for Newcastle as a whole, in these wards a high proportion of women were economically inactive. Among them, almost a quarter were permanently sick or disabled.

Women within the area were also far less likely to be qualified, with particularly high rates of young women with no qualifications. Even when they were qualified they were less likely to be in employment. In these wards over a quarter of employed women worked in elementary or low-skilled occupations. The study found that the shift towards more service sector employment in the city had resulted in many low-paid and poor-quality jobs, and that although there had been significant public and private investment in the area, many women in these communities continued to experience economic disadvantage. Local organisations, as well as women living in the area, felt local residents were not benefiting from employment opportunities, including higher-skilled and better-paid employment opportunities available in Newcastle (Escott et al, 2006c). Detailed analysis suggested that the policy priorities needed to be interventions relating to health, housing, education and training, coupled with a focus on transport, support with caring roles, and confidence building. This would enable women living in these wards to access the wider range of jobs that are within relatively easy reach in Newcastle.

## Infrastructure

As well as considering local employment indicators when developing, implementing, monitoring and assessing labour market policies, it is also important to consider broader local labour market conditions, such as the availability and quality of public transport, and local provision of affordable, appropriate childcare. As a high proportion of both women and men work within five kilometres of where they live (Buckner et al, 2004a), local data are critical in revealing the drivers of men's and women's labour market engagement (or lack of it), such as access to public transport, the availability of affordable, appropriate childcare, and the extent to which the jobs on offer locally provide opportunities for flexible working and a living wage. As seen in Chapter Two, these factors are extremely important in enabling people, especially women, to escape the 'benefits trap' and move from welfare to work (Escott and Buckner, 2006; Grant and Buckner, 2006). Although some of these factors will be common across many different local areas, with the need for affordable childcare perhaps the most important example, others (such as transport systems and the gap between the cost of housing and pay) will be very area specific. These topics are discussed in further detail in Chapter Six.

A key issue for parents, particularly those with young children and who are trying to access employment or who are already in work, is the local availability of affordable childcare. The type of care needed, and how it fits with the working lives of parents, will vary considerably according to local patterns of family and household structure, household income and occupational opportunity. With the launch of the National Childcare Strategy in 1998 and the introduction of free nursery places for children aged 3 and 4, much has been done in recent years to increase local provision. However, these free places are only available in term time, and very few jobs offer term-time-only contracts (Buckner et al, 2004a–i, 2005a, 2005b, 2006). At the time of the GELLM research programme there was much variation in the provision of childcare places across the GELLM areas, ranging from 236 places per 1,000 children in Wakefield to 743 in Trafford. There was also considerable variation in the type of childcare on offer, with out-of-school provision ranging from 43 places per 1,000 pupils in Wakefield to 327 in Southwark.

A further significant difference between men and women in the labour market is in how they get to work and the distance they travel. Women who travel to work are much more likely than men to work near to where they live (over half live within five kilometres of their place of work), although men are more likely to work at or from home (10%, compared with 8%) (see Table 4.2). Across the GELLM areas this ranged from 43% of women living within five kilometres of their place of work in Thurrock to 78% in Leicester, and for men from 28% in Thurrock to 64% in Leicester. These differences were even greater for men and women who lived in households with children. Nationally, 56% of women aged 30–44 who live in households with children worked less than five kilometres from where they lived (41% of women in households without children), compared with only 35% of men (and 33% of men in households without children) (2001 SAR, ONS, 2006c).

Women are also far less likely to drive to work and are more likely to travel by public transport (train, metro, tram or bus), or to walk. For the GELLM areas, the highest rates of public transport use were seen in Camden (54% of men and 60% of women) and Southwark (53% of men and 62% of women). In the GELLM areas outside London, 22% of men and 33% of women in Newcastle travelled to work by public transport, compared with just 2% of men and 4% of women in Somerset. The driving to work figures ranged from 74% of men in East Staffordshire and 65% of women in Somerset to 20% of men and 13% of women in Camden. These differences between the way men and women travel to work and the distances they travel inevitably affect the types of occupations and industries in which they work, and need to be considered when employment initiatives are developed and implemented locally.

## Conclusion

This chapter has sought to highlight the importance of considering gender and other dimensions of diversity, as well as locality, when developing, monitoring and analysing employment policies. A direct consequence of this is the significance of the availability of accurate, timely disaggregated data at the local level. At present, gender disaggregated labour market indicators are available at a local level through sources such as the Annual Population Survey. However, these are rarely available by gender and other aspects of diversity such as age, ethnicity, religion, sexuality and disability (Brook, 2004). Although data from the Census can be used to cover some of these dimensions, output is only available every ten years and other sources therefore need to be developed to cover the inter-censal periods. These data are essential if flexible and effective labour market policies are to be developed that are capable of promoting greater fairness in the operation of the labour market in a range of different localities.

It is important to note that analysing labour market indicators at the local level shows that not all labour markets work equally well for all people. For example, a high proportion of men and women in Camden work in higher-level occupations, yet this is not true for the Bangladeshi men and women who live there (Buckner et al, 2004e). Also, data presented here and in Chapter Five show that not all men and women in a particular ethnic group are disadvantaged.

Using local data to analyse labour market engagement also shows the geographical clustering of people from some ethnic groups and of men and women in particular economic situations. This highlights the need for local data to enable local policy makers to target effort and resources more effectively. However, it is not just a case of creating local jobs that often cannot be accessed by local people, as seen above (and in the GELLM study in Newcastle (Escott et al, 2006c)). Areas where employment rates are low also tend to be areas where a high proportion of residents are in poor health, are providing unpaid care and/or have no qualifications. Thus a more holistic approach is required, which encompasses not just job creation, but also the provision of good quality local employment that can be accessed by local people. The approach should include tailored support to increase the confidence and skills of disadvantaged local residents, and policies to ensure local childcare and good public transport are readily available and of high quality.

# FIVE

# Discrimination and disadvantage in local labour markets: issues affecting Black and minority ethnic women

*Sue Yeandle and Lisa Buckner*

## Introduction

This chapter considers the labour market situation and labour force participation of ethnic minority women, focusing on three topics: the local labour market situation, in two locations, of Indian women, numerically one of the most important minorities in the English labour market; the position of two much smaller ethnic minority groups (Pakistani and Bangladeshi women), again in two specific local labour markets; and the relationship between changing levels of qualification, different family circumstances and labour market participation among Black Caribbean women.

The evidence presented is drawn from several sources: statistical analysis of the local labour market situation of ethnic minority women in 12 localities (Buckner et al, 2004a–i, 2005a, 2005b, 2006), the GELLM study of ethnic minority women and the labour market in five local authorities (Stiell and Tang, 2006a–e; Yeandle et al, 2006j) and an examination of local authority district-level data, focusing on the geographical distribution of unemployment and economic inactivity among women of different ethnicities (Buckner et al, 2007). The research involved extensive statistical analysis, explored local understandings of key issues using documentary sources, and drew on new qualitative research in the selected localities, using innovative methodologies (Stiell et al, 2006). It was developed as a contribution to the literature on ethnic minority women and to inform public policy at the national and local levels.

The labour market disadvantage experienced by some ethnic minority groups is well established (Daniel, 1968; Smith, 1974; Brown, 1984; Modood et al, 1997; Robson and Berthoud, 2003; Berthoud and Blekesaune, 2007), with some writers emphasising the multiple disadvantages experienced by ethnic minority women (Noon and Hoque, 2001; Bradley et al, 2002; Hall et al, 2004). These studies have identified a range of factors that may restrict labour force participation among ethnic minority women: domestic responsibilities and childcare, limited knowledge of English, lack of formal qualifications, family or community pressures against working outside the home, racial discrimination in the labour market and the geographical location of jobs (Brah and Shaw, 1992).

Qualifications have sometimes been highlighted as particularly important, as ethnic minority women have historically had poorer access to these. Some studies have found that some ethnic minority women need better qualifications than White job applicants to stand a similar chance of success, noting that having both qualifications and English language fluency is strongly related to whether a woman was educated in the UK (Dale et al, 2002; Shields and Wheatley Price, 2002, 2003; Hall et al, 2004). Frequently, cultural factors are invoked in explaining the labour market situation of Pakistani and Bangladeshi women, some researchers finding that the decision to seek employment has to be justified to other family members (Thewlis et al, 2004). However, there is also evidence of change across generations, with well-qualified ethnic minority women demonstrating confidence, determination and motivation in relation to paid employment (Dale et al, 2002). Other writers have drawn attention to factors such as low awareness of job opportunities, difficulties with travel and financial problems (Hall et al, 2004), and have shown that many ethnic minority women work in insecure or precarious employment (Reid, 2002).

Analysis of the demographic and family situation of ethnic minority women has mostly been undertaken at national level. This has shown that Black women are more likely, at each stage of family formation, to be in full-time employment, while White women and Indian women are more likely to be in part-time work. It has also revealed that young Pakistani and Bangladeshi women with a partner are less likely to be economically active than those without, and that economic activity is lowest among young Pakistani and Bangladeshi women with both a partner and children (Holdsworth and Dale, 1997; Dale et al, 2002; Lindley et al, 2004). However, few studies have analysed the complex interplay between the structural, contextual and attitudinal factors in women's lives and the opportunities and conditions in the local labour markets where they live. This has made it hard to know how much variation there is between women of the same ethnicity in different places, or how policy should respond to the inequity and disadvantage observed.

Evidence-based policy guidance is particularly challenging in this field because of the uneven geographical distribution of different groups within the ethnic minority population. Thus even in the 12 GELLM localities, the percentage of the population from non-White ethnic minority groups varied from barely 1% (Somerset) to over a third (Leicester). Among women aged 25–59,[1] both the numerical size and the percentage share of specific population groups varied enormously. Indian women represented 5% or more of women aged 25–59 only in Birmingham, Leicester and Sandwell; Black Caribbean women 5% or more only in Birmingham, Sandwell and Southwark; Pakistani women 5% or more only in Birmingham; and Black African women 5% or more only in Camden and Southwark.

—

Thus, many local labour markets were drawing on an overwhelmingly White supply of local female labour. Among women aged 25–59, White British women represented 90% or more of local residents in six of the GELLM localities, and over 78% in two others. Only in the two London boroughs, with their access to the wider London labour market (and its distinctive features in relation to female employment, described in Chapters Four and Seven) did the White British share of the female population aged 25–59 fall below 51%. However, there were two major cities in the GELLM study – Birmingham and Leicester – where White British women represented only 68% and 59% of the age group respectively. These cities had particularly diverse female populations, and it is here that we focus some of our detailed analysis in this chapter.

## Indian women in Birmingham and Leicester

In 2001, there were almost 14,000 Indian women aged 25–59 in Birmingham (as well as about 19,000 Pakistani women and 13,000 Black Caribbean women). Leicester's 18,000 Indian women aged 25–59 represented 28% of women in this age group, and were by far the largest minority.[2] The two cities both had similar local labour market patterns and structures. Between 1991 and 2002 both experienced a net loss of full-time jobs (losing just over 1% of female full-time jobs and around 7% of male full-time jobs in both cities) and marked increases in part-time employment (plus 13% female part-time employment in Leicester and plus 24% in Birmingham, with the number of male part-time jobs more than doubling in both cities). These changes represented a net gain of almost 5,000 jobs in Leicester and of about 20,000 jobs in Birmingham. Under equality legislation (see Chapter Two), these additional jobs were theoretically available to both men and women and to people of any ethnicity; however, there was marked clustering in industries and occupations (see also Chapter Four), associated with both gender and ethnicity.

In both cities Indian women had full-time employment rates only a little lower than those of White women (35% for Indian women, and 39% for White British women). The disparity was a little greater for part-time employment, but again figures were almost identical in the two cities (17% among Indian women and 25% among White British women in both). Unemployment rates were also similar in both Leicester and Birmingham (close to 5% for Indian women; 3% for White British women), as were the percentages of women looking after their home and family full time (Indian women 21% in Leicester and 18% in Birmingham; White British women 15% in both cities), or economically inactive because of permanent sickness or disability (Indian women 9% in Leicester, 8% in Birmingham; White British women 7% in both cities). These data on economic activity thus suggest that women in these two ethnic groups encountered a broadly comparable structure of labour market opportunity in both places.

Yet examination of the occupations in which Indian and White British women worked in the two cities reveals some notable differences. In both places, about a third of White British women worked in higher-level jobs (30% in Leicester and 33% in Birmingham); 46% in both cities were in middle-ranking jobs and only 23% in Leicester and 17% in Birmingham were in lower-level jobs. The situation for Indian women was different. Only 17% of Indian women in Leicester were in higher-level jobs, compared with 31% in Birmingham, and while the percentages in middle-ranking jobs were similar (41% in Leicester, 44% in Birmingham), far more Indian women in Leicester than in Birmingham were in lower-level occupations: 41%, compared with only 25% in Birmingham.

Can these differences be explained by differences in the industrial structure of employment in the two cities? Recent trends in the sectoral distribution of employment in Birmingham and Leicester (Buckner et al, 2004f, 2005a) give only a small clue to this puzzle. In 1991 90% of female employment in Birmingham was in four sectors: public administration, education and health (39%); distribution, hotels and restaurants (19%); banking, finance and insurance (19%); and manufacturing (14%). The pattern in Leicester was broadly similar: public administration, education and health 37%; distribution, hotels and restaurants 18%; and banking, finance and insurance 13%. However, in 1991 Leicester's manufacturing sector accounted for 22% of all female jobs.

By 2002 the loss of 14,000 manufacturing jobs in Leicester (7,500 of these were female jobs) and 37,000 in Birmingham (women losing 10,000 jobs) had reduced these shares, from 22% to 12% in Leicester and from 13% to 8% in Birmingham (Buckner et al, 2004f, p 26; Buckner et al, 2005a, p 26). In Leicester this pushed the share of all female jobs in the public administration, education and health sector up to 43%, with small increases in the share of jobs in banking, finance and insurance and in distribution, hotels and restaurants as well. In Birmingham, where the scale of female job losses in manufacturing was not so great, there was a small increase in the share of female jobs in banking, finance and insurance and in distribution, hotels and restaurants, while the share of jobs in public administration, education and health was relatively stable (falling to 38% in 2002 from 39% in 1991).

The more disadvantaged situation of employed Indian women in Leicester may in part be attributable to the size and pace of the decline of women's employment in manufacturing, a major point of difference between the two cities. However, manufacturing comprises a range of sub-sectors in which the structure of jobs is different. Historically, Birmingham's manufacturing sector has been dominated by engineering jobs: metal fabrication, motor vehicle and parts manufacture and mechanical and electrical engineering (Birmingham City Council, 2006). By contrast, only very few manufacturing jobs in Birmingham (2%) have been in textiles, clothing and leather manufacture – the sub-sector that has been such an important feature of the Leicester economy, both historically and in the recent past (Felstead et al, 2002). This segment of the labour market, traditionally important for women's employment (Bradley, 1989; Wigfield, 2001), has had fewer jobs designated as 'skilled' than engineering, which has always been dominated by male employment and has had a different history of unionisation and collective bargaining (Walby, 1986, 1988).

Thus, comparing employment in the manufacturing sector in the two cities is not really comparing like with like. Employees in manufacturing in Leicester, especially women, work mainly in the textile and related industries, while employees in manufacturing in Birmingham work in a wider range of sub-sectors, dominated by engineering (Birmingham City Council, 2006). Another difference between Birmingham and Leicester may be the occupational level of manufacturing jobs, with Birmingham having fewer lower-level jobs than Leicester.

However, examination of the evidence suggests this is not the case. Most employment in Leicester's manufacturing sector in 2001 was in lower-level jobs. Almost two thirds (63%) of jobs held by White British women were low-graded positions, compared with 49% held by White British men, 69% held by Indian men and 85% held by Indian women. Meanwhile, 17% of White British women and 19% of White British men were in higher-level jobs; for Indian men the percentage was 13%, yet among Indian women it was only 3%. In Birmingham's manufacturing sector, Indian women were similarly concentrated at the lower level (83%, compared with 47% of White British women, 69% of Indian men and 49% of White British men, held low-graded jobs). While more men and White women in manufacturing held higher-level jobs in Birmingham (24% of White British men, 20% of White British women and 22% of Indian men), here, too, only 3% of Indian women were in these grades (2001 Census CAM, ONS, 2006d). Thus while the percentages of jobs in low-graded positions were almost identical (and high) for Indian women in the two cities (as for Indian men and for White British men), there were notable differences between the cities at the top end of the jobs spectrum. In manufacturing, a much higher proportion of White and Indian men, and of White women, occupied the highest-graded jobs in Birmingham than in Leicester (especially among men); but in both cities only a tiny minority of Indian women working in the sector had managed to secure jobs at this better-rewarded level.

Thus Indian women, in both cities, experience clustering in the manufacturing sector, and disadvantage in terms of job level within it. Although requiring explanation in both cities, from the point of view of either employment or equality policy, this is particularly important in Leicester where, despite forming only 25% of all women of working age, Indian women represented 48% of all women employed in manufacturing. By contrast, in Birmingham, only 6% of women of working age were Indian, and just 12% of them worked in manufacturing. In Leicester, Indian women accounted for 55% of all women working as process, plant and machine operatives in the manufacturing sector (compared with 18% in Birmingham), placing many Indian women in Leicester in a precarious labour market situation, as the textile sector faced particularly intense global competitive pressures and continuing job losses (2001 Census Standard and Commissioned output, ONS).

These patterns and structures in the local labour market have clear consequences for women, with Indian women losing out in terms of labour market status and rewards. However, there are also other factors to consider if a fuller understanding of women's participation in the labour market and its impact on their lives is to be achieved. The disadvantaged position of Indian women in Leicester compared with those in Birmingham, primarily attributable to the nature of its local labour market, may in part be explained by differences in personal and family circumstances and backgrounds.

As noted in Chapter Three, skills and qualifications are important predictors of status and progress in the labour market, so differences between the two groups of women in the two cities in terms of qualifications are relevant considerations. Indian women in Leicester were indeed less well qualified than White women: in 2001, 35% of Indian women had no formal qualifications (compared with 22% of Indian women in Birmingham, 25% of White British women in Leicester, and 19% of White British women in Birmingham (ONS, 2006e)). In addition, many Indian women in Leicester had been born outside the UK (69%, compared with 54% in Birmingham and – unsurprisingly – less than 2% of White British women in either city). In both cities, over 93% of Indian women of working age who lacked any formal qualifications had been born outside the UK, and, of all Indian women of working age born outside the UK, 47% of those living in Leicester, compared with only 37% of those living in Birmingham, had no qualifications.

There are also some notable features relating to family and household circumstances. In Leicester, 55% of Indian households[3] contained dependent children (compared with only 26% of White British households) and of these 12% were extended families (compared with just 4% of White British households). Furthermore, within the city Indian women and their families (like most other minorities) were highly concentrated in certain wards, two of which (Stoneygate and Spital Hills) were studied in the GELLM research programme (Stiell and Tang, 2006c). Over a quarter (28%) of all Indian women in Leicester lived in these two wards (compared with less than 5% of White British women), and within them 57% and 60% of Indian households contained dependent children, including 14% and 13% that were extended families (Stiell and Tang, 2006c, p 23, Figure A4). While the Indian female population in Leicester did not contain a large number of dependent children (25% of Leicester's Indian female population were aged 0–15, compared with 47% in England), this figure too was considerably higher than for the city's White British female population (18%); and as there were also fewer women over state pension age in Leicester's Indian population (11% compared with 24% for White British women), it is not surprising that a higher percentage (49%, compared with 43% of White British women) fell within the 25–59 age group.

The 2001 Census also revealed that in Leicester 16% of Indian women of working age were carers (providing unpaid care for a relative or friend needing help because of illness, disability or frailty associated with old age), and that this compared with a lower figure (13%) among White British women. Among

Indian women in this age group, 7% provided 20 or more hours of care each week, compared with 4% of White British women. In Birmingham, although White British women (15%, with 2% caring for more than 20 hours per week) were more likely than those in Leicester to be carers, among Indian women the opposite was true (15%, with 5% caring for more than 20 hours per week). It is likely, too, that working parents with dependent children living in Leicester had more difficulty finding a day care place than those living in Birmingham, as in 2002 Birmingham provided 201 full day care places per 1,000 children, compared with only 70 in Leicester (Buckner et al, 2004h, 2005a)).

Like Indian women in England as a whole, Leicester's Indian population contained women of different faiths (in England, 45% were Hindu, 29% Sikh and 13% Muslim; in Leicester 55% were Hindu, 15% Sikh and 25% Muslim).[4] However, the religious composition of the Indian women living in the Stoneygate and Spital Hills wards was rather different: fewer were Hindu (41% and 25% respectively); 19% and 6% respectively were Sikh; while many more were of Muslim faith (36% and 66% respectively). At the national level, Muslim women in almost all ethnic groups have lower employment rates and higher unemployment rates than non-Muslim women (ONS, 2006e).

Although a large minority of Indian women in Leicester were born in the UK (42%, compared with 44–45% both in England and in the Stoneygate and Spital Hills wards), a further group (22% in the city, 21% and 18% in the two wards, 16% in England) were born in Africa, while most of the rest originated in India (34% in Leicester, 32% and 37% in the two wards, and 36% in England). Leicester also had a particularly mobile population (in part related to its two universities). The 2001 Census showed that while in England as a whole 12% of all people had moved during the year, this was true for 15% of people in Leicester and for 18% and 13% respectively in the Stoneygate and Spital Hills wards.[5] And, although in England 86% of these migrants moved within their local area, this was true of only 54% in Leicester (and of just 16% and 27% in the two wards).

This evidence about qualifications, households, religion, birthplace and migration indicates some of the distinctiveness of the Indian female population in Leicester. Key factors in 2001 were that Indian women of working age in Leicester, when compared with White women in the city and (on some variables) with Indian women in Birmingham, were 'clustered' in especially disadvantaged ways: in terms of their occupations, the industries in which they worked and the wards in which they lived. They were also more likely to have been born abroad, to be of the Muslim faith, to be carers and to live in households containing dependent children (at a time when the city had lower levels of childcare than were available in Birmingham).

Thus Indian women in Leicester faced particular challenges in accessing and engaging with the labour market; policies to support them in achieving fair access to labour market opportunities therefore needed to take account of these differences, but rarely did so. In the context of the kinds of job opportunities available in the city, this complex interplay of factors made it particularly difficult for Indian women in Leicester to secure their fair share of the better-paid or more secure jobs available locally. Their own perspectives, crucial to a rounded understanding of how these different factors play out, highlighted some of the policy responses required. The GELLM study of ethnic minority women (Yeandle et al, 2006j; see also Appendix A), which included group work with a small number of Indian women in Leicester, showed that:

- Some had English language difficulties, which they felt limited them to manual work, usually in Asian-run businesses; these were hard to overcome when access to suitable training (including language training) was so limited.
- Support was available from voluntary sector groups for some women, helping them to access employment opportunities, but in practice this often meant access to low-level jobs in the precarious hosiery and textile sectors.
- Experience of racism, discrimination and harassment was common; many participants felt unsafe on the street and vulnerable to unfair treatment in employment and when accessing services.
- Although many very much wanted to improve their skills, requalify or gain recognition of qualifications obtained abroad, their difficulties and frustrations in achieving this had sapped the confidence of some and limited the aspirations of others (Stiell and Tang, 2006c, pp 13–14).

Together, this research evidence suggests the need for carefully targeted support for this group of women, and indicates the importance of detailed local level analysis of the factors that hold back the attainment of particular groups of women. Two other groups of women of Asian origin, again considering those living in Leicester, but in this case comparing them with their counterparts in Newcastle, the largest city in England's North East region, are now discussed.

## Pakistani and Bangladeshi women in their local labour markets

As we saw in Chapter Four, although the numbers of women in these two groups are quite small (in 2001 there were just 207,000 Pakistani women and fewer than 79,000 Bangladeshi women of working age living in England), both are groups that experience disadvantage in the labour market. As shown below (and elsewhere in this book), their disadvantage seems to be at least partly the result of discrimination, and their low employment rates do not merely reflect their own preferences.

Using the 2001 Census, and drawing on relevant GELLM publications (Buckner et al, 2004a, 2004c, 2004f, 2005b; Stiell and Tang, 2006a, 2006c, 2006d, 2006e; Yeandle et al, 2006j), their labour market situation in two localities, chosen because Bangladeshi and Pakistani women were resident in numbers large enough to permit statistical analysis, are discussed. In each case their position in the labour market is compared with that of White British women in the same place. Bangladeshi women in two London boroughs, Camden and Southwark, and Pakistani women in two major cities, Leicester and Newcastle, were chosen. Because of the small size of these two ethnic minority groups, detailed data about their participation in their local labour markets, relating to their age, sex, economic activity and occupational and industrial distribution, is only available from the Census. We saw in Chapter Four that this source has not often been interrogated with regard to comparison of the situation of women in specific localities. Here this is addressed, comparing the circumstances of both younger and mature women, and considering how far the labour force participation of these two groups of women is affected by their place of residence and ethnicity.

Camden and Southwark both have access to the comprehensive public transport system linking different parts of London, and to the capital's large and complex labour market. Although very different places, as shown in the GELLM gender profiles, in 2001 each of these boroughs was home to a substantial number of Bangladeshi residents, among whom about 3,660 in Camden and some 1,072 in Southwark were women aged 16–59.

Leicester and Newcastle are 'university towns', each with two large universities providing a major source of employment, as well as opportunities for higher education. Both cities have struggled in recent decades with the consequences of economic restructuring. Newcastle has responded to major job losses in shipbuilding and heavy engineering in the later 20th century; Leicester, as seen above, is only now emerging from its reliance on textile and clothing manufacturing, where employment has declined sharply in recent decades. Both cities saw significant job growth in the 1990s in other sectors, however – most notably in part-time employment – and by 2001 each had a small population originating from Pakistan, in each case comprising about 1,400 female residents aged 16–59.

Thus in all four locations, the women considered here were part of very small minorities. In Leicester, as seen earlier, there is also a large Indian population, and while most residents are White, in some parts of the city the Indian population forms the majority of local residents. Newcastle has far fewer non-White residents, and several other small minorities; here in 2001 the Pakistani community represented only about 2% of the population. In Camden, minorities represent about half of all residents, and about a third of the population is non-White; the Bangladeshi community represents about 5% of all people living in the borough. In Southwark, where in 2001 again about half the population was from ethnic minority groups, the Bangladeshi community formed only a very small part of this, as most ethnic minority residents in the borough were from the Black African and Black Caribbean groups.

## Pakistani women in Leicester and Newcastle

In 2001, just over half (54% in both cases) of all young Pakistani women in Leicester and Newcastle (those aged 16–24) were in full-time education at school, college or university. This compared with 46% of White British young women in Leicester and 57% in Newcastle, so on this measure access to study (and the achievement of educational qualifications) seems not to be a particular problem for young Pakistani women. Even at this young age, however, more than 1 in 8 of young Pakistani women (13% in Newcastle and 14% in Leicester) were looking after their home and family full time (compared with just 6% of young White British women in Newcastle and 10% in Leicester). They were also considerably less likely than young White British women to have a paid job; about 1 in 3 White British young women in the two cities had paid employment, compared with only about 1 in 5 of young Pakistani women in both places.

Among the mature female working age population (women aged 25–59), only about 3% of Pakistani women were students in either city (close to the figures for White British women), and a large minority (43% in Newcastle, 38% in Leicester) looked after home and family full time – a very much higher percentage than found among White British women in either city (14%–15%). Consequently, far fewer Pakistani than White British women were in paid work; in Leicester just 33%, among whom only 18% worked full time, and in Newcastle only 29%, among whom just 12% worked full time. Similar proportions of women in both ethnic groups and in both cities were permanently sick or disabled (though in both cities the figure for White British women was slightly higher than for Pakistani women). However, among those economically active in this age group, 11% of Pakistani women in Newcastle (compared with just 4% of White British women) and 11% of Pakistani women in Leicester (compared with 5% of White British women) were unemployed. These figures indicate that there is a significant problem for Pakistani women in both cities in accessing paid employment.

Among those Pakistani women who were in paid work (and remembering that these women were the minority in their ethnic group), we find both similarities and differences in occupational and industrial distribution. In Leicester, 27% of Pakistani women and 30% of White British were in higher-graded jobs; while 31% of Pakistani women, but only 23% of White British women, were in the lowest-graded jobs. There were similar proportions of women in both personal service and sales and customer service among both groups of women. Pakistani women in Leicester were somewhat clustered in the manufacturing sector (where 26% worked, compared with 12% of White British women) and rather under-represented in public sector jobs (30% compared with 40%). Similar proportions of women of both ethnicities worked in the wholesale, retail, restaurants and hotels sector (23% compared with 25%). In Newcastle, Pakistani women were also under-represented in public sector jobs (37% compared with 44%), but here they were clustered in the wholesale, retail, restaurants and hotels sector (33% compared with 24%), and very few women of either ethnicity worked in the manufacturing sector (5% in both cases). Pakistani women were, though, over-represented in sales and customer service work (24% compared with 14%).

Among Pakistani women in Newcastle, 42% held higher-graded jobs (compared with 35% of White British women), but White British women were far more concentrated in the city's administrative and secretarial jobs than Pakistani women (21% compared with 13%). Here it is important to note the numerical differences between these groups of women; in Newcastle, the 42% of employed Pakistani women occupying higher-graded jobs were only about 175 in number, compared with over 15,000 White British women in this type of work in the city.

Comparison of the circumstances of Pakistani and White British women in these two cities thus shows that while young Pakistani women had reasonably equitable access to education, even at this age they were much more likely than White British women to be working unpaid within the family. This situation intensified among older women, with Pakistani women much more likely than White British women to have full-time family roles. In both cities, however, we found much higher rates of unemployment among economically active Pakistani women, indicating that some wish to enter paid work but cannot do so. Among those in paid work, Pakistani women were under-represented in public sector jobs in both cities, while in Leicester they were over-represented in manufacturing jobs and in Newcastle in the wholesale, retail, restaurants and hotels sector.

## Bangladeshi women in Camden and Southwark

In the two London boroughs where Bangladeshi women and White British women were compared, differences between the two groups of women are considerably more marked. Again, the proportions of young women in full-time education were similar – 45% for Bangladeshi women aged 16–24 in both boroughs, compared with 49% in Camden and 41% in Southwark for young White British women. However, in this age group, Bangladeshi women in both boroughs were only half as likely as White British young women to have paid jobs (20% in both cases for Bangladeshi women, compared with over 40% in both cases for White British women), and among young Bangladeshi women, about 1 in 5 in both locations was looking after home and family full time, compared with just 7% in Southwark and only 3% in Camden among young White British women.

Among mature women of working age, these differences intensify. In both boroughs, well over half of all Bangladeshi women aged 25–59 looked after their home and family full time (56% in Camden and 52% in Southwark), compared with just 10% and 14% among White British women. Again, similar percentages of women in this age group were permanently sick in both ethnic groups and in both boroughs (between 5% and 8%), and very few (under 3%) were students. Most notably, however, although the employment rates of White British women in both boroughs were very high by national standards (72% in Camden and 68% in Southwark), suggesting that London offers adequate employment opportunities for this group of women in both localities, Bangladeshi women clearly either could not access the same opportunities or did not choose to do so, as their employment rates were very low: 12% in Camden and 17% in Southwark. Unemployment among economically active Bangladeshi women in Camden was extremely high

(18% compared with 9% in Southwark and with 5% for White British women in both boroughs).

Stark differences emerge too when those who are in employment are compared. In Camden, just 19% of Bangladeshi women were in higher-graded jobs, compared with 66% of White British women; the situation was similar, though less marked, in Southwark (30% compared with 54%). In Camden, a remarkable 40% of Bangladeshi women worked in sales and customer service jobs (compared with less than 5% of White British women), while in Southwark the percentages were 20% and 6%. Accordingly, in Camden 53% of Bangladeshi women worked in the wholesale, retail, restaurants and hotels sector (compared with 12% of White British women) as did 28% and 15% in Southwark. A third (33%) of White British women in Camden (and 28% in Southwark) worked in the finance and real estate sector (compared with just 11% and 19% of Bangladeshi women). However, the share of employment in public sector jobs was rather similar for both groups (27% for Bangladeshi women in Camden, compared with 29% for White British women, and 38% compared with 35% in Southwark).

Thus, in these two London boroughs, although many young Bangladeshi women had succeeded in accessing educational opportunities, mature women in this group were living lives very different from those of White British female residents. Despite the high employment rates seen in these boroughs among White British women, Bangladeshi women had very low rates of employment, and in Camden they were more than five times as likely as White British women to look after their homes and families full time. Those who were economically active had much higher rates of unemployment than White British women, and when employed were strongly concentrated in the lower-paid segments of the labour market.

## Educational attainment, family circumstances and age

As mentioned in Chapter Three, the percentage of women achieving higher-level qualifications has increased significantly in recent years. In 2001, among women aged 25–44, 37% of Indian women, 28% of both Black African and Black Caribbean women, 20% of Pakistani women and 13% of Bangladeshi women – compared with 25% of White women – had acquired graduate-level qualifications (Yeandle et al, 2006j, p 17; ONS, 2006c). These figures are particularly impressive when compared with the situation 10 years previously. Then, only 8% of Indian women, 5% of Black Caribbean women, 12% of Black African women, 4% of Pakistani women and 9% of White women were qualified at this level (Yeandle et al, 2006j, p 17; ONS, 1993). This sharp upward trend in higher-level qualifications reflects the extension of educational opportunities in universities and polytechnics, quickly taken up by many women, who, from the 1980s began to 'catch up', in educational terms, with men. This is important, because graduate women have higher employment rates than other women. In 2001, among graduate women aged 25–44, 84% of White women, 77% of Indian women, 83% of both Black

African and Black Caribbean women, 53% of Pakistani women and 57% of Bangladeshi women were in employment.

Education and qualifications open up more and better opportunities for participation in the labour market, and the state's investment in higher education is at least in part intended to achieve this. So it is desirable, in policy terms, to know how having qualifications affects the labour market situation of ethnic minority women, and to explore differences between groups of ethnic minority women and those living in different places. However, in most localities the small size of the ethnic minority population hampers investigation of these questions. Even using the Census, accessed via its specialised data sets (here we use the Census SAM and Census CAM, drawn from samples of Census returns), analysis of these topics at local authority district level is possible only in larger districts that have relatively large numbers of ethnic minority residents. Because of this, this section begins with some national-level data about ethnic minority women's education, family circumstances and labour force participation, before turning to comparison of two groups – Black Caribbean and White British women – in two specific local labour markets: Birmingham (where Black Caribbean women represented 6% of the female population of working age) and the London borough of Southwark (where the figure was 9%).

## National-level comparisons: Black Caribbean, Pakistani and Bangladeshi women

As noted earlier, among women there are marked differences by ethnicity in both economic activity and unemployment rates. There are also important differences in women's employment rates and in their family situations. At the national level, Black Caribbean women had the highest full-time employment rates (45%, compared with 36% for White British women, 13% for Pakistani women and 10% for Bangladeshi women), but their part-time employment rates were lower (15% compared with 23% for White British women and with 8% for Pakistani and 6% for Bangladeshi women).

Perhaps the first point to note is that among those in any type of paid employment in 2001, White British women were much less likely to be mothers than the other groups of women considered here. Thus while 70% of Black Caribbean women in employment had dependent children, with similar figures found among Bangladeshi (65%) and Pakistani women workers (68%), only 50% of employed White British women were in this situation. This arises from a range of factors – including delayed motherhood among younger White British women (Robson and Berthoud, 2003), an older age structure among working age White British women and higher rates of childlessness among White British women – but because motherhood is associated with part-time employment and with reduced or stalled career progress for many women (as shown in Chapters Three, Seven and Eight), it is an important factor in understanding the differences in the labour market situation of these women. There were points of differentiation among employed mothers, too. For while the large majority of White British (82%), Bangladeshi (85%) and Pakistani (84%) working mothers lived in dual parent households, Black Caribbean mothers who were in paid work were split equally between lone parents and those living with a partner (ONS, 2006c).

When the labour force participation of women in only those households where there were children is considered, Black Caribbean women, despite being much more likely to be lone parents, were among the most likely to be economically active. In these households, the difference that qualifications make to women's labour force participation is also readily apparent. Among Black Caribbean mothers, 83% of those who were graduates, compared with 60% of those who had a very low level of qualification (below Level 2) were either in a paid job or seeking work. The figures were very similar for White British women (who, as just noted, were more likely to have a partner in the household as well as children); but they were much lower for Pakistani and Bangladeshi women – although among those who were graduates 47% of Pakistani women and 50% of Bangladeshi women were either in employment or seeking work. Among the least well-qualified Pakistani and Bangladeshi mothers, however, barely 1 in 8 (15% and 12% respectively) were participating in the labour market.

Turning to those households where there were no children (where, as shown above, about half of all White British women were living, compared with fewer than 1 in 5 women in the other groups under consideration), for poorly qualified women there was still a marked disparity between White British and Black Caribbean women on the one hand (70% and 74% of whom were economically active) and Pakistani and Bangladeshi women on the other (only 22% and 24% of whom were economically active). Among qualified women (visible among those with Level 2 qualifications and above, and especially among graduates) this gap really narrowed. In those households without children, and among those women who were graduates, 88% of White British women and 86% of Black Caribbean women were economically active, compared with 68% of Pakistani and 69% of Bangladeshi women (ONS, 2006c).

Thus, while the accelerating pace of qualification among ethnic minority women was clearly raising their participation in paid work, as shown elsewhere (Yeandle et al, 2006j, p 17), this effect was much more muted among those who had children. However, if in the future more women in these groups choose, as so many other women have done in recent decades, to delay childbearing or limit their family size, it seems very likely that this too will raise their participation rates.

So far this section has looked at economic activity; but what is the relationship between ethnicity, qualifications and employment/unemployment for women in different ethnic groups, and how is this related to age? In 2001, in England and Wales, 362,000 White British women aged 16–59, along with some 12,000 Black Caribbean women, over 9,000 Pakistani women and about 3,500 Bangladeshi women were unemployed (ONS, 2003). As shown in Chapter Four, these figures represented very much higher rates of unemployment among ethnic minority women than among White British women. In the case of Pakistani and Bangladeshi women the rates were three to four times higher at national level and even higher in some local labour markets.

Young women (those aged 16–24) had unemployment rates in 2001 of 6% among White British women, 13% for Black Caribbean women, 17% for Pakistani women and 16% for Bangladeshi women. For those young women with few qualifications (below Level 2), the rates were even higher, still showing the same disparity by ethnicity (14% among White British young women; and 24%, 30% and 27% respectively for young Black Caribbean, Pakistani and Bangladeshi women). Among young graduates, the figures were lower but again showed marked differences (3% for White British women, 7% for Black Caribbean women, 12% for Pakistani women and 9% for Bangladeshi women) (ONS, 2006c).

When all unemployed women of working age are taken into account, 28% of the White British women, and a similar proportion of the Pakistani and Bangladeshi women (29% and 30%) had no qualifications, but this was true of only 16% of the Black Caribbean women. In all three of these ethnic minority categories, the percentage of unemployed women who had qualifications at Level 3 and above was much higher (25% of Black Caribbean women, 23% of Pakistani women, and 18% of Bangladeshi women) than among White British women (17%).

## Black Caribbean women in Birmingham and Southwark

In England in 2001 Black Caribbean women had high full-time and rather low part-time employment rates compared with White British women, but their situation in our selected localities differed. In Southwark, Black Caribbean women had lower full-time employment rates than White British women (41% compared with 45%), while the opposite was true in Birmingham (where 41% of Black Caribbean women and 37% of White British women worked full time). However, Black Caribbean women in Southwark had higher part-time employment rates than White British women (14% compared with 12%), with the opposite true in Birmingham (where 17% of Black Caribbean women, but 21% of White British women had part-time jobs). In both places, Black Caribbean women were more likely than White British women to be students or to be unemployed, but less likely to look after their home and family full-time (Buckner et al, 2005a, 2005b).

There were also some differences in age structure. In Southwark, more women were in their 20s than in Birmingham, especially among White British women, and among Black Caribbean women fewer in Southwark were in their 30s and 40s (54% compared with 62% in Birmingham, contrasting with 48%–49% in both places for White British women) (ONS, 2006e).

Employed White British women of working age in Southwark were much better qualified than those in Birmingham (49% held Level 4/5 qualifications, compared with 23%), but this pattern was reversed among Black Caribbean women (24% held Level 4/5 qualifications in Southwark, compared with 29% in Birmingham). However, more Black Caribbean women were poorly qualified (no qualifications, or only Level 1) in Southwark (43% compared with 35% in Birmingham), although the opposite was true of White British women (among whom 35% in Southwark, but 47% in Birmingham, had very low levels of qualification) (ONS, 2006e).

Of those in employment, in both places White British women were more likely to hold higher-level jobs. Among White British women in Southwark, 18% worked in the top two occupational categories ('larger employers and higher managerial occupations' or 'higher professional occupations'), compared with just 5% of Black Caribbean women in Southwark, and with 8% of White British and 4% of Black Caribbean women in Birmingham. Many White British women in Southwark were in lower managerial and professional occupations too (40% of all employees, compared with 29% in Birmingham and 33% for Black Caribbean women in both places). While this in part reflects differences in qualification, as discussed in the next section, this was by no means the whole story.

If we consider only employed graduate women, interesting contrasts emerge (Table 5.1). At national level, just 15% of Black Caribbean women graduates are in top jobs, compared with 29% of comparable White British women. However, Black Caribbean women were far more likely to be in lower managerial and professional posts (such as schoolteachers, nurses, social workers, librarians and pharmacists). This pattern was seen in the selected localities, too, but with differences. In Southwark, 11% of White British women held jobs in the large employer/higher managerial category, yet no comparable Black Caribbean women occupied these high status posts. In Birmingham, where only 6% of White British women were in these jobs, the figure for Black Caribbean women was just 3% (ONS, 2006e).

In both places large minorities of White British women (17% in Birmingham and 19% in Southwark) had jobs in the 'higher professional' category (which includes doctors, lawyers, scientists and university teachers), although these figures were well below the national average (29%). Among Black Caribbean women, however, while 18% of those in Southwark were in this type of work, only 6% in Birmingham had secured similar positions.

In both places the percentages of women graduates who held 'lower managerial and professional' jobs – the main occupational category for Black Caribbean women graduates – also differed from the national average (61%). In Birmingham 65%, but in Southwark only 50%, were in this category. Among White women, where the national figure is just 38%, the figures were much higher for both groups of women in Birmingham (58%) and in Southwark (52%). Few graduate women of any ethnicity occupied the lowest-level jobs, but at national level, Black Caribbean women were more often found in 'semi-routine' positions, while their White British counterparts were slightly more likely to be in 'lower supervisory and technical' occupations.

Why do similarly qualified women, living in the same localities, with (in theory) access to the same local labour markets, have such different occupational profiles? Clearly significant numbers of higher managerial jobs are accessible in Southwark,

**Table 5.1: Employed women qualified to degree level: Birmingham, Southwark and England (%)**

| Socio-economic category | Birmingham | | Southwark | | England | |
|---|---|---|---|---|---|---|
| | White British | Black Caribbean | White British | Black Caribbean | White British | Black Caribbean |
| Large employers and higher managerial occupations | 5 | 3 | 11 | 0 | 14 | 5 |
| Higher professional occupations | 17 | 6 | 19 | 18 | 29 | 10 |
| Lower managerial and professional occupations | 58 | 65 | 52 | 50 | 38 | 61 |
| Intermediate occupations | 11 | 19 | 10 | 24 | 6 | 14 |
| Small employers and own account workers | 2 | 0 | 3 | 0 | 6 | 1 |
| Lower supervisory and technical occupations | 2 | 1 | 1 | 2 | 4 | 2 |
| Semi-routine | 4 | 4 | 3 | 4 | 2 | 5 |
| Routine occupations | 1 | 1 | 1 | 2 | 1 | 1 |
| ALL | 100 | 100 | 100 | 100 | 100 | 100 |

*Source:* 2001 Census SAM. The 2001 SAM is provided through the Cathie Marsh Centre for Census and Survey Research (University of Manchester), with the support of the ESRC and JISC. All tables containing Census data, and the results of analysis, are reproduced with the permission of the Controller of Her Majesty's Stationery Office and the Queen's Printer for Scotland.

since 11% of White British women graduates are in them. Likewise, since 17% of White British women graduates in Birmingham occupy higher professional positions, we need to ask why these posts are available to so few Black Caribbean graduates living in the same city.

White British women of working age living in Southwark in 2001 had a particularly young age profile. Those in employment were also much less likely to be lone parents (16% compared with 55% for Black Caribbean women), and much more likely to live with a partner but to have no dependent children (47% compared with 15%). However, there is also well-established (national level) evidence that Black Caribbean girls are particularly career oriented (Bhavnani with PTI, 2006; Bradley et al, 2007, p 10), and among those under 35 surveyed by the EOC, Black Caribbean and White British women had similar aspirations to secure senior managerial or professional positions.

Black Caribbean women were more likely than White women to see opportunities for progression as important when choosing a job, but had also had more difficulty finding a job; they had more often had to take a job below the level for which they were qualified and they had more frequently seen less well-qualified people appointed above them (Botcherby, 2006). The Black Caribbean women surveyed by the EOC nevertheless placed great importance on pay, opportunities for progression and 'a job that people look up to', scoring more highly than White British women in all these categories. Thus Black Caribbean women's labour market attitudes and aspirations, far from explaining their lower levels of attainment, directly contradict them.

Black Caribbean women are more likely to work full time and to be family breadwinners, an observation also highlighted in other analyses (Dale et al, 2005b; Platt, 2006, 2007). In Southwark, some of the differences between the women may arise from their different life stages and family circumstances. Many young managers and professionals spend the early part of their careers living in London, and London has a particularly transient population (Travers et al, 2007). However, even the best-qualified Black Caribbean women seem to face additional barriers to progression at work and to securing high-level jobs, especially in the education and business services sectors (Adams and Carter, 2007), where in 2001 one third of Southwark's female employment was located (compared with only one fifth in Birmingham).

## Conclusion

The focus on ethnicity in this chapter has shown that women's participation in the labour market is complex: affected – but not determined – by local labour market opportunities and conditions; influenced by family situation, but in different ways for different groups; and patterned according to educational background and attainment. Rates of unemployment among ethnic minority women are almost always much higher than those of White British women, and among women in work the distribution of jobs and occupations tends almost always to leave ethnic minority women clustered in lower-level jobs, sometimes in very disadvantaged and insecure positions. Such local-level evidence about ethnic minority women's labour market participation is essential for effective policy making and interventions, both at the national and the local level.

The analysis presented here has important implications for policy makers, and calls for a fine-grained approach to understanding the kinds of support needed by women from different backgrounds, facing varied barriers to work, in different places. The experience of women of differing ethnicities indicates, as we have seen, that living in the UK when young and educational achievement within the UK system both raise economic activity and employment rates. For some groups of women, there is also a need to understand better the relationship between religious affiliation, family circumstances, migration history and cultural practices, since assumptions that one or more of these factors *fully* explain low participation or employment rates in a given locality may in fact conceal weaknesses in the structure of local labour market opportunity, or discrimination; factors that call for very different kinds of action at the local level. More detailed qualitative research is undoubtedly needed to explain fully the variations described in this chapter, with an emphasis on listening to women's own descriptions of their aspirations and experiences in accessing and progressing within the labour market. But already in this analysis there is strong evidence that local labour markets are not operating efficiently or fairly with regard to ethnic minority women, and that – for reasons of good business sense as well as of social justice – new local strategies are needed to address this situation.

## Notes

[1] Data for the 25–59 age group were commissioned, to eliminate any effects of working after state pension age.

[2] For further information about the cities and localities referred to in this chapter, see Appendix A.

[3] Households are identified here by the ethnicity reported by the 'household representative person' who completed the 2001 Census return.

[4] In addition, 5% of Indian women in England are Christian (1% in Leicester) and 7% either have no religion or did not state a religion (4% in Leicester).

[5] These data are not available by ethnicity and gender for small geographical areas.

# SIX

# Accessing the labour market

*Karen Escott*

## Introduction

In this chapter, we argue that the difficulty some women face in accessing employment opportunities has been poorly understood by those designing and implementing employment policies. We examine why this is a problem and explore the position of women who are on the margins of the labour market. For this group of women, and for those women who are, in effect, excluded from the labour market, access to local employment is crucial. If labour market analysis and policy are to be effective, we need to understand why routes into the labour market work so inadequately for many women, and why, even in areas of employment growth, many women living in poor neighbourhoods remain either disconnected from sustainable employment opportunities or concentrated in poor-quality jobs.

Women's patterns of work, their relationship to the labour market over the life course, and gendered occupational segregation in many workplaces are known to lead to a concentration of women in low-valued jobs, but the reason why some women remain on the margins of the labour market is less well understood. Chapters Two and Three showed that the existing literature on gender and the labour market provides an incomplete understanding of the experience of women who are disengaged from the labour market. Reshaped tax, benefit and employment interventions designed to transfer people from welfare into work have focused on factors related to individual and family situations that are thought to impede them in accessing employment. Child welfare and the barriers faced by lone parents have been central themes of New Labour's welfare policy (Finch, n.d.), but there has been much less emphasis on the availability of jobs and on employment opportunities that can fit their other responsibilities.

The local dimension explored in this chapter is especially important for women, as it is well established that women living in poorer areas include disproportionate numbers of lone parents, older women and those on low wages, most of whom lead tightly circumscribed and highly localised lives (Hanson and Pratt, 1995; Yeandle et al, 2003). Women's use of local services is different from that of men, and the 'lived experience' of local labour markets plays a crucial role in shaping communities (Raco, 2007). At the local level, as discussed earlier in Chapter Four, patterns of mobility, housing provision, childcare services and the location of workplaces are all important facets of policy making that also have a gender dimension, (Massey, 1993; Law, 1999; Hamilton and Jenkins, 2000; Booth et al, 2004; Greed, 2005; Hamilton et al, 2005).

If we can understand the various processes at play in women's access to the labour market, we can begin to solve two of the puzzles set out in Chapter Three. Questions we need to answer include: why are women's employment aspirations not being met? Why is poverty such a persistent problem for women on the margins of the labour market? To explore these puzzles we need a deeper understanding of the characteristics of the women for whom labour market access is most difficult. This raises questions about the effectiveness of welfare policy and calls for analysis of what is missing from existing theories and policies on labour market activation and regeneration. The chapter concludes by developing ideas about more workable policies, capable of improving women's access to the labour market, which can address economic disadvantage and labour market inequality in the longer term.

## The significance of 'access' in the context of labour market inequality

The GELLM studies found large numbers of women struggling to connect with their local labour market despite a range of policy interventions, in a period of significant job growth and when women's participation in the labour market was increasing. It raised a number of questions. What specific problems do women face in accessing the labour market? What measures have been taken to support economically inactive women into work, and with how much success? How significant is the local neighbourhood and the local labour market?

The first theme – exploring the problems that women face in accessing the labour market – needs to be discussed in the light of broader labour market issues and the gendered divisions in the labour market (Curran, 1988). Some aspects of women's difficulty in accessing employment can be attributed to the major changes affecting the labour market in the last decades of the 20th century. They include the demise of traditional industries and the growth of new sectors requiring different types of skill and experience. Deindustrialisation and the parallel growth in service sector employment are associated with important differences in the experience of those living in 'uncompetitive communities' and on the margins of the labour market (Gordon and Turok, 2005, p 243). This has resulted in a more polarised labour force where divisions between higher-paid and lower-paid employment opportunities are much more stark, and poverty makes it more difficult for those who are unemployed to return to work (Gallie et al, 2003; Goos and Manning, 2003). Poor labour market conditions, including high unemployment rates, are known to discourage some women from participating in the labour market and spatial barriers have been identified as important, particularly for those women actively seeking paid employment (Van Ham and Buchel, 2006).

Recent industrial and technological trends have created particular challenges for women without the skills, qualifications and work experience required in new sectors of employment. Many of them find it difficult to access jobs and remain disconnected from the labour market as they cannot afford to live on the low wages on offer (Toynbee, 2003; Escott and Buckner, 2006). Access to paid work is also known to be particularly problematic for unskilled employees, often reproducing patterns of inequality in the workplace itself and thereby making it more difficult to progress within the labour market (Rainbird, 2000).

As we saw in Chapter Three, access to work is often influenced by the uncertainties people feel about an insecure labour market. Insecurity, often related to low-paying, short-term and temporary jobs, is a further feature influencing transitions to work, affecting potential workers in different ways (Theodore and Peck, 2000). Many residents in poorer communities make a direct connection between individual worklessness and the nature of jobs on offer (Lupton, 2003). Their feelings of insecurity relate not only to the workplace and the labour market but also to their households and domestic arrangements (Dean and Shah, 2002; Charles and James, 2003).

The second theme is concerned with the effectiveness of measures designed to support people into work. We noted in Chapter Two that since 1997, the New Labour government has promoted paid employment as the best route out of poverty, and has set a target of an 80% employment rate overall. Key policy developments introduced since 1997 include the New Deal programmes, which provide different amounts of support and compulsion to join the labour market; the introduction of tax credits for low-paid earners with children, as incentives to enter paid work; and the introduction of the national minimum wage (NMW).

Public investments in childcare and schemes to assist women into paid work have focused on the poverty of low-income mothers, especially lone parents. National programmes aimed at these women are the New Deal for Lone Parents (NDLP), the New Deal for Partners of the Unemployed (NDPU) and Pathways to Work (Walker and Wiseman, 2003; DWP, 2008). Fears about an ethnic penalty and concerns that middle-class women in employment are benefiting more than women who are living in poorer households raise questions about whether labour market activation programmes benefit the most disadvantaged communities (Platt, 2007). Evidence that employment among lone parents has been no greater in areas of high unemployment, and that the take-up of tax credits by lone parents has increased more in areas of low than of high unemployment adds to this argument (Webster, 2006).

The promotion of affordable childcare provision to support women into work is now recognised as an essential aspect of access to work. But the issue of which women benefit most from services designed to support women in employment is also important in the discussion of access to jobs. For example, low-income families are more likely to use informal sources of childcare, 'rather than the more expensive formal arrangements that are available to higher-paid families' (Dean and Shah, 2002, p 77). The impact of financial incentives has been limited since tax credits do not cover the full costs of childcare, and wider support is only available to those households on the lowest incomes (Daguerre and Taylor-Gooby, 2003).

The third theme centres on the significance of the locality and of neighbourhood policy interventions in enabling labour market access. Initiatives that have sought to improve labour market participation through welfare and regeneration investment in localities that experience significant deprivation are central to this analysis. The unevenness of local labour markets in the context of structural employment changes and growing evidence about its local impact (Peck, 1996; Lupton, 2003; Gordon and Turok, 2005; Helms and Cumbers, 2006) is evident in research on the influence of geography on access to work (Green and Owen, 2006). But existing research has not fully explained why so many women living in communities where there has been significant public and private investment continue to find access to employment difficult.

The remainder of this chapter examines 'access to employment' issues for women living in England's poorer communities by exploring: the scale of the problem, the types of women for whom access is most difficult and the constraints they face, from both an individual and a wider labour market perspective.

## What is the nature and scale of the problem?

Labour market accessibility is often measured through official employment statistics. In Chapter Two we noted that while there is agreement that women's employment and economic activity rates have increased in recent decades, measuring unemployment and economic inactivity (considered analytically distinct categories in labour market analysis) remains more difficult, as these are especially complex topics when applied to women (Coyle, 1984; Martin and Wallace, 1984; Yeandle, 1996; Beatty et al, 2007). This section shows that the invisibility of women's unemployment has resulted in a poor understanding of gendered differences in accessibility at the interface between local people and their labour market.

### Women's disconnection from the labour market

Across England, the GELLM studies found large-scale and persistent disconnection from the labour market among women that had not been addressed by policy makers.[1] In 2001, 4% of women in England indicated on their completed Census return that they were 'unemployed', and 29% of women were classified as 'economically inactive'. This latter category is particularly significant for women, since if they are fully occupied doing household work, or caring for others, they are classified as economically inactive and not available for paid work. Taken together, there were over 4.7 million economically inactive and unemployed women of working age in England in April 2001, representing a third (33%) of working age women. From our GELLM research we know that they include women who:

have been made redundant, have looked for work but been unable to secure a job, have found work but struggled to stay in their jobs, and have taken a break to care for children or for an older, sick or disabled relative.

In our studies, low levels of labour market engagement were particularly notable in the major cities, including the two inner London boroughs (Table 6.1), with unemployment rates among economically active women as high as 7%, and economic inactivity rates verging on 40% among women of working age in these districts. Despite variations in labour market engagement, influenced by past industrial history and changing sectoral conditions, these women faced similar problems in accessing employment in all these areas.

**Table 6.1: Economic inactivity and unemployment among women of working age: England and selected districts**

|  | Number of women aged 16–59 | Number of economically active women aged 16–59 | Unemployed women (as % of those economically active) | Economically inactive women (as % of all women) |
|---|---|---|---|---|
| Birmingham | 287,518 | 176,410 | 7 | 39 |
| Camden | 70,785 | 45,218 | 7 | 36 |
| East Staffs | 30,264 | 21,887 | 4 | 28 |
| Newcastle | 79,748 | 50,162 | 5 | 37 |
| Sandwell | 81,520 | 53,426 | 7 | 35 |
| Somerset | 139,330 | 103,197 | 3 | 26 |
| Southwark | 81,518 | 54,088 | 8 | 34 |
| Thurrock | 43,865 | 31,890 | 5 | 27 |
| Wakefield | 93,662 | 64,953 | 5 | 31 |
| West Sussex | 212,237 | 159,632 | 2 | 25 |
| England | 14,064,350 | 10,332,809 | 4 | 29 |

*Source:* 2001 Census Standard Tables, Crown Copyright 2003.

While unemployment as measured in official statistics fell between 1991 and 2001 at national level and in most localities, the GELLM research showed that despite significant regeneration investment, unemployment among economically active women in most of the poorest wards studied (Figure 6.1) remained much higher than in the districts within which these wards were located (Escott and Buckner, 2006).

The GELLM studies also found that during the decade 1991–2001, a period of considerable job growth, in some wards women's economic inactivity rates increased, against the national trend. Thus in Birmingham, although the city recorded a 24% increase in female part-time jobs (alongside a very small fall – minus 1.3% – in female full-time jobs), in these poorer wards within the city there were significant increases in female economic inactivity rates. For example in Birmingham's Soho ward, women's economic inactivity rates increased from 41% in 1991 to 52% in 2001 (Escott et al, 2006).

These data, illustrating the scale of disconnection from the labour market for women living in deprived neighbourhoods, raise important policy issues about access to the labour market, particularly when, as we show below, many women in these localities have a very strong desire to work.

**Figure 6.1: Unemployment as a proportion of economically active women*: England and selected localities**

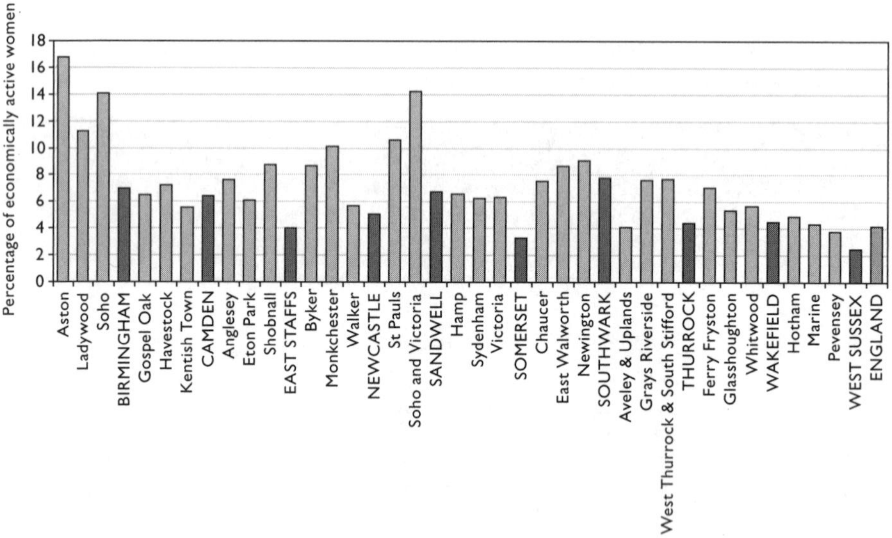

*Source:* 2001 Census Standard Tables, Crown Copyright 2003.

* Data in this figure are for all women of working age.

## Aspiration to work

One of the myths we identified in Chapter Three was the argument that most women who are outside the labour market, particularly those living in poor communities, do not aspire to enter paid employment. The GELLM studies found evidence that contradicted this view, and showed that there are many women on the margins of the labour market (Escott and Buckner, 2006; Grant and Buckner, 2006). These women often had very low incomes and experienced a range of labour market disadvantages; they included women who moved in and out of the low-wage sector of the economy.

In our reports of these studies (Escott et al, 2006a–f; Grant et al, 2006b–f), we demonstrated that many of these women have a desire to engage in paid work and have experienced periods of labour market engagement as well as periods of labour market disconnection. The extent of their desire to work can be measured both quantitatively and qualitatively. In England there are an estimated 1.5 million women of working age who are not only outside paid employment but who say they want to work; that is, they are either formally unemployed or are economically inactive but want to work (ONS, 2006a). Shockingly, this represents 10% of all women of working age, and 24% of all economically inactive women of working age.

In the GELLM focus group discussions with women, many participants expressed strong aspirations to gain paid employment. Their views were often influenced by their social situation, but were also affected by the employment structure of the locality, by the types of jobs available and by their experiences of the labour market. Young women were often motivated by a desire to move beyond the poverty faced by their parents and grandparents: 'I don't want to live like that, and in order not to I have to develop myself and get qualifications' (Focus group participant, Birmingham).

Women with children explained that they wanted to set an example and provide for their children.

> 'My partner's family were against me going out to work. They said, "Oh no, you can't do that, you've got two kids." And that's made me even more determined to prove them wrong. When the kids are older, I want to have something for myself and I want to do it for them. I want to make things better for my kids.' (Focus group participant, Thurrock)

Nevertheless, many women, particularly in the younger age group, felt despondent about their opportunities and their employment potential in relation to the labour market. Most were looking for work in the retail industry or in childcare, but they feared they were competing in a crowded labour market. Their aspirations were often influenced by awareness of low wages in the local economy, by limited qualifications and by their lack of recent work experience.

## Which women find it difficult to access sustainable employment?

To gain a greater understanding of which women find it most difficult to access the labour market, we need to consider the social and personal characteristics that are most likely to influence women's labour market behaviour, including their qualifications, ethnicity, age and health. These factors are all known to have a bearing on women's connection to or disconnection from the labour market, and involve processes that often reflect the wider class and income differences experienced (Escott and Buckner, 2006; Grant et al, 2007).

For those living in poorer communities, qualifications – one of the strongest predictors of labour market engagement – have limited influence in accessing employment. The GELLM studies found considerable variation in labour market connection for women of working age with similar levels of qualification. In the poorer localities fewer qualified women were in paid work, and there was considerable variation in the percentage of women with higher-level qualifications who were in employment (Grant et al, 2007). For example, across our study areas the employment rate for graduate women ranged from 88% in Eton Park in East Staffordshire, to 57% by Byker, Newcastle. Unqualified women were also less likely to be in employment; in Aston, Birmingham, for example, just 19% of women with no qualifications were in employment, well below the national rate of 50%. Elsewhere, one woman commented: 'I've done so many courses, I've got loads of certificates at home, but the opportunity of getting a job isn't available. There aren't any jobs around' (Focus group participant, Southwark).

Young women's relationship to the labour market is different from that of young men and subject to a range of gendered processes and structures. Young women without qualifications have greater problems than young men in accessing the labour market,[2] but for many of those living in poorer areas there are added challenges. Among young women with similar levels of educational attainment, the marked variation in their connection with the labour market appears to be strongly associated with the type of local labour market in which they live (Escott and Buckner, 2006). Many young women also feel very let down by the education and welfare system.

Among young women, their own health and care responsibilities had more importance than we expected. We found particularly high rates of ill health among young women living in some (not all) of the deprived wards studied. For young women living in poor communities who have caring responsibilities this is clearly another factor that contributes to economic inactivity. Many young women aspire to work, but face considerable constraints, with the result that they often have limited horizons, influenced not only by their own experiences but also by the nature of the job market.

The GELLM studies confirmed that lone parenthood has a stronger negative impact on access to the labour market than age or qualifications (Grant et al, 2007). However, the picture is more complex than first appears. In disadvantaged areas, employment rates among lone parents were particularly low. For example, in Newcastle's Byker ward only 9% of lone mothers were in full-time employment (compared with 16% in the city). This suggests that lone parents living in disadvantaged communities face additional barriers to engagement in the local labour market.

For women from ethnic minority backgrounds, labour market access can be particularly challenging, as discussed in Chapter Five. The GELLM studies found that, while unemployment rates for White British women were well above the national rate in poor communities, the unemployment rate for women from some ethnic minority groups was far higher – but that this varied considerably. Indian women and Black Caribbean women have similar rates of unemployment to White British women, but local data show that Pakistani, Bangladeshi and Black African women who actively seek work suffer from particularly high rates of unemployment. For example, within the London borough of Southwark, in Chaucer ward, 16% of Bangladeshi women and 13% of Black African women were unemployed, compared with 4% of White women of working age living in the same ward (Escott et al, 2006f). Our qualitative research also found that many women from ethnic minority groups felt excluded from any type of engagement in the labour market.

> 'If they actually listened, they would find that we don't want to be unemployed, we don't want to sit inside. We all have brains, we all have ambitions – but after a while you go there and they look at you and it starts to make you feel like, what's the point? I'm useless. That's why a lot of people get depression who sign on.' (Focus group participant, Southwark)

This complex picture of variability across localities and across ethnicities suggests that it is not only labour market barriers affecting access, but that direct or indirect discrimination also plays an important role. Black and ethnic minority young women in particular felt that they faced race discrimination in gaining a foothold in the labour market: 'You don't get feedback. They won't tell you the truth, will they? They'll say someone is better qualified, or has more experience than you' (Focus group participant, Camden).

For many women living in poor communities, caring responsibilities also contribute to lower employment rates. The GELLM studies found that women with unpaid caring responsibilities were less likely to be in paid work (either full time or part time) in these areas than in the wider district or at national level. Some women seeking access to the labour market explained that they had very significant unpaid caring responsibilities, with little support from statutory agencies (Escott and Buckner, 2006). Part-time employment rates were particularly low for women with unpaid caring responsibilities in some poorer localities with high ethnic minority populations, perhaps also reflecting the additional problems they face in gaining paid work that will produce sufficient income to support their household and combine paid work with their caring role, and reflecting unintentional disincentives in the benefits system (Burchardt, 2003, pp 50–1). Ill health has a well-established role in labour market detachment (Yeandle and Macmillan, 2003), and is strongly associated with poverty (Rowlingson and Berthoud, 1996; Sly et al, 1999), so it was not surprising that rates of limiting long-term illness among women of working age were relatively high in the poorer communities we studied (Escott and Buckner, 2006). Problems in accessing paid employment can in themselves contribute to high levels of poor health: 'That's why a lot of people get really ill from depression. Sitting at home with their kids and they've got nobody to talk to. It's really, really hard' (Focus group participant, Birmingham).

Variations in levels of labour market access suggest that while social characteristics are an important influence on how women access the labour market, other processes at the local level are also important. Our qualitative research revealed a number of additional factors that contributed to their poor prospects, including the quality of local employment, discrimination, inadequate organisational support and poor job seeking experiences.

## What are the access issues for women?

The GELLM studies, which highlighted the views of women living in poor communities, showed that access is influenced by a number of economic and social factors. These include a growing demand for their labour in the context of particular local industrial structures, alongside a number of significant constraints that influence women's ability to participate in the labour market. We also found that the geography of their local labour market was important for these women, including the location of employment, and the quality and affordability of local services such as transport and the proximity of schools and nurseries.

### Sources and types of employment

The type of job opportunities in or close to the neighbourhoods studied had a major impact on women's ability to engage with the labour market. Many women saw their local labour market as discrete and bounded, needing to be close to their home, family and children's schools. This made the availability of local jobs particularly important for them. Young women and Black and minority ethnic women in these deprived neighbourhoods found their access to the labour market was further constrained by their age and race and by 'postcode discrimination' (Grant et al, 2007). Thus although there had been strong employment growth in the local economies in which these neighbourhoods were located (see Table 6.2), many women who wanted to work in secure, sustained, paid employment found they were unable to access suitable work.

Much of the employment growth in the districts and cities where the wards were located had been in female part-time jobs, reflecting the more general expansion of service sector employment, including new jobs in distribution, banking and finance. However, the limited range of jobs available in this part of the job market, and the affordability of working part time in poorly paid employment, were issues for many women living in low-income households.

As shown in Chapter Four, the national growth in full-time jobs among women (up 12.7% between 1991 and 2002) disguises considerable variability in female full-time employment, with substantial increases in some districts and decline in others, indicating that in some areas the types of full-time employment available are more limited now than a decade ago. The loss of female full-time jobs in Birmingham, Newcastle and Wakefield, much of it in the manufacturing sector, was in part responsible for recent problems in accessing the labour market among women living in the poor communities we studied.

**Table 6.2: Changes in employment 1991–2002, by full-time/part-time status and sex: England and selected localities**

| | Change in the number of jobs | | | | |
|---|---|---|---|---|---|
| | ALL jobs | Female full-time jobs | Male full-time jobs | Female part-time jobs | Male part-time jobs |
| *Numbers* | | | | | |
| Birmingham | +20,679 | −1,657 | −17,661 | +20,588 | +19,409 |
| Camden | +56,970 | +12,478 | +15,838 | +17,968 | +10,686 |
| East Staffs | +11,235 | +1,418 | +1,766 | +5,457 | +2,594 |
| Newcastle | +18,628 | -126 | +4,332 | +6,891 | +7,531 |
| Sandwell | +1,058 | +1,509 | −5,447 | +1,358 | +3,638 |
| Somerset | +36,947 | +4,843 | +4,220 | +19,558 | +8,326 |
| Southwark[1] | +19,438 | +5,991 | +1,996 | +6,412 | +5,039 |
| Thurrock | +16,869 | +3,527 | +4,207 | +6,208 | +2,927 |
| Wakefield | +12,152 | −891 | +3,074 | +5,368 | +4,601 |
| West Sussex | +93,447 | +13,559 | +44,047 | +21,821 | +14,020 |
| **England** | **3,566,931** | **+632,389** | **+819,143** | **+1,231,606** | **+883,793** |
| *Percentage increase/decrease* | | | | | |
| Birmingham | +4.5 | −1.3 | −7.6 | +23.8 | +115.7 |
| Camden | +28.2 | +17.1 | +15.5 | +97.7 | +117.6 |
| East Staffs | +26.8 | +14.4 | +8.1 | +61.5 | +171.3 |
| Newcastle | +12.2 | −0.3 | +6.7 | +20.7 | +118.2 |
| Sandwell | +0.8 | +5.2 | −7.5 | +6.0 | +89.1 |
| Somerset | +24.1 | +13.0 | +5.9 | +52.5 | +107.8 |
| Southwark[1] | +15.8 | +16.0 | +3.0 | +44.0 | +105.9 |
| Thurrock | +43.5 | +45.3 | +19.9 | +73.4 | +214.0 |
| Wakefield | +10.9 | −3.1 | +5.8 | +20.9 | +116.3 |
| West Sussex | +35.7 | +19.0 | +38.9 | +34.5 | +98.1 |
| **England** | **+19.2** | **+12.7** | **+9.3** | **+30.8** | **+103.1** |

*Note:* [1] Southwark data are for 1991–2003.

*Source:* 1991 AES Census of Employment, 2002 ABI, Crown Copyright.

Occupational and industrial segregation also affects labour market access. Clustering in a limited range of jobs and sectors was found to be particularly pronounced in some neighbourhoods, limiting the options for women (particularly young women) seeking to move into paid work.[2] In some of the poorer areas of East Staffordshire, Thurrock and Wakefield, one third of all young women in employment were 'clustered' in the wholesale and retail sectors, considerably above the national, and in some cases district, average. Focus group discussions with women revealed how significant the limited structure of employment opportunity was for them in further distancing them from the labour market. Low pay, poor employment conditions and unattractive jobs all featured strongly in their own perception of the problems confronting them.

These concerns were also expressed in localities where the local labour market was very buoyant. Many women (and the local agencies supporting them) were frustrated by the emphasis in policy initiatives on low quality jobs and 'entry-level' employment (Escott and Buckner, 2006, p 25). The jobs held by women living in these deprived localities were often filled through agencies and were frequently part-time and temporary positions. 'Yes, there are skills shortages, but people shouldn't have to accept low paid, anti-social jobs just so they have a job' (Local stakeholder, Birmingham).

## Understanding local circumstances

The uneven patterns of labour market access evident in the GELLM studies indicate a range of different local circumstances, each requiring appropriate policy interventions. First, even in areas where there has been very significant job growth (such as Inner London), for many women the obstacles to accessing employment remain, including affordability and the poor quality of local support services. Second, where the only accessible employment opportunities are in low-paying sectors and occupations, problems of access are likely to persist. Third, particular labour market problems arise for women in more dispersed and rural communities, where the major employers are in sectors (for example, tourism, agriculture and care) offering low-paid or seasonal work and where most positions are 'entry-level' jobs. Here a wider range of opportunities within these sectors is required. Fourth, for many women living in poorer areas of major cites, where new jobs have been created to replace major, long-term job loss in local traditional industries, many residents, including well-qualified women, are excluded from them.

## The role of local employers

In the GELLM research programme we also found that some employers' approaches to working practices limited the options available in the local job market. Women living in poorer wards often felt disillusioned by their past work experiences and told us that their employers had, generally, not been flexible in relation to hours of work, training, childcare and school holidays. In the workplaces they had known, few had any experience of work–life balance policies or of career development opportunities, as some of those advising them readily acknowledged: 'One of the main barriers for women with children is the lack of management accepting flexible working' (Local stakeholder, West Sussex).

While it seems ironic that many public sector and statutory agencies cannot fill vacancies in areas of high unemployment, this is a key part of understanding the complexity of the puzzles surrounding access to the labour market. Thus the GELLM studies highlighted the potential for local employment in the education, health and care sectors, where many agencies were struggling to fill vacancies, but it also found that – with some exceptions, very recently introduced – the employment and recruitment practices of public service agencies and providers did not reflect the local community or utilise their experience or skills (Yeandle et al, 2006a–g). 'Statutory organisations have created barriers themselves to specific groups, and these groups have not engaged with them' (Local stakeholder, Birmingham).

## Skills and work experience

Alongside limited employment options, particularly for women wanting to work flexibly or part time in or near poorer neighbourhoods, a range of other issues caused problems for women in looking for work. First, women who had failed to access the labour market often felt constrained by their lack of recent work experience. Added to this, an employer's requirement that job applicants must have a specified level of formal qualifications affected the types of jobs women considered applying for. Job advertisements often stated higher qualifications and training than was, in practice, needed for the job. A narrow view of skills means that many women without qualifications or recent experience would be unlikely ever to find employment. As some local project workers pointed out, previous work experience may not be relevant or useful, and can be dated. Yet, coping on low incomes with demanding family circumstances may have equipped some women with skills they do not recognise or know how to present when applying for jobs. 'You've got to be skilled, you've got to have lots of qualifications. You can't get experience until you get qualifications. It's a vicious circle' (Focus group participant, Newcastle).

## Support in the local labour market

Services designed to assist women into employment have long been recognised by policy makers as an essential component of effective labour market engagement. The GELLM studies found that many of the services making up this support system were inconsistent and expensive for those women for whom access to the labour market was most difficult (Escott and Buckner, 2006). Over the past decade, government has invested heavily in developing an infrastructure of childcare support services (HM Treasury, 2004a, 2004b) and this has assisted many women. Yet although there have been improvements in the availability of provision for pre-school children, formal childcare remains prohibitively expensive for those in low-paid and part-time occupations. 'Women are very keen to work, but they need to be able to earn a decent wage without being crippled by childcare – it has to be affordable to help most women out of poverty' (Local stakeholder, Southwark).

More flexible childcare is needed too, and can be developed to accommodate part-time hours, shift-work requirements and school days (Formby et al, 2004). Women were acutely aware that local childcare provision was patchy for school age children, especially those in the early years of secondary education, and school holiday periods often posed a major problem for women in, or wishing to enter, paid employment. 'The lack of breakfast clubs and after-school facilities limits not just children's education, but prevents further work on raising self-esteem and expectation for parents' (Local stakeholder, West Sussex).

Recent initiatives, including Sure Start and the work of family centres, are important for many poor communities, as local women recognise that there are now more opportunities for them to be involved in education and training activities offered by the centres, as a stepping stone to employment (Ranson and Rutledge, 2005; Escott and Buckner, 2006, p 27).

For women living in poorer neighbourhoods, proximity to work is a particularly important factor in considering employment (Escott and Buckner, 2006). As well as travelling time (a particular consideration for women with care responsibilities), transport choices for women in poorer localities also depend on wages, time, car ownership and public transport. Inadequate public transport and distance from schools hindered efforts to seek employment beyond the immediate locality, and could have long-term effects on perceptions of local labour market opportunities. 'Physical barriers can create mental barriers in looking for employment' (Local stakeholder, East Staffordshire).

The characteristics of localities as experienced by women seeking to connect with the labour market are important in understanding how future improvements may be achieved, and go beyond purely economic and employment concerns. Among both local women and stakeholder interviewees in the GELLM studies, there was a lack of confidence that this type of analysis of the locality had been undertaken or planned for.

## Policy limitations

Given that the women on whom our studies focused live in areas with high levels of worklessness, it would be expected that state welfare policies would be of considerable benefit to them in improving their access to local labour markets. However, the GELLM studies found that welfare policy largely fails to support these women (Grant and Buckner, 2006). One of the reasons for this is that only those women with a connection to the benefit system are drawn into welfare programmes. In addition, women outside paid employment lack a relationship with mainstream service providers. Our studies found that job search services were not grounded in an understanding of women's specific circumstances or aspirations, and that service providers tended to channel women into low-paid, low-skilled jobs. This had the effect of intensifying women's marginality in the labour market (Grant et al, 2007). Because mainstream services are designed – and to a large degree managed – at national level with limited local flexibility, it is difficult for a genuine understanding of, and response to, local circumstances and conditions to develop.

At the same time, the tax credit system offers many women an inadequate incentive to make the step from welfare to work. Many women are unconvinced that they can secure paid employment that will provide them and their family with an income sufficient for their needs, even with the support of tax credits. In spite of numerous recent changes in welfare policy aimed at assisting working families (Bennett and Millar, 2005), the GELLM studies confirmed that many women felt paid employment would offer little advantage to household incomes: 'I hate benefits, it's a stigma. I'd like to move off, but what can you do?' (Focus group participant, Somerset); 'As long as the benefits trap exists and there isn't a clear way out for people, it is very hard, because the wages are so low in the area' (Focus group participant, West Sussex).

Many women claiming benefits felt very anxious about losing the financial stability they had secured, or possibly risking lower household income if they took up work in employment sectors with low earnings. The short-term, transitory nature of many local jobs contributed to their fears, as the length of time needed to apply for benefits can leave women short of income. Some of those advising them pointed out that understanding the interaction between wages and benefits was difficult, too: 'I think one of the major problems is fear of coming off benefits. What they don't realise is that with tax credits and Child Tax Credits, they can be better off by going back to work' (Local stakeholder, East Staffordshire).

In spite of this, many women wanted to look at employment options and expressed the desire for greater understanding and support in finding work. The GELLM studies also found that many women who did interact with the welfare system, for example lone parents claiming Income Support, were highly critical of the nature and quality of the services provided. As well as a paucity of information about job opportunities in their locality and inconsistent professional support, they also complained that mainstream services lacked an appreciation or understanding of their specific circumstances, their labour market needs and aspirations, and their employment histories. In their experience, mainstream employment services often failed to offer the one-to-one advice, support and understanding they needed in their search for work.

> 'I thought they'd be more about sitting you down and looking at what you want to do, a plan or something, something constructive. But all they're doing is looking on the internet and getting jobs up. You can do that yourself.' (Focus group participant, Birmingham)

For women seeking to return to work after having a family, practical help in overcoming difficulties such as lack of recent work experience, lack of up-to-date qualifications, or loss of confidence after a period outside work was often missing in mainstream services:

> 'It's not just about filling in an application form. It's how you come across when you do get an interview. It's about bringing the best

of us out, letting us recall that before we had all these kids we were somebody. It's about bringing our individuality back.' (Focus group participant, Birmingham)

The general failure of the welfare system to support many women who are looking for sustainable employment is related to limitations in policy measures themselves. It is now recognised that tailored and personal approaches to providing services and work incentives are required to address pockets of worklessness in deprived localities (DWP, 2006, 2008). Nevertheless, failure to find work for people living in these communities continues to be blamed on individual inadequacies and deficiencies, without adequate understanding of the complex set of problems many women living in poorer areas face. 'There's a huge gap between who we are and the way people on the other side are seeing us' (Focus group participant, Camden).

By channelling women into the lowest level of the labour market, where progression opportunities are very scarce, welfare policy in effect establishes further barriers to employment:

> 'The jobs that go through the Job Centre tend to be crappy security jobs, retail jobs that are here today and gone tomorrow, minimum wage, 40-hour week jobs— and you never see your kids. These are not the jobs women want. The jobs might be entry-level jobs, but they need to be jobs where people can progress.' (Focus group participant, Camden)

> 'I don't think the area is expected to be aspirational. You get everyone talking about basic skills – skills needed for low-paid, low-quality jobs. It's all about getting them a job, not about the type of job.' (Local stakeholder, Birmingham)

Most of the localities that were the focus of our research on women's access to employment were also areas where major regeneration investment and funding to support local residents, including a plethora of employment and training schemes, had been put in place. Here our study found significant limitations, since there was rarely an explicit gender dimension to regeneration initiatives, and links between labour market activation and regeneration policy tended to be poor (Escott, 2007). When interviewed, regeneration project managers revealed that very little attention had been given to understanding women's problems in accessing the labour market: 'We never really considered gender issues' (Local stakeholder, Somerset); 'We target ethnic minority groups, but have not done any monitoring by gender, because we are not required to' (Local stakeholder, Birmingham).

Regeneration programmes typically emphasised the skills needed to acquire employment, but did not identify local economic characteristics or link up with other labour market and service initiatives when planning and delivering projects. Many of our interviewees were concerned that problems of economic exclusion continued, despite substantial investment. They felt limited targeting of women in regeneration interventions in part explained some of the persistent problems they faced in accessing employment. 'The problem for this ward was that it should have benefited from city centre developments, but local residents simply didn't' (Local stakeholder, Birmingham).

There were few incentives for local employers to recruit local residents or, as part of regeneration schemes, to support them in securing longer-term employment opportunities. Local stakeholders questioned the value of many regeneration schemes: 'We don't want flashy newsletters, we want solid information on jobs and training, better communication, and information points directing people on how to access employment' (Focus Group participant, Southwark).

## What works in supporting women's access to local employment?

What will assist women in accessing the labour market? What types of approaches are most effective in sustaining women's labour market participation and ensuring that progression within the workplace is possible? Policy has been pragmatic in this field, and practitioners have struggled to focus on effective solutions for poorer communities. Strategic, locally relevant welfare and regeneration investment and delivery plans that take into account diversity and gender equality are extremely rare. Consideration of the quality of local employment, including conditions of employment (hours, flexibility, tenure, family friendliness) as well as pay and progression opportunities, needs to be central in policy formulation. New sustainable employment opportunities that link up labour supply and labour demand also need to recognise that women's employment aspirations are varied.

Improving access to local labour markets for women depends on approaches that appreciate the distinctions between men and women, but also between women of different ages and ethnicities. Strategies encouraging more women to gain paid employment need to understand the nature and scale of women's non-participation and their 'distance' from labour market opportunities. Understanding and responding to women's particular circumstances has resulted in some effective employment initiatives. Successful intermediate labour market (ILM) projects, where participants are given paid work experience on a temporary basis, offer work experience in expanding sectors, involve close employer engagement and allow trainees to apply for permanent jobs once their training ends (Grant and Buckner, 2006). Such projects also provide intensive personal support to trainees, including mentoring and advice on other aspects of women's lives, such as childcare facilities and financial benefits. The most effective and sustainable employment projects are located in workplaces that offer potential progression routes and in-house training and support in the longer term.

Access to employment is much more likely where training is linked to transferable skills and to permanent jobs. This may involve listening carefully to women and working in local communities to develop a detailed understanding of the particular needs of women at different stages in their lives. A physical presence within a locality is more likely to work, often starting in places where women are most likely to be, which for many communities includes schools, nurseries and community centres.

Employer involvement in employment projects that offer good-quality local jobs with flexible hours of work is an essential aspect in supporting women's access into employment. The business case for this is part of a broader argument about economic competitiveness, about meeting future labour requirements and being much more strategic about local labour market interventions. Some local employers have introduced schemes to raise skills levels and to attract more women into employment by changing shift patterns, but examples of this are limited (Escott et al, 2006 a–f).

In some localities, voluntary sector organisations have developed with a specific focus on women who are out of work. Such projects are often an invaluable support to local women but, by virtue of their voluntary nature, they are usually small-scale projects, with insecure funding.

## Conclusion

Women's access to employment has improved significantly in recent decades, but this trend has been of limited benefit for women living in England's poorer communities. In focusing on women living in these areas, this chapter has highlighted a number of tensions between the desire of many women to work in satisfying, well-paid jobs, supported by effective local services and close to family and to local networks, and the demands of employers, including expectations that many women are able and prepared to work in low-status and poorly paid jobs.

Policies designed to inspire labour market activity have generally overlooked the significance of the gendered employment characteristics of the locality, and have not acknowledged the wider employment aspirations of women living in these areas. Our analysis points to the failure of policy at the local level, both in terms of the services available to support women who are looking for work, and in many of the regeneration schemes involving training and skills that women living in deprived areas are being offered.

Qualifications, ethnicity and health are important in shaping women's relationships with the labour market. Access to the labour market is also influenced by caring responsibilities, which for women living in poor communities is a particularly important factor. Other factors that are especially important in these areas include: transport problems in accessing jobs outside the immediate locality and finding affordable childcare in the context of a low pay economy. But the problems women face in accessing the labour market are not solely attributable to their individual and social characteristics, as policy often tends to suggest.

Structural inequalities in employment have a particularly severe impact on women who are on the margins of the labour market, and poor-quality employment influences the propensity for women living in poorer communities to have access to local jobs. Much of the job growth close to these poorer areas is in a narrow range of jobs that are often part time and low paid. Occupational segregation is a particular problem for these women, who are often directed to low-value jobs in a very limited number of employment sectors. Employers offer few concessions to the employment potential of women living in these areas, and for some women access to the labour market is further damaged by discrimination.

Finally, our evidence underscores the importance of locality in understanding women's access to the labour market. Their financial problems and the practical constraints they face in accessing the labour market are magnified by limited employer engagement. For many women living in poor neighbourhoods, where the labour market is defined in a particularly localised way, the quality of local jobs and the potential for flexible working to meet their household responsibilities is especially important. Strategies that enhance women's employment potential and directly address the constraints many women face in accessing sustainable jobs will, in the longer term, contribute to social development and economic growth. But building stronger local economies depends on fundamental changes in labour market activity that take into consideration the lived experience of local labour markets. New approaches to develop proactive labour market policies alongside economic and social regeneration investment need to reflect the complex needs of women in poor communities. Investment to address low income and inequality must not only support initiatives that improve access to employment for the most deprived women, but also work on longer-term strategies designed to strengthen labour market demand for high-quality jobs, located in deprived communities.

### Note
[1] This chapter draws on two of the studies within the GELLM research programme, LRS2 and LRS5 (see Appendix A).

[2] In 2006, unpublished research for the YWCA (Oxford) – 'Young women's employment: growing up poor in England and Wales', by K. Escott and L. Buckner – showed that 18% of young women without qualifications were in employment, compared with 31% of young men.

# SEVEN

# Job design and working hours: key sources of gender inequality

*Linda Grant*

## Introduction

This chapter explores formal approaches to job design and more informal workplace decisions, processes and practices relating to the structure and content of part-time jobs. It shows that these factors increase the tendency for women to experience economic disadvantage and poor-quality working lives, and play an important role in sustaining and reinforcing gender inequalities in employment. The chapter demonstrates that in many workplaces employers approach the design of part-time jobs, in a range of aspects, in a distinct way; the chapter seeks to explain the reasons for this. It also shows that there are more informal workplace processes, practices and decisions that influence job design and limit the range of part-time job opportunities, reproducing the association between part-time jobs and low-status employment. Because the majority of part-time jobs are held by women, this contributes to gender inequality.

By combining a discussion of working time with a consideration of job design and informal workplace practices we can reach a deeper understanding of the sources of disadvantage associated with part-time employment. In addition, there is a locality dimension to this discussion. One outcome of variations in occupational and industrial structure between local labour markets is that the spread of jobs in terms of working time also varies, with diverse implications for gender inequality. It also suggests that the feasibility of constructing more higher-level part-time jobs is much greater than is currently realised.

In Chapter Three we set out a key puzzle associated with women's part-time employment. Part-time jobs tend be of poor quality and typically characterised by low pay and limited opportunities for training and promotion. Yet there has been significant growth over the past decade in the number of women who work part time. This is particularly important because part-time employment is a typical and long-term form of employment for many women in their 30s, 40s and 50s. Thus, millions of women in the prime years of their working lives are affected by the poor quality of part-time jobs. During the period 1991–2002 the total number of part-time jobs held by women rose by 31%. Part-time job growth was very marked in the labour markets of all the localities in the GELLM research programme (as discussed in more detail in Chapter Four). In a number of these labour markets the proportion of jobs that were part time had grown from about one quarter of all jobs in 1991 to about one third in 2002. The percentage of jobs held by women that were part time had also been growing across the labour markets. In some of these, part-time jobs accounted for one half or more of women's jobs (Grant et al, 2006g, pp 5–6).

There are a number of dimensions to the poor quality of part-time jobs. First, working conditions tend to be poor for part-time jobs: hourly pay tends to be low (Harkness, 2002; Manning and Petrongolo, 2004); access to training – including access to training that would enhance opportunities for progression – is restricted (Francesconi and Gosling, 2005); and promotion opportunities tend to be limited (O'Reilly and Fagan, 1998; Women and Equality Unit, 2003; Jenkins, 2004; Grant et al, 2005, 2006g–l). These aspects of part-time jobs are, in part, outcomes of employers' approaches to job design, albeit approaches that, in some workplaces and industries, are mediated by trade union intervention and collective bargaining.

Second, other dimensions of job design are also important in understanding the poor quality of part-time jobs. This relates to job content and employee autonomy and responsibility, including: the amount of flexibility allowed with respect to hours of work, including daily start and finish times; the range and variety of tasks; the range of responsibilities undertaken by workers; and the degree of independence and worker autonomy permitted. Compared with working conditions, these aspects of job design have been less widely explored and discussed, yet they form a vital element in understanding why and in what ways part-time employment is a source of gender inequality.

Third, although part-time workers do occupy senior level jobs in some workplaces, these jobs are rarely advertised on the open labour market (Grant et al, 2005, 2006g). Thus the availability of senior level part-time jobs is important, but this varies considerably between local labour markets.

## Part-time working and low-level jobs

There is a strong relationship between part-time working and low-level jobs, which has been noted in many studies (Warren and Walters, 1998, p 106). Recent research shows that 30% of all those working part time work in the bottom 10 jobs in terms of pay, compared with only 7% of full-time workers (Jones and Dickerson, 2007, p xiii).

Figure 7.1 reveals the concentration of part-time women workers in low-paid occupations, showing that in 2001, 70% of women employed in elementary occupations, 65% of women in personal service jobs and 54% of women in sales occupations worked part time. In contrast, in higher-paid occupations part-time female employees made up a much smaller percentage of the workforce. In the same year only 19% of women managers and just 26% of women professionals worked part time. It is also noteworthy that in the elementary and personal service

**Figure 7.1: Occupation by hours worked: women aged 16-74, England, 2001**

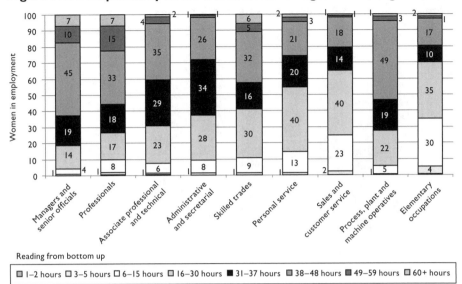

Reading from bottom up

☐ 1–2 hours ☐ 3–5 hours ☐ 6–15 hours ☐ 16–30 hours ■ 31–37 hours ☐ 38–48 hours ■ 49–59 hours ☐ 60+ hours

*Source:* 2001 Census Standard Tables, Crown Copyright 2003.

occupations many women worked relatively short part-time hours, exacerbating the problem of the low income from part-time work. About one third (34%) of female elementary workers and 25% of female personal service workers worked 15 hours or less.

Overall, in 2001 just 19% of all part-time women employees worked in the three highest-paid occupational groups, while 59% worked in the four lowest-paid occupational groups. In contrast, 45% of full-time women employees worked in the three highest-paid occupations, while just 26% worked in the four lowest-paid groups (Grant et al, 2006g, p 11).

One important outcome of the association between low-level jobs and part-time working is, as the GELLM study and reports show, that despite strong growth in the number of part-time jobs, a large proportion of women working part time (around 50%) are working 'below their potential', that is, they are employed in jobs that fail to use their skills, experience or qualifications (Grant et al, 2005, 2006g). As already noted in Chapter Three, follow-up research by the Equal Opportunities Commission, based on the GELLM findings, revealed that nationally 2.8 million part-time women workers are in this situation (Darton and Hurrell, 2005).

Despite this general pattern, not all part-time jobs involve poor conditions of work. Some women working part time are employed in occupations associated with higher pay and with good working conditions, including some in managerial, professional and some technical jobs. This means that the availability of better-quality part-time jobs is a key issue, given the extent to which women are working 'below their potential' in low-paid part-time jobs and the percentage of working age women in part-time employment (80%) who express a preference for part-time hours (Warren, 2001; ONS, 2006a). Here variations in the occupational and

**Figure 7.2: Distribution of part-time women employees by occupation: women resident in England and selected localities**

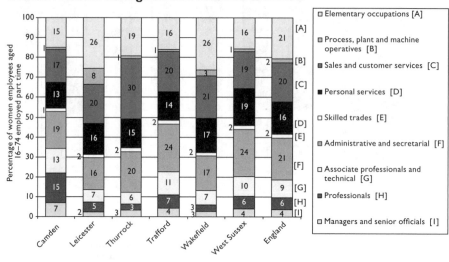

*Source:* 2001 Census Standard Tables, Crown Copyright 2003.

industrial structure of local labour markets are important. Because of this, in some local labour markets women have a much greater likelihood of being in, or of being able to find, a good-quality part-time job than in others. This means that they also have a reduced tendency to be 'working below their potential'.

## Labour market variations in occupational structure

One way to explore the variation in occupational structure with regard to women's part-time employment is to look at the distribution of women part-time workers in different occupational groups across labour markets. This is shown for the localities where part-time work was studied in Figure 7.2, revealing that women living in Camden and working part time were much more likely to be employed in a higher-paid, better-quality part-time job than women working part time and living in the other localities in the study. While over a third (35%) of part-time women workers in Camden worked in the top three, higher-paid, occupations (managers and senior officials, professionals, and associate professional and technical occupations), in Thurrock and Wakefield barely one eighth (12% and 13%) were in this situation.

At the other end of the occupational hierarchy, while 34% of part-time women workers in Leicester, and 29% in Wakefield, were employed in the two lowest-paid occupational groups (elementary occupations and process, plant and machine operatives), only 16% of part-time women workers worked in these two occupational groups in Camden, and only 17% in Trafford. These kinds of variations between labour markets are also apparent in the middle-ranking jobs, such as administrative and secretarial jobs. In Leicester, just 16% of part-time women workers were employed in these jobs, compared with 24% in Trafford.

Indeed, if we look at the distribution of women working part time in the top four occupations in terms of pay (that is, including the administrative/secretarial group), while 54% of part-time women workers worked in these four occupations in Camden, in Leicester the figure was only 30%. If we focus on the bottom four occupations in terms of pay, we find that in Leicester 70% of women part-time workers worked in the bottom occupations, compared with only 51% in Trafford. Thus, in different local labour markets, women working part time are distributed across the occupational groups in very different ways.

Variation in the distribution of part-time women workers across occupations provides only one aspect of the picture, however. We also need to consider the proportion of women workers who work part time in the localities and in various occupations. This is shown in Figure 7.3.

**Figure 7.3 Proportion of women employees who work part time, by occupation: England and selected localities**

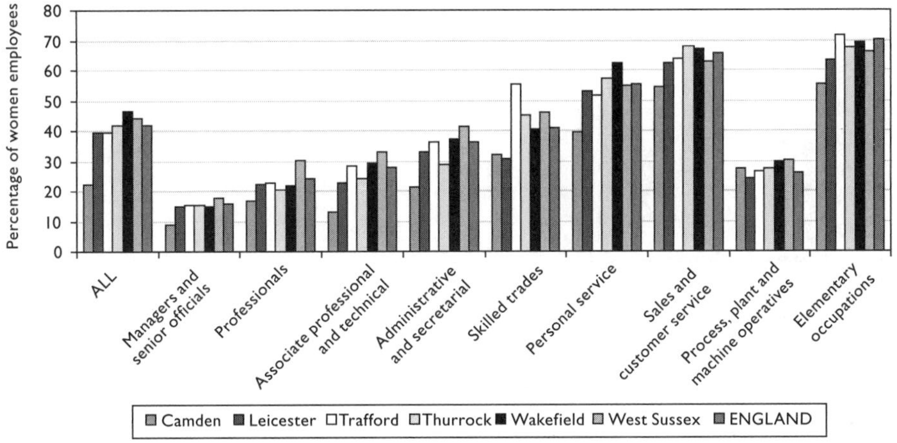

*Source:* 2001 Census Standard Tables, Crown Copyright 2003.

Again, there is considerable variation. In Camden, the proportion of women workers who work part time is considerably lower than the proportion in the other localities in the GELLM study or in England as a whole. Only 22% of Camden's women employees worked part time in 2001, compared with 42% in England. This is reflected in the figures for different occupational groups. In Camden, just 9% of women managers worked part time, compared with 15% in Leicester. Only 17% of women professionals worked part time in Camden, compared with 30% in West Sussex. At the lower end of the occupational hierarchy similar variations are evident across the localities. In Trafford, 72% of women working in elementary occupations worked part time, compared with 63% in Leicester. And in Wakefield, 30% of process, plant and machine operatives worked part time, compared with 24% in Leicester. Thus, it appears that in different local labour markets women seeking part-time employment have a very different range of job opportunities available to them.

## Labour market variations in industrial structure

One of the factors underpinning the differences in part-time job opportunities, and the availability of good-quality part-time jobs, is industrial structure, which varies across local labour markets. There are a number of dimensions to this. First, the tendency to create part-time jobs varies by industry, with part-time jobs forming a much higher proportion of women's jobs in, for example, the wholesale and retail sector than in manufacturing or transport, as shown in Figure 7.4 for the GELLM localities.

**Figure 7.4: Proportion of women employees who work part-time in selected industries, England and selected localities**

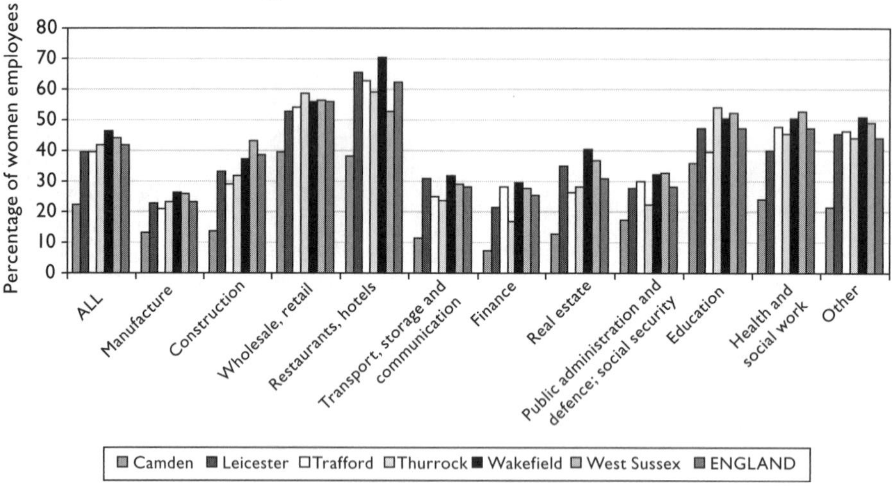

*Source:* 2001 Census Standard Tables, Crown Copyright 2003.

Thus the industrial structure in a particular locality has an important bearing on the availability of part-time jobs. Second, across localities the proportion of women's jobs that are part time in a particular industry also tends to vary. For example, in Wakefield 70% of women working in hotels and restaurants worked part time, compared with just 59% in Thurrock. And while 54% of women who worked in education in Thurrock worked part time, in Trafford only 40% did so.

Third, across local labour markets there are important variations in the distribution of part-time jobs in the industrial structure, as shown in Figure 7.5 for the GELLM localities. While just 30% of part-time women workers in Thurrock worked in the industries associated with the public sector (health, social work, education, public administration and social security), in Trafford this sector accounted for 41% of part-time women workers. In Wakefield, 27% of part-time women workers worked in the wholesale and retail sector, while in

Thurrock 38% were employed in this sector. Similarly, 10% of part-time women workers in Leicester worked in manufacturing, but in Trafford only 3% worked in this industry. Finally, the availability of part-time jobs at senior and management levels also varies by industry. Overall, variation in industrial structure across the localities and variation in the proportion and distribution of part-time workers by industry are key factors underpinning the availability of part-time jobs in general, and good-quality part-time jobs in particular.

The discussion above reveals that the distribution of part-time jobs in different occupations and industries varies across local labour markets. It also shows that the proportion of part-time jobs in different industries and occupations varies across local labour markets. Thus we are more likely to find part-time jobs in some industries and in some local labour markets than in others. In turn, there is greater availability of good-quality part-time jobs in some industries and in some local labour markets than in others. Overall, this suggests that the scope to construct part-time jobs, and, more importantly, good-quality part-time jobs, is much greater than is currently realised, as it is clearly not simply an outcome of industrial structure.

In the next section we draw on the qualitative research in the GELLM study of part-time work (Grant et al, 2006g–l). This relates to 22 workplaces in six different localities (see Appendix A for a description of the study). Our aim here is to explore why it is that only certain jobs tend to be designed as part time, and why part-time jobs are typically designed with particular characteristics that mark them out as poor-quality jobs. It also seeks to explain the limited availability of senior level part-time jobs on the open labour market.

**Figure 7.5: Distribution of part-time women employees by industry: women resident in England and selected localities**

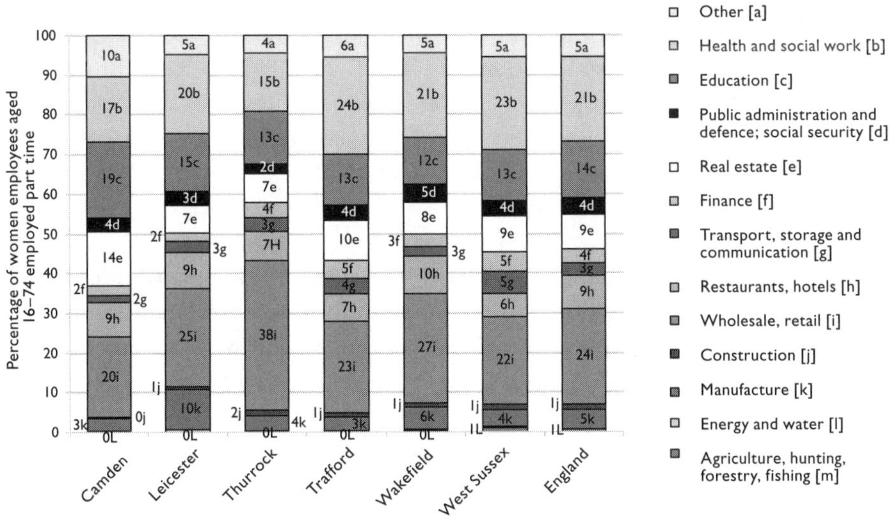

*Source:* 2001 Census Standard Tables, Crown Copyright 2003.

## Managers' reluctance to construct senior-level part-time jobs

The GELLM study found that many women seeking part-time work are unable to find jobs on the open labour market that use their skills, qualifications or labour market experience. One consequence of this is that women are forced to work 'below their potential' in low-level part-time jobs. This is a key contributor to gender inequality as it limits women's ability to maximise their earnings or progress in their careers. The GELLM study explored the processes that lead to the restricted availability of senior level part-time jobs, and found that this is often an outcome of informal management decisions, prejudice and workplace culture.

In many workplaces the balance between full-time and part-time jobs remains much the same year on year. Part of the reason for this is that, over time, line managers tend to replace 'like with like', part time with part time and full time with full time, without always conducting a thorough review of labour needs.

> 'I think, over the years, we've pretty much replaced like with like and we've not really thought, is this role worth splitting in two? Would it give us a bit more variation to re-evaluate the position and, say, there's a bit more focus needed in that area? I guess no one has ever sat back and thought, is there a different way of doing this?' (Manager, Camden)

The importance of managers' informal decision making in specific workplaces, and its capacity to enhance or limit opportunities for part-time workers, has also been noted in relation to line managers' reluctance to adopt new policies (Tomlinson, 2006, p 70). The disinclination to design senior-level jobs as part-time thus appears to stem, in some circumstances, from an unintended inertia in decision making. But it can also be an outcome of a more conscious rejection of part-time working at senior levels. Some managers argue that the tasks involved in such jobs cannot be undertaken on a less-than-full-time basis. Employing part-time workers in these posts would, it is believed, lead to a situation where uncompleted tasks would fall to other managers to complete and essential decisions would not be taken. Managers can thus be unwilling to contemplate changing existing structures and systems to accommodate part-time workers.

> 'It would be very difficult to justify a part-time role, say, as a duty manager ... because they are all on a three-week shift rota ... If you introduced a part-timer into that it's going to throw them out ... and it couldn't be done as job share ... Where would you get the continuity and the decisions that are made? Every senior management team meeting that we had, you'd have to have both of the people doing that job in all the meetings ... It wouldn't, it couldn't work.' (Manager, Thurrock)

Broader workplace cultures are also important (Jenkins, 2004). In many organisations the association between long hours of work and seniority is deeply embedded, and thus even where strategies exist to encourage part-time working, individual managers can be resistant to the adoption of new approaches when filling senior jobs, again highlighting the importance of informal decision making.

> 'I think sometimes the managers are fairly closed to new ways of doing things. Maybe they can't see the opportunity ... there is a bit of our HR strategy which hasn't been finalised ... And I do think sometimes I need to say, would it be better as a job share which still meets the needs of the service? When I joined here there was a real anti-job share approach, but now we have got a lot more job shares – and they work.' (Manager, Thurrock)

This thinking, which resists part-time working at senior levels, can manifest itself across entire workplaces, as noted by a human resources manager seeking to extend part-time working in her current workplace.

> 'There is a view in other organisations that part-time is OK, but only for jobs "down here". I've never come across that here. There is a push here to get the work–life balance correct. There is a push against the long hours culture.' (Manager, West Sussex)

Other research has suggested that employers' reluctance to create more senior-level part-time jobs may be an outcome of employers' calculations about the costs of hiring, training and administering workers. These costs are likely to be as much for part-time as for full-time workers, but for part-time workers returns are lower because they work fewer hours (Manning and Petrongolo, 2004, p 28). Tomlinson (2006) suggests that employers' prejudices against part-time workers have an impact in restricting certain jobs to full-time employees. This was also evident in the GELLM study. Some employers complained that part-time workers were less loyal, less flexible and less reliable than full-time workers, even where part-timers and full-timers are occupied in similar jobs (Grant et al, 2006g, pp 30–1).

> 'We seem to get more problems with the part-time staff and I think that is because they are trying to balance more things ... There is more absence, being late, sometimes reliability about what they are doing whilst they are here. I think the quality and the calibre of the full-time staff is higher than the part-time staff.' (Manager, West Sussex)

Concern was expressed that if senior posts were advertised as part time on the open labour market the calibre of candidates might decline: 'We're not going to get such a good field if we advertise for someone four days a week ... the field won't be as good as it would be for full-time' (Manager, Camden).

That individual prejudice against part-time workers, and against women seeking part-time work, is more important in explaining the dearth of senior level part-time jobs than genuine organisational barriers is further confirmed by the fact that most of the managers interviewed were willing to consider requests from senior post-holders to reduce their hours of work. The key problem resides in the resistance to designing senior posts as part time, and advertising them as such on the open labour market.

Unintended inertia, informal management decision making, workplace culture and prejudice all appear to play a part in restricting the availability of part-time jobs at more senior levels. In effect, qualified and experienced women workers seeking part-time jobs on the open labour market are excluded from particular levels of employment, with implications for gender equality. At the same time, employers have specific reasons for designing certain jobs as part time. This contributes to the clustering of part-time jobs at the lower levels of workplace hierarchies.

## Managers' thinking and the clustering of part-time jobs at lower levels

One reason given by managers interviewed in the GELLM study for designing specific jobs as part time reflects their views about the particular tasks involved in a job. There are certain tasks that, employers argue, can be completed in a limited number of hours and in less than a full working day or less than a full working week. Thus employers' perspectives on the nature of certain tasks are important in understanding why some jobs tend to be constructed as part time. Jobs that fit into this category of 'task-based part-time jobs' include care assistant, cleaner, learning support worker, catering assistant and administrative worker. Many employers evaluate the length of time required to fulfil a particular task – for example to clean the ward of a hospital, to provide personal care services to an individual, or to offer a support service to students in a classroom setting – and design jobs on this basis. The aim is to use part-time employment as a means of avoiding unnecessary wages costs by not paying for time in the day when the task is not being performed.

> 'If you're simply supporting in the classroom, as a learning support assistant, putting it bluntly, if they are not needed they are not paid. Their hours fit in with the time the students are here, when they are needed. Obviously teachers work much longer days than that ... With support staff we are just paying people when they need to be here. The bottom line is saving money.' (Manager, Camden)

This is partly about the way in which the range of tasks associated with certain jobs is restricted; an issue to which we will return later. Not all 'task-based part-time jobs' are filled by employees on part-time contracts. Full-time employees can carry out more than one 'task-based part-time job' in a workplace. However, 'task-based part-time jobs' tend to be occupied by part-time employees, and overwhelmingly by women. The association between these jobs and 'women's work' is widespread and deeply embedded.

Another set of jobs tends to be designed as part time because, employers argue, the worker is only required during a part of the working day or working week. The jobs that fit into this category of 'demand-based part-time jobs' include: checkout operators, production and assembly workers in manufacturing, library assistants, security workers and bar workers. Part-time employees working in 'demand-based part-time jobs' tend to work alongside people employed on full-time contracts doing a similar job.

Sometimes 'demand-based part-time jobs' are constructed to fill a shortfall in the labour available to deliver a service or produce a product. Using full-time employees would not fill these gaps cost effectively, as the additional staffing is not needed for a full-time period. Gaps can be specific hours in the day or whole days. For example, one retail organisation had extended its opening hours and the additional hours were being covered by employees on part-time contracts. Similarly, one of the manufacturers had experienced an increased demand for its products, which had led it to extend the production hours each day and across the week. The additional hours and days were covered by employing people on part-time contracts. 'We just started taking on part-timers to cover gaps. We were trying to meet the demand for products. There were no altruistic or work–life balance reasons for it. It's purely for the commercial needs of the business.' (Manager, Leicester).

'Demand-based part-time jobs' also enable employers to boost the number of workers at particular times of the day or week in response to a heavy workload or trading period. Thus demand-based part-time jobs provide employers with numerical flexibility (Fagan and O'Reilly, 1998). 'Part-time workers are boosting the staff available at that time of day' (Manager, West Sussex).

The GELLM study also revealed that a third set of jobs are constructed as part time in order to ease recruitment in tight labour markets. For some employers a combination of low unemployment in a locality and the low pay offered for a specific job creates significant recruitment problems. The construction of 'recruitment-based part-time jobs' is one solution. These are jobs designed to attract women workers looking for part-time work. 'We were scratching around for ideas to get people in. We haven't always been madly keen on them as a group' (Manager, West Sussex). A number of key features, taken together, mark out the jobs that employers are willing, or eager, to construct as part time, and to advertise as such on the open labour market.

First, the tasks involved in these jobs have been limited to a narrow range and classed as unskilled and quickly learned. In other words, there is little worker autonomy in defining or creating job-related tasks. Second, the jobs can easily be time-limited by the employer. Third, there is variable demand for the worker, over the course of the day or week. Fourth, because the tasks associated with part-time jobs can be quickly learned, workers are regarded as easily replaced:

'The less complicated the job (the more) it lends itself to part-time, because you are just looking for a bum on a seat as opposed to the continuity of the individual' (Manager, Trafford). Fifth, managers invariably expect to recruit women to these jobs. Finally, potential recruits are perceived as second earners, whatever the reality of household circumstances: 'There are a lot of people who want to work for pin money' (Manager, West Sussex).

This analysis contributes to and develops previous discussion on employers' reasons for constructing part-time jobs and highlights the heterogeneous nature of part-time employment. For example, Tilly (1996) identified two types of part-time job: 'secondary' and 'retention'. 'Secondary part-time jobs' are low-skill jobs that offer little opportunity for advancement, while 'retention' part-time jobs are skilled jobs created to retain valued employees occupying senior positions. The part-time jobs identified in the GELLM study fall into Tilly's 'secondary' category, but our analysis differentiates this category further, into three distinct sets of part-time jobs: 'task-based', 'demand-based' and 'recruitment-based'. The 'retention part-time jobs' identified by Tilly, which are more highly paid, also exist and represent an additional category (not explored by our research because it focused on low-paid part-time employment). However, the existence of 'retention part-time jobs' is important to our analysis overall, since it suggests that senior-level jobs could more readily be occupied by part-time workers than is currently the case. The problem remains employers' unwillingness to advertise such jobs on the open labour market.

There are a number of features of part-time jobs that, taken together, contribute to their poor quality. The following discussion explores why part-time jobs tend to be designed with a particular set of characteristics.

## Pay and pay determination

One critical aspect of the generally poor design of part-time jobs is low pay. In 2005, at the time of our study, the average hourly pay for part-time women workers in England was £6.75, compared with £9.98 for full-time women workers and £11.63 for full-time male workers (Grant et al, 2006g, p 22). Women who worked part time earned on average 27% less per hour than women who worked full time, a gap that had changed little in the previous 25 years (Hurrell, 2005). One of the main explanations for this pay gap is the segregation of part-time jobs into the lowest-paid occupations and sectors of the industrial structure. Women experience a 'pay penalty' for working part time and, as we saw in Chapter Three, the prevalence of women working part time in the UK is a key factor affecting the gender pay gap (Grimshaw and Rubery, 2001; Harkness, 2002; Manning and Petrongolo, 2004). Working part time also has a longer-term detrimental impact on women's earnings. Women who move to full-time employment after only one year of part-time working in a 15-year period can earn 10% less per hour than those who worked full-time for all 15 years (Francesconi and Gosling, 2005, p x).

Given the clustering of part-time jobs in low-paid occupations and sectors, the GELLM study explored employers' approaches to pay setting for part-time jobs. The research was focused on a wide range of part-time jobs, including: catering assistant, cleaner, administrative worker, receptionist, care assistant, learning support worker, library assistant, bar worker, leisure facility attendant, swimming pool attendant, supermarket checkout worker, supermarket stock replenisher, assembly line worker, postal worker and security worker. For the majority of the jobs, pay was at or just above the level of the national minimum wage (NMW). In interviews with managers it emerged that in the pay-setting process the NMW was an important benchmark. Wage rates above the NMW were invariably characterised as generous. For example, a rate of pay of £5.78 an hour offered in one workplace for administrative staff (at a time when the NMW was £4.85) was described as 'at the top end', yet would yield, for a lone mother with two children working 30 hours a week, a weekly income below the official poverty line of 60% of median earnings in 2004/05 (CPAG, 2005).

It became clear, also, that private sector employers typically sought to keep wages and wage increases in line with those in their industry and in their locality, with employers effectively colluding to contain pay within certain limits.

> 'The way we set pay is looking at the roles and responsibilities of the job, and then looking at what other similar companies are doing. We belong to an association of similar [employers]. We get together and meet regularly and we share and exchange information. That's how the rates are set.' (Manager, Thurrock)

In the public sector, pay-setting processes build on well-established pay scales developed through national collective bargaining. Although the placing of specific jobs on these pay scales appeared to be subject to some local decision making (for example, care assistants working in different local authorities received different rates of pay), the differences in hourly pay were small and the jobs were typically located towards the bottom of these scales. This is an outcome of decisions taken over long periods of time about the relative value of certain jobs.

Critically, for the jobs studied, pay setting in both the public and private sectors usually involved only minor adjustments to pay rates year on year, in effect locking the part-time jobs involved into the lowest wage layers of the economy. As discussed earlier, this is partly an outcome of employers' thinking about the tasks involved in the jobs themselves. Jobs that are typically occupied by women tend to be constructed as of lower value than jobs typically occupied by men, reflecting views about the skills involved in 'women's work' (Grimshaw and Rubery, 2007). Thus while pay at or near the NMW level was regarded as poor by most managers, a pay rate just 50 pence above the NMW was considered a major step forward.

'We pay above the national minimum wage but I don't think it's enough. The company is looking at ways to boost that up ... By the end of this year we hope to get all our staff just above £5.00 an hour ... because you can't give 100% if you're worried about keeping body and soul together.' (Manager, Leicester)

It also reflects employers' thinking about why part-time women workers are working. Typically, managers did not expect part-time workers to be breadwinners or even to be making significant contributions to family income: 'A typical part-time worker is somebody who has got outside commitments ... probably supporting the family income ... to help support the holiday and really more on the social side of life' (Manager, Trafford).

At the same time, the skills and qualifications held by part-time women workers were largely invisible to managers; they were unaware that many part-time employees were working below their potential: 'We may have one or two who are over-qualified' (Manager, Leicester).

Employers' comments about the pay-setting process are revealing, as they provide clues about the thinking applied in the job design process more widely. The jobs were described by employers as 'unskilled' and were regarded as capable of being performed by people who are 'easily replaced'. Employers also had a fairly clear idea of the type of person they expect to recruit: someone who is not a breadwinner and who is likely to be a woman with few skills or qualifications, a finding that reinforces the argument presented over 20 years ago in Beechey and Perkins' (1987) study of part-time employment: 'You've got this group of people, waiting until their partner comes in and then they're coming out for a bit of pocket money' (Manager, Trafford).

This reminds us that pay setting is subject to gendered thinking and is an outcome of workplace cultures, norms and structures. As Grimshaw and Rubery (2007) have argued:

> ... the setting of wages is far from a precise science and in practice reflects a compromise between a range of influences. Labour market and production cost factors are clearly one set of influences, but wages are also fixed in relation to long established social norms and with regard to internal organisational hierarchies. (pp 2–3)

A range of factors affect the levels of pay typically associated with part-time jobs. The NMW clearly sets a benchmark against which employers assess the wages offered. It is also the case that employers collude with each other to maintain pay levels in the low wage economy. However, employers' thinking about part-time jobs and part-time workers plays an important role in maintaining low pay and thus in perpetuating gender inequality.

## Training and promotion

Low pay is one key aspect of the design of part-time jobs that has a wider impact on gender inequality. A second aspect concerns the opportunities for training and promotion associated with part-time employment. Previous research has shown that part-time workers have poor access to training – particularly poor access to training that might enhance their chances of progression or promotion – and few opportunities for promotion. This was strongly reinforced in the GELLM study:

> 'I'd like to be doing something at the higher level, but it's quite regimented in terms of the level that people are at. You can't just get trained for the higher-level work. They tend to want to keep it all separate. I've never had a chance to prove myself.' (Part-time worker, Camden)

> 'I'd like to be a section supervisor ... they've advertised it externally now ... it would not be available on the hours I work'. (Part-time worker, Leicester)

These limitations associated with part-time jobs were confirmed by managers: 'If you want to work part time the opportunities for promotion are limited' (Manager, Leicester). In many organisations, low-paid, part-time jobs are designed as 'self-contained jobs' with no obvious career paths attached to them. These are jobs that are not integrated into organisational progression opportunities and structures, making low-paid, part-time jobs the 'dead-end jobs' of popular parlance.

> 'They won't train me on the machines because I am only part time ... I said I'd like training on basically anything that would need any training ... and I've never heard anything at all. I just said, "Well, I'm not going to pursue it, because I know it's because I'm part time." And if I wanted to go up the ladder to a supervisory role, I'd have to go full time.' (Part-time worker, West Sussex)

There are a number of reasons why training is limited and promotion opportunities rare for part-time workers. It is partly an outcome of broader changes to internal labour markets across organisations, whereby intermediary jobs that previously provided a stepping stone to higher-level jobs have tended to be removed from workplace hierarchies, trapping those occupying lower-level jobs at this level (Grimshaw et al, 2002). 'I feel I'm trapped. You feel you want to move on, but you're stuck on this level. You want to advance to the next level but you can't' (Part-time worker, Trafford).

Poor access to training and promotion for part-time workers also stems from assumptions about part-time workers themselves. Often managers assume that part-time workers are incapable of working at a higher level; they know little about the employment histories of workers occupying low level jobs: 'The managers on the floor have no idea of our past and they don't talk to you to find out ... They don't tap into anything you've ever done, which is sad. It's sad. It's a totally wasted resource' (Part-time worker, West Sussex).

Managers also make assumptions, disputed by our evidence from part-time workers, that this group of workers is not ambitious.

> 'It's people's personal preferences if they want to come back to work how much they want to commit themselves ... You get to a point where you still need the mental stimulation but don't want to give the 140% you are required to give in a full-time job in today's society.' (Manager, Trafford)

In many organisations managers simply fail to accept that their own jobs could be done by part-time workers: 'My role is too important to be part time. It's a full-time position' (Manager, Leicester).

The limited opportunities for training and promotion available to part-time workers are, in part, an outcome of broader changes in organisational structures. But, as with the tendency to low pay, this aspect of job design also stems from managers' thinking about part-time jobs and their assumptions about part-time workers.

Overall, the design of part-time jobs and the location of part-time jobs in workplace hierarchies are outcomes of a range of formal and informal management decisions and practices. Informal management decisions sometimes stem from workplace culture, but they also arise from individual prejudice against part-time work and part-time workers, and from gendered thinking and assumptions. More formal management decision making also contributes to part-time job design and the positioning of part-time jobs in the occupational structure. Management perspectives on particular tasks, cost considerations, including the importance of numerical flexibility and recruitment difficulties, all play a part.

## Job content, employee autonomy and responsibility

There is another set of dimensions of part-time jobs that also underlines their poor quality. These include, in particular, the limited job content and limited worker autonomy and control associated with part-time work. Less is known about these aspects of part-time jobs; however, the GELLM study provides some insight into why they arise.

In the first place, part-time jobs are often presented as jobs that offer 'flexibility' to workers. Yet, in practice, as the GELLM study confirms, this is sometimes far from the reality. Part-time workers rarely fix or choose their total hours of work, their start and finish times, or their working patterns. On the contrary, all these aspects of flexibility are usually controlled by managers. Indeed, part-time workers are valued by employers precisely because their hours of work and their start and finish times can be changed at short notice; as one manager commented: 'you can juggle their hours'.

> 'One week they might do 10 hours, another 20 hours and one week they may not have any work at all ... They work up to 30 hours a week but the idea is to maintain it between 20 and 30 hours over the month.' (Manager, Leicester)

> 'We have lots of cashiers on flexible contracts where they work, for example, "20 hours flexible" ... Their rota may change on a weekly or monthly basis. So one Thursday they might work between 10 and 4 and another Thursday they work between 2 and 8.' (Manager, Thurrock)

The reverse, where employees seek to use opportunities for flexible working to their own advantage, can be challenged by managers and firm action taken to eradicate it.

> 'We had a long hard look at our business and we noticed that a lot of part-timers were working five days a week. They had a one-day contract but they were working five days one week and three days the next and two days, or whatever. And we said, right, you can have a choice of a five-day contract or no contract ... So we have tried to move away from part-time working now and gaining more flexibility through the week by altering our shift patterns.' (Manager, Leicester)

This resistance by managers to workers exercising more choice in their hours of work is indicative of the wider features of lower-level part-time jobs and the lack of control and autonomy enjoyed by most part-time workers. Because of the location of part-time jobs at the lower levels of the occupational hierarchy, they tend to be jobs that entail a limited range of tasks, in which workers are offered few responsibilities, and where the pace and intensity of work is often closely supervised. The consequences for women workers, particularly where women are 'working below their potential' can be boredom and frustration.

> 'You're not using your skills. To be an input clerk – am I allowed to use the word boring? I feel like you're a robot and you're just part

of a production line … how can I put it? You're literally just being passed something and asked to process it and you've got no particular thought other than making sure you're inputting it correctly … and there's no other involvement.' (Part-time worker, Leicester)

Yet the potential to enrich task-based, demand-based and recruitment-based part-time jobs by extending responsibilities, widening the range of tasks and offering workers greater independence is rarely grasped by employers.

'In terms of responsibility, this job is a lot more interesting than it was when I started. But, you know, I ran a company and we had about 25 staff. If there were part-time jobs that were able to use my experience it would appeal to me, but they're basically not there. I'd like a higher level of responsibility but I know that kind of job doesn't exist.' (Part-time worker, Camden)

In essence, part-time jobs are largely trapped in a particular segment of the occupational structure. This serves to deny women who work part time the possibility of realising their potential or extending their skills. Part-time jobs are overwhelmingly repetitive and limited in their scope to engage in independent thinking, to exercise control and to determine flexibility.

## Conclusion

The availability of part-time job opportunities and the tendency for part-time jobs to be restricted to lower-level jobs varies by workplace, industry and locality. Local industrial structure is important in explaining the range of part-time job opportunities and the availability of higher level jobs in particular local labour markets but it is not the entire explanation. There is variation by locality in the distribution of part-time women workers across industrial sectors, but there is also variation by locality in the proportion of part-time women workers in particular industries. This is because, regardless of local industrial structure, the construction of part-time jobs is an outcome of decisions taken in workplaces and larger employing organisations.

Current approaches to the design of part-time jobs and the structuring of part-time job opportunities are an outcome of management decisions in workplaces and organisations. There are clearly a range of business and cost-related reasons why some jobs are designed as part time and others as full time. But these are not the only reasons. Both formal and informal management decisions regarding the proportion of part-time jobs, the proportion of higher-level part-time jobs, and the design of lower-level part-time jobs in a workplace or organisation are often based on factors unrelated to business or cost imperatives. Inertia and prejudice against part-time jobs and part-time workers also play a part. Such prejudices can stem from the views of individual managers or from the wider workplace culture.

The typical design features of low-level part-time jobs: low pay; limited opportunities for training and promotion; restriction of tasks; limited responsibility, independence and autonomy; and lack of flexibility in working hours all highlight the poor quality of part-time jobs. But the key problem with these jobs is that women who occupy them are trapped at the lower level. Notwithstanding the contemporary tendency to 'de-layering' in organisations, these jobs are purposely disconnected from internal progression structures and opportunities. This is the major factor that contributes to the association between part-time employment and gender inequality. It may well be the case that, for some people, the routine nature of part-time jobs and the limitations in tasks, responsibility and control associated with them are what suits them and perhaps what they desire at particular points in their lives. The problem remains, however, that – if a worker's aspirations change, or their skill levels do not correspond to the requirements of a typical part-time job – as long as they wish to work part time, or experience constraints which force them to work part time, their opportunities will be limited.

That there is scope to break out of the current tendency to design low-level part-time jobs in particular ways, and to break down the tendency to limit part-time jobs to lower levels of the occupational structure, is shown by the example of 'retention part-time jobs'. These are jobs at higher levels of the occupational structure occupied by workers working part time who previously worked full time in the job. Many have negotiated reduced working hours while retaining their seniority. This is a practice that has been growing as a result of new legislation introduced in 2003, and extended in scope in 2007; it offers parents of young and disabled children, and some carers of adults, the right to request flexible working (Yeandle and Buckner, 2007). The problem is that the vast majority of part-time jobs are designed in a way that restricts the scope of the job and confines part-time working to lower occupational levels.

To address the current situation, part-time jobs need to be integrated within wider employment structures and opportunities within workplaces and organisations, and this requires new thinking by managers and employers. First, it requires recognition that most jobs can be undertaken on a part-time basis. Second, it requires an acknowledgement that many part-time women workers are 'working below potential' and thus have skills, qualifications and experience that are under-utilised in part-time jobs. Third, it requires an understanding that many women workers do have aspirations to occupy more senior-level jobs whilst continuing to work part time.

There is also scope for the enrichment and enlargement of low-level part-time jobs. Job enlargement would involve extending the range of tasks associated with a job; job enrichment would involve extending the range of responsibilities offered to part-time workers and the amount of independence they exercise in their job. Here the benefits for women employees would include both more satisfying jobs and opportunities to improve their pay and promotion prospects.

Employers could also offer greater flexibility to all workers to enable them to alter their hours of work over the course of their working lives, from full time to part time, to full time, and so on, whilst retaining their status and not closing down progression opportunities. This is in the interests of employers and managers, as well as women workers, as the current separation of part-time and full-time jobs within workplaces, and across industries leads to a massive waste of talent and skills, and often involves poor use of organisational investments in staff development and training.

At particular points in their lives millions of women either prefer to work part time, or are constrained by wider circumstances to search for part-time work. But the way most employers and managers currently design part-time jobs and locate them within workplace hierarchies is a basis for widespread gender inequality. To overcome this, part-time jobs need to be released from the 'low level' trap.

# EIGHT

# Tough at the top: women's career progression – an example in the local government sector

*Cinnamon Bennett and Ning Tang*

## Introduction

This chapter takes up the issues facing women with the skills and qualifications to progress to the most senior levels in the labour market. Research by employers and academics shows that women are very poorly represented in the boardroom and in senior management teams, despite over three decades of legislation and policy interventions on their behalf. Herein lies the puzzle. Do women themselves lack commitment to their jobs and to earning their own money, and are they uncomfortable wielding power, as some have suggested? Or are structural explanations, and the indirect discrimination found in workplace cultures and processes of advancement, more compelling explanations? To explore these issues, we discuss the experiences of qualified women in the local authority sector, a sector that has been in the vanguard of the development of family-friendly and equal opportunities policies. All the women whose experiences we discuss here had attained jobs that were judged to have promotion prospects, earning upwards of £18,000 pa in 2005.[1]

The GELLM study discussed here was concerned with women's advancement within the workplace (Bennett et al, 2006a). It focused on women with educational qualifications who were in jobs, paid above the national average, with career development potential. Women's work–life preferences and their perception of the choices they had to make to achieve these preferences were at the heart of the investigation. Data were collected about their aspirations and attitudes towards their current career, the value they attached to employment, and to their own job in particular, and their perceptions of the opportunities and challenges facing them when considering applying for promotion within their organisation.

As described elsewhere, the policy agendas of the local authorities involved in this study fed into and guided the research design (Bennett, 2008). Four local authorities chose to examine women's career progression within their own organisations and gave the team access both to their employees and to their workforce data. The research design, carried out in the same way in each participating local authority, incorporated both quantitative and qualitative research methods (described in Appendix A).

The study discussed here is based on 1,370 structured questionnaire responses from female employees in these four organisations and focus group discussions with 106 of these same women, grouped according to their age, caring responsibilities and career stage. With all groups we explored women's career aspirations and future plans. We also asked those in the oldest age group to reflect on the extent to which their youthful career aspirations or plans had been met. To conclude the discussion, participants were invited to complete an open-ended questionnaire that asked about their attitudes towards their job and career and the types of support they could draw on (or pay for) to help them sustain their work and non-work roles.

## Women's employment in the local authority sector

Local government accounts for 9% of the workforce in the whole economy, with other public sector agencies accounting for a further 11% of all employees (Employers Organisation, 2005a). The sector is a significant employer of women, who make up 70% of its workforce, in contrast to the whole economy where women make up 49% of the national workforce (LGAR, 2007a, p 14). In 2005, 1.65 million women were employed in local authorities' education, social services, corporate and customer-facing functions, compared with around 580,000 men (LGAR, 2005).

Part-time work is a prominent feature of women's employment in the sector. Of female employees in English local authorities, 60% (925,512 women) were contracted to work part-time hours in June 2005 (LGAR, 2005). Part-time working among women is more prevalent in county councils (54% of the county council workforce) and lowest in the London boroughs (35% of the LB workforce).[2] As women's employment dominates the sector, the impact of part-time working on wages and the gender pay gap is smaller in local government than in the economy as a whole (LGAR, 2007b, p 23). Figures for the public sector in 2006 show that the gender pay gap for full-time employees (13.5%) was almost 9 percentage points closer than for private sector employees (22.3%) (LGAR, 2007a, p 10). However, this difference masks a decade of unsettled pay claims in local government arising from the 1997 National Joint Council (NJC) Single Status Agreement (agreed by the employers and trade unions), which aimed to end pay discrimination through the introduction of a unified national pay spine and harmonised terms and conditions for part-time staff (Fuller, 2007).

Over the last decade the public sector[3] has been a stable employer for women and men, in terms of the total number of full-time and part-time jobs it has offered (Bennett et al, 2006a, p 7). The Improvement and Development Agency (IDeA), in its role supporting future workforce development, has championed the benefits of employment in local government promoting its: 'flexible working opportunities; generous annual leave; good training and development; pension scheme and good pay' that currently accrue as service lengthens (IDeA, 2007). Research on workforce turnover suggests that many of these incentives are effective (Yeandle et al, 2002). Local analysis suggests that approximately 30% of an authority's staff will have 10 years or more of continuous service (Stockton-on-Tees Borough Council, 2007). Consequently the local authority workforce has an older age profile than the economy as a whole. Figures for January–March 2007 show that 34% of local authority employees in England and Wales were aged over 50, and that 31% were aged 40–49 (compared with 25% for both these groups in the economy as a whole) (LGAR, 2007a, p 14).

In local government, relative stability in the size of the public sector workforce conceals the extensive reorganisation that has taken place, mainly in response to central government guidance and policy, and the outsourcing of many direct services starting in the 1980s and occurring again in the late 1990s.[4] The Local Government Pay and Workforce Strategy 2005 noted that rising demand for and levels of sub-contracted delivery in local authority children's, education and adults' services would have the most important influence on the size and composition of the directly employed local authority workforce in the future. In the same year, large losses were recorded among teaching staff (both full and part time, 14,000 jobs), and in services delivered directly to the public (11,000 jobs). However, in contrast, employment in corporate functions increased by 7,000. Overall, women bore the brunt of these job cuts, losing 15,000 full-time jobs (compared with 5,000 full-time and 3,000 part-time jobs lost by men) (Bennett et al, 2006a). Women nevertheless benefited from the rise of better-paid jobs in corporate functions, linked to the evolving role of local authorities as commissioners of services, which required staff qualified in law, procurement, client management and performance monitoring. This trend may in future be eclipsed by the growing importance of local strategic partnerships in the planning of local services, however, as more local authority positions are being paid for out of central or regional funds.

Recent structural reorganisation has been predicated on the Local Government Modernisation Agenda (LGMA), introduced by the Labour government in two White Papers in 1998 and 2001. It aimed for improvement in quality and cost, primarily through new arrangements in the way that services were planned, implemented and monitored.[5] More than 20 policy initiatives[6] have strengthened community and customer choice and increased the involvement of stakeholders in the sub-contracted delivery and scrutiny of services (Martin and Bovaird, 2005). These changes have been brought about through law and through organisational incentives such as the national and local targets set by politicians, and through the adoption of 'payment by results'.[7] Local Public Service Agreements reward local authorities on the achievement of national targets, with bonuses of up to 2.5% of their total revenue budgets.

As well as a change in the number of jobs in its different functions, another effect of the modernisation agenda on the workforce, and in particular the greater emphasis on performance management, has been a rise in long hours among more senior officers in the sector. In 2006, local government officers were identified alongside senior civil servants, directors and CEOs in the TUC's Managers Top Long Hours League Table as working the longest hours of all managerial groups (TUC, 2006b). Of these managers, 45% were averaging 12 hours' unpaid overtime per week, 2 hours 12 minutes per week more than they were averaging in 2005 (TUC, 2006a). Concerns have also been voiced by the Local Government Employers Organisation and others about the impact on productivity of increasing levels of absence linked to work-related stress and morale within the sector.[8]

These changes are significant in explaining women's career development in the sector, as they provide the context for the way individual women express their preferences and make their job choices. As 90% of the labour pool for senior officer positions is drawn internally from existing employees (Bennett et al, 2006a), the majority of those who aspire to reach the very top positions are required to perform effectively (and indeed to out-perform others) in the middle-ranking managerial grades that, arguably, have been the positions most affected by the changes described above (Simpson, 1998; Boyne, 2001).

Locality is also an important factor. Outside London and the conurbations of Birmingham and Manchester, the local authority is the largest employer in the majority of local labour markets. In districts with large central government headquarters or health trusts, recruiting local authority staff is less difficult, as these organisations create a large, dynamic local workforce moving between public sector job opportunities (Public Sector Review, 2008). For many local authority employees elsewhere this will not be the case, however, and promotion may rely on an ability to be mobile, either within a region, or to make a permanent relocation elsewhere, as local prospects tend to rely on natural workforce turnover and rates of retirement.

As its workforce profile suggests, the local government sector has been very successful in attracting and retaining women employees. This success can partly be explained by its history of commitment to and implementation of equal opportunity and family-friendly employment practices, which began in the 1980s. At this time, socialist feminist officers within local government, and women's organisations outside, lobbied politicians to improve local women's employment opportunities and services (Bennett, 2000). These early developments were subsequently strengthened by European and national equality and employment legislation and a growing consensus in organisational and human resources theory that managing the diverse situations and talents of the workforce brings business benefits.

The LGMA has formalised many of the sector's equality commitments: setting targets on race and sex equality at all levels of the organisation as part of its best value performance assessment;[9] introducing the equality standard for local government in England in 2001 to monitor progress towards the systematic mainstreaming of equality into public service delivery and employment practices (IDeA, 2007) and placing a duty on local authorities to actively promote sex equality as part of the public sector gender duty outlined in the 2006 Equality Act. At the local level, some authorities (including Wakefield, one of our study authorities) have been proactive in their approach to women's employment, developing women-only management training, networks and mentoring schemes.

Yet, despite these legislative and policy initiatives and women's numerical superiority in the sector, women do not command the upper strata of local government hierarchies. Female employees are clustered at the lower end of occupational structures, and in job roles associated with traditional 'women's work'. In 2006, only 21% of the 410 chief executives in the English and Welsh local authorities, and only 25% of approximately 7,000 chief officers, were women (Local Government Employers, 2007). Women made up only about a third of local government's top 5% of earners (Audit Commission, 2007). Even in functions that can be described as feminised, men continued to dominate senior management. For example, in the social care sector, men made up 56% of those in professional care occupations, compared with 79% of women in the care workforce as a whole (Jagger, 2005, p 25; Yeandle et al, 2006c). There has been much debate among academics and practitioners about the reasons for the absence of women from senior levels in all parts of the economy. These analyses generally agree that structural factors, including how work is organised and the practicalities of combining work and family responsibilities, are very significant (Grimshaw and Rubery, 2001). Some theorists, more controversially, have also emphasised that women's own choices and preferences relating to paid work and family orientations also play a significant role.

## Explanations of women's absence from senior positions

Although flexible working has become more widespread as more organisations attempt to respond to fluctuations in customer demand, the use of part-time and casual arrangements has mainly been adopted for the benefit of employers (Tam, 1997; EOC, 2005c). As we saw in Chapter Seven, some employers have deliberately structured these low-wage jobs to appeal to women with caring responsibilities, for example by offering term-time working or part-time hours that fit around school times (Yeandle et al, 2006c). More recently, policy innovations and new employment legislation has further encouraged these practices (Yeandle and Buckner, 2007). Recognition of the costs of failing to retain trained and experienced staff has also encouraged some employers to extend flexibility to full-time employees, in some cases offering compressed working weeks, annualised hours and flexi-time (Yeandle et al, 2002; Kersley et al, 2005). These arrangements, facilitated by technological advances that allow off-site remote working, are also beginning to be used as inducements when recruiting new employees, particularly if there is pressure on employers to keep wages and office overhead costs down (Yeandle et al, 2006b). However, this trend towards greater flexibility, which has assisted women's labour market participation, has occurred against the continuing and well-established practice of privileging full, day-time commitment to paid work over unpaid work performed in the domestic sphere and at home: as

Hochschild (1997, p 93) has commented: 'to work part-time was to renege on an agreement to do a whole, complete job'.

Management-level jobs have long been identified as a marked and particularly visible area of organisational gender relations and as a key site of male power and exclusionary practice (Cockburn, 1991). More recently, Junor (1998) has argued that these senior jobs have been almost completely unaffected by the wider use of flexible working, claiming instead that they have become even more demanding in terms of hours of work and the attendance they expect of post-holders. As discussed in Chapter Seven, the position often taken is that the tasks and roles associated with management jobs make them 'too important' to be performed on a part-time or flexible basis. Most organisations do not advertise any of their senior jobs as being part time, and it is rare for organisations to encourage senior post-holders to work part time (Fried, 1998; Grant et al, 2006g). Furthermore, there is often an organisational cultural expectation that those who hold these senior posts should work 'whatever hours it takes' to complete the tasks. This has been described as 'extreme working' (Saner, 2007).

These problems are particularly acute in the UK, where full-timers work the longest hours in Europe (Kodz et al, 1998; Grimshaw and Rubery, 2001; Cousins and Tang, 2004), and where management roles often include extensive unpaid overtime (Harkness, 1999) and under-utilisation of annual leave allowances (Carvel, 2006). Men and women in management-level jobs elsewhere have reported that this 'long hours' culture has increased in recent years (White et al, 2004; Gillan, 2005; Cooper and Sutherland, 2006).

In local authorities, the LGMA, new statutory requirements, in-sector restructuring and a focus on 'efficiency savings' have changed both the experience and the working conditions of many employees. Participants in our study reported increased workloads alongside static or reduced staffing levels, leading to even longer hours for senior-level staff as they struggled to fulfil their job remits. Echoing other research findings (Simpson, 1998; Worrall and Cooper, 2000; Sheridan, 2004), senior women in our study described their frustration at being unable to bring value to their role, as they found themselves covering for staff absences, taking on lower staff functions, fulfilling new and increasing monitoring requirements and working to the point of exhaustion to meet the expectation that they alone are responsible for service delivery and performance:

> 'You only need a couple of people to be ill long term – holiday, training, whatever – and suddenly because the operation has to keep going you're doing their jobs as well as yours.' (Local government employee, Wakefield)

> 'As a result of the last review, we all became managers of our buildings – but what was hidden was that we were also health and safety officers and premises officers, which was added on to your other job.' (Local government employee, Leicester)

'[Statutory] procedures have changed every year for the last three years. This year it's been particularly bad. We've had four major releases in about four months, whereas we normally have two a year.' (Local government employee, Leicester)

Junior women were under no illusion as to what would be expected of them if they were to advance to a senior level.

'We had a middle tier. The managers got rid of the section head tier and put in a management strata tier. So that one manager – first on the rung – is doing the jobs of the section head and the management. So that's a stressful position to be in.' (Local government employee, Wakefield)

'It seems like there's a level of management where work has to be your life. It's that mid-level manager that does hours and hours of work and then you get past that and suddenly you get to cruise again.' (Local government employee, Leicester)

As the GELLM study and other investigations have concluded, it is very hard for women with child or adult care responsibilities to sustain management positions as these are currently configured (Connolly and Gregory, 2007). Organisational systems and processes (including assessment and reward systems and promotion criteria) uphold and reinforce the 'privileged' status of full-time, long hours work as the normal working time regime of managers (Crompton, 1996). Furthermore, the pace and unpredictability of the workload in many occupations has also increased through the use of portable information technology, used to communicate new work demands as they occur. In preferring those who are willing to be constantly 'on call', organisations indirectly privilege male employees, who are less likely to have both paid and unpaid work to attend to (Halford et al, 1997), a point also highlighted more recently by Bunting (2007a), who has argued that the 'cost' women are willing to pay: '... depends entirely on the individual woman, her own understanding of motherhood and the kind of engagement she wants with her own children'.

The role of women's own preferences in explaining why many highly educated and ambitious young women do not reach senior-level positions has been hotly debated (Fagan, 2001; Crompton, 2002). Hakim's preference theory (Hakim, 2002) uses 'person-centred' longitudinal data on attitudes to demonstrate that some women's individual preferences for a certain type of family role – combined with their desire to undertake market work primarily for job satisfaction rather than the income it brings – determines their commitment to labour force participation. Preference theory insists that women's 'lifestyle preferences' or attitudes are a more significant predictor of their labour market activity than educational attainment (Hakim, 2005, p 68).

>Lifestyle preferences predict work rates, but [full-time] employment does not predict women's lifestyle preferences and core values. Lifestyle preferences are not simply a rationalisation of employment decisions already made. The causal impact is essentially one way. (Hakim, 2005, p 67)

Hakim identifies three essential female 'identities'. Seventeen per cent of women are 'home-centred or family-centred'. These women want gender role segregation in their households, and choose to focus their time and energy on managing home life; their husband or partner is the primary breadwinner. A second group, 'work-oriented' women, regard themselves as the primary or joint main earner (in a dual-earner household),[10] but nevertheless have a 'non-financial' commitment to work. These women are most likely to be childless and prefer symmetrical rather than gender-segregated household roles. The third and largest group, making up almost two thirds of all women, is 'adaptive' women, who want to combine work with family life, but are not totally committed to a work career. This group includes women who see themselves as 'secondary' earners, and those preferring symmetrical gender roles but who work as a primary or joint main earner out of financial necessity rather than as their preferred identity (Hakim, 2005, p 62).

As we saw in Chapters Three and Seven, this theorisation of women's orientations to work has been widely criticised and debated. However, most of this criticism has not been grounded in new empirical evidence, or in studies that combine qualitative and statistical analyses. Our GELLM study of women working in the local authority sector in England, together with the other GELLM studies that also collected relevant evidence, has provided an important opportunity to subject preference theory to new empirical examination and assessment, and discussion of this is the main focus of the rest of this chapter.

## Women in the local authority workforce

In the study we sought to understand the career choices and ambitions of a particular sub-set of women: those who had made an academic investment in their working lives and who had already secured above-average financial reward. Twenty-four per cent of female participants in the study were aged 25–34, 35% were aged 35–44 and 33% were aged 45–59. More than half (56%) had one or more dependent children and 74% had an annual salary of over £18,000. Among them, 24% were in the £27,000–£34,999 salary band, 7% had an annual salary between £35,000 and £41,000, and almost 6% had an income over £41,000 p.a. (Bennett et al, 2006a, p 44).

A large majority of women in the study, all in jobs that were, or could become, part of a career, placed a high value on their employment. For them, their paid work was an important source of satisfaction and income security, and provided a context for fulfilling their personal values. Women in the focus groups held in each of the four local authorities told a similar story, emphasising that paid work represented important 'personal' time and that they valued the challenge of developing an independent reputation and identity. They were committed to their work because it served local communities, improving the lives and circumstances of local people. Their commitment to their career was also indicated by their choice of contractual hours: 74% of those with children and 85% of those with unpaid caring roles for sick, frail or disabled relatives or friends were working 31 hours or more per week (Bennett et al, 2006a, p 12). Almost half the women with children also reported that they routinely worked beyond their contractual hours, 47%, compared with 55% of women with no dependent children (Bennett et al, 2006a, p 23).

By focusing on mid-career women (in their 30s and 40s) who had the potential to reach more senior levels in their organisation, we aimed to understand the preferences of women who could exercise a degree of choice about their career progression, and to explore their reasons for changing or maintaining their work orientation. Older women already at a senior level, both with and without dependants, were also included in the study to provide an insight into the strategies they had employed, and the 'price' they felt they had been required to pay to become 'work-centred' at the high level they had achieved.

## Mid-career women: aspirations, choices and preferences

The women who most closely corresponded to Hakim's 'adaptive' category had many different reasons for prioritising their family lives. For some, unforeseen family circumstances, such as the illness or frailty of a family member, had prompted them to reconsider their work commitment. As demonstrated elsewhere (Yeandle and Buckner, 2007), although most carers voluntarily accept their role and gain satisfaction from it, they pay a penalty for doing so in terms of their own health and social lives. For carers who also have a paid job the pressures of sustaining both roles can be very difficult to manage unless there is good support, including support at work:

> 'My parents-in-law are old and ill, needing more support. It's coming to the point where I have started to consider whether I need to reduce my working hours as I cannot deal with this extra pressure.' (Local government employee, Wakefield)

Among those who had chosen to alter their commitment to work because of motherhood (or grandmotherhood), several admitted being surprised by the strength of their feelings and by the range of tasks involved; they had not planned to put their career in second place to a childrearing role. A shift towards more active, time-consuming parenting, which has intensified parents' (especially mothers') sense of responsibility for meeting all their children's social and educational needs, with accompanying emotional investment, has been noted by a number of commentators (Coward, 1993; Bunting, 2007b). As women in our study put it:

'I don't want my daughter to be picked up by a childminder every day. I want to do it, and that's really important to me, because I had her quite late.' (Local government employee, Sandwell)

'I'd like to do compressed hours, so [in] that way I get the pleasure of spoiling my grandson one day a week, and childcare for my daughter will only cost her three days.' (Local government employee, Leicester)

As the last example shows, putting their family role first did not necessarily mean reducing working hours and earnings. Many women in the study had sought greater flexibility in the organisation of their working time. For some, 'adapting' meant ruling out further promotion while their children were most dependent, and 'treading water' at their current level. They feared that any 'step up' might threaten the small but important concessions they had negotiated, which enabled them to satisfy their own, their children's, and their current managers' needs.

'If I took on something else [a higher position], I would barely see the children, so you have to say – well I'm not going to do it until they get to an age where they are more independent.' (Local government employee, Wakefield)

'It depends on flexibility. My biggest worry at the moment – before I accept [a higher level job], is I have to say, "Will you let me drop my daughter off at school at 9 o'clock? Which means that I won't start with you until quarter to 10, but I will work through into the early evening etc – that's fine – but I need to start at quarter to 10 rather than at half past 8."' (Local government employee, Wakefield)

Likewise, women's reasons for reducing their working hours or moving to a part-time contract were not based exclusively on their desire to fulfil the identity of mother. Rather, they simply found the practicalities of sustaining two demanding and often competing roles too physically and mentally difficult:

'Before [having children] I wanted to get as high as possible. Now I just want reasonable pay, but I will not take on excessive pressure.' (Local government employee, Leicester)

'I realised that the pace I was operating at before my child was a pace I couldn't keep up with a baby. She's 3 now, but I've taken that choice to stand back. I know I felt grateful when my boss said that I could go job share.' (Local government employee, Sandwell)

'I want to be able to give my children my love, time and support but also give my job my all, and sometimes I end up exhausted as a result.' (Local government employee, Wakefield)

For some women, moving into part-time work had been a difficult decision: many voiced their concerns that in choosing to work reduced hours they were 'giving up' the possibility of future career progression, since the impact of this decision would be 'irreversible': to be perceived as 'work–centred' meant meeting the full-time, long hours model of an ideal senior officer or manager, and doing so continuously.

'I've never gone part time, because you'd worry that once you go part time, it's very difficult then to come back full time and get that respect from your colleagues.' (Local government employee, Sandwell)

'What I do find that stifles me is that, time and time again, you come up against barriers – and barriers specifically around the fact that you're a parent. If you're not prepared to work full-time, it's, like, well, forget you. There's nothing there for you at a higher level, unless you want to work full-time.' (Local government employee, Leicester)

'I'm just about to go on maternity leave and I'm not clear at all about how things will change. I imagine that coming back part time will block me immediately in terms of career, because service managers don't work part time or job share, so that will be it.' (Local government employee, Southwark)

Among those who had negotiated part-time hours and maintained their existing organisational grade there was a huge desire to remain in contention for promotion. These women were working additional unpaid overtime (often hidden at home) to cover their workloads, which they felt had not been adjusted to reflect their new contractual hours. Many believed they could not refuse a manager's request, even when it meant extra work, as they feared this would confirm others' perception that they lacked commitment.

'I don't like to say no – perhaps that's my fault. But then I don't want it to hinder me. Because they might think – she's part time, she can't deliver what she's supposed to deliver.' (Local government employee, Sandwell)

'I don't get to do flexi, because I only work Monday to Thursday, but I've always been asked to come in on a Friday for team leader meetings, and you say, "Well I don't actually work Fridays" – "Well, you are a team leader now, you have to come in, if you don't come in,

I'll expect that you don't want the job."' (Local government employee, Southwark)

Unlike the 'adaptive woman' described by Hakim, the women in our study who worked part time continued to pursue training opportunities and to gain the qualifications required in more senior jobs, with an eye to achieving promotion in the future. Some explained that they had sacrificed their own, personal time to do this – sometimes damaging their own health and well-being – to avoid becoming 'blocked'.

'The final year [of my degree] was the hardest, because any leave I took was to study. So I never had any time for myself or for my family. I became so run down because I was only getting 3–4 hours' sleep each night that I just kind of collapsed, and the doctor said, "Well, you're going to have some time off now."' (Local government employee, Sandwell)

Senior jobs in this sector have become increasingly focused on performance management tasks, which – in the eyes of our research participants – detract from the expression of skill and creativity within individual occupations and from the public service ethos, which is about improving the lives of local people and was what had attracted many women into the sector. For some women their currently 'adaptive' stance towards promotion was linked to a desire to remain work centred at a level where, in their opinion, the value of their contribution really could be about 'making a difference'.

'Look at our Heads of Service, the things they have to put up with. There's just all this hassle from elected members, from service managers. It's not just about the number of hours that you are working, it's about actually being able to enjoy those hours and not spending them in a permanent argument.' (Local government employee, Southwark)

'I very rarely get the opportunity to do anything proactive, this recent piece of work I've done was the first proactive piece of work that I've done for several months. Most of my job is 'fire-fighting' or maintaining what we've got.' (Local government employee, Leicester)

Preference theory claims that, while social, economic and institutional factors affect women's employment patterns, contributing to gender differentiation in the labour market as a whole, women's 'motivations and aspirations are independent factors with causal powers' (Hakim, 2002, p 454), and it is these that carry the greatest weight in determining their work orientation. The evidence about those women in our study who were poised to advance to senior level does not support this. These women are very concerned about structural and institutional factors, since to be 'work centred' at the next level above them is to meet a very demanding commitment in terms of the hours and intensity of work, and to accept alongside this a deterioration in the quality of work, too, which shows no sign of abating.

## Experiences and preferences of 'work-centred' senior women

Turning to the experience of senior women in our study, and taking this group as perhaps corresponding to Hakim's category of 'work-centred' women, our study again allows us to look beneath the surface of how they maintain work as their main priority. We have been able to examine the resources they draw on and to see how their working lives fit with their personal circumstances. In Hakim's analysis, these women are responsive to economic opportunity. Many had progressed in their careers by moving between different local authorities in search of promotion. As a result, some women commuted long distances each day from a home base that, for family reasons, they were reluctant to relocate: 'I am still 30 miles from work, but I'm closer to my elderly parents now' (Local government employee, Wakefield).

The majority of women in senior roles had dependent children and emphasised the equal importance they attached to their family life. They seemed to have the same feelings of guilt about the compromises their jobs forced upon them and their families as their younger and more junior counterparts:

> 'If I'm out monitoring, I'm there at 7.00. I know my children are feeling it, my daughter especially. But you then try to reward them, because I've worked longer hours. But I need that job, for me, because I know they're going to grow up and find their own way.' (Local government employee, Wakefield)

These women highlighted the fact that their partners or parents played a key role in enabling them to commit all the hours and energy they wished to give to their work.

> 'I still want to see the kids at some point. For an 8 o'clock meeting I have to get up an hour earlier. My husband does a lot of the childcare, but there are things I like to sort out, like their clothes, whatever. It just eats into your personal time ... there's just not enough hours in the day.' (Local government employee, Sandwell)

> 'When I had children, I knew I could not work elsewhere ... because I could not work without the extensive family support. My parents still live here, so when my child is sick, it's not me that takes the time off, I ring my parents up.' (Local government employee, Wakefield)

They were also aware that in choosing to 'opt out' of the role of primary carer of their children they differed from most other women: 'I am still made to feel guilty, not by my husband but by other women. A lot of my friends don't work or do part-time jobs' (Local government employee, Wakefield).

Yet to operate effectively at senior level – to complete their workload and meet the expectation of continuous responsibility – these women had shunned flexible working, either because they were reluctant to ask for 'favours' that might single them out as different from the rest of senior management, or because they could not imagine how the job could be done in less time.

> 'The main frustration for me is that senior managers don't benefit from work–life balance, we don't do flexi, we're expected to go to evening meetings in our own time – and we go to a lot of them – and I find that exhausting. I understand that at a senior level you need to be flexible, but they are long hours and we could benefit from a little bit of work life balance and they'd probably end up with a healthier lot.' (Local government employee, Southwark)

> 'Flexible working policies for me are important for everyone else wrapped round me, and I do encourage people to go home early, spend time with their children. But I don't apply the same policy to me … I don't see how I can – the expectation above me [for me] to be there constantly is I think worrying, really, because if you have a normal life you just couldn't possibly do that.' (Local government employee, Wakefield)

Their reluctance to challenge the status quo was strongly indicated by their descriptions of how they managed family commitments, giving an impression that they felt these needed to be hidden from view:

> 'I care for my elderly mother – I get up at 6.30, leave at 7.30 for work until 5.30. Go and cook mum's tea, do the housework – then I've got to take her washing home. I get home at 9 o'clock at night, and I've got to put the washing machine on – and I am doing that four days a week. It's exhausting.' (Local government employee, Sandwell)

> 'They know that I'm a single parent and that I haven't got a partner, and one guy turns around to me [at an evening work event] and says, "So who's looking after your child tonight then?" and I said, "Don't worry, I'll make my arrangements. Who's looking after your kids anyway?"' (Local government employee, Southwark)

## Reappraising preference theory

In her discussion of the rising importance of lifestyle preferences in determining women's employment patterns, Hakim acknowledges that the qualitative questions she has used to determine the centrality of work in research participants' lives may need modifying for different labour markets and cultural settings (Hakim, 2005, p 71). In our study we have looked in detail at the labour market within the local government sector, and considered how well preference theory works when subjected to empirical testing in this setting. We aim to show why women's preferences and choices arising from real experiences in this sector call for modifications to Hakim's theory.

First, Hakim's categorisation of women has been rejected by many academics who argue that women's orientations to work change during their life course according to their personal circumstances and the organisational structures they are part of, and cannot therefore be 'fixed' (Ginn et al, 1996; McRae, 2003). Our research participants, too, were constantly reappraising their work orientation in the context of life and organisational changes; their attitudes were not fixed, but responsive to a range of structural changes. If we treat Hakim's categories purely as 'ideal types' or theoretical constructs, and recognise that individual women may move between them during their life course, however, they are useful in developing an analysis of organisational cultures and in highlighting where policy interventions could address some of the inequalities women experience.

Second, evidence in our study relating to those women in mid-career who are poised to move into senior and executive roles in local government suggests that Hakim's 'work-centred' category is too restrictive. These women have certainly made a significant investment in their career development and they say that they want, and are capable of, more. Many have accepted the need to work full-time hours and already sacrifice their personal time in order to sustain caring and work roles simultaneously; they also face a high degree of pressure at work, experience work spill-over into their home lives, buy in help at home and rely on partners, parents and friends to help with childcare. Nevertheless, at the same time this group of women say that work and family are equally important. In Hakim's theorisation, our research participants should fit one or other of her categories. In common with other studies, we find that this categorisation does not adequately describe them (Houston and Marks, 2005). A second modification is needed to include a new theoretical category, 'women in contention', since in our study many women had found themselves grappling with their (conflicting) aspirations to have both a satisfying and committed personal and family life and to pursue a rewarding, successful career in the public sector. Their deliberations were shaped by the organisational practices and behaviour of people they observed around them and the context of sectoral restructuring, over which they had no control. Being 'in contention' is neither a permanent nor a momentary phase, but in many cases involves a longer period of consideration, to explore different options of accommodation.

The final modification relates to Hakim's argument that policy makers, by failing to recognise the 'polarisation of lifestyles', have developed policies, particularly around the reconciliation of work and life, which assume a preference among all employees for: 'a single, universally-attractive model of the family and the good life' (Hakim, 2005, p 73).

Preference theory contends that, since the contraceptive revolution, sex differences in attitudes to work and family are being replaced with equally profound divisions between 'adaptive' people and 'work-centred' careerists, who do not necessarily divide along gender lines, and whose different life trajectories are not being catered for. This position is not supported by the evidence in our study. Rather than using theoretical categories to demonstrate the sexless nature of individuals' preferences, we use them to understand the gendered barriers and prejudices that persist, and are strengthening. Far from dispelling sex differences, the 'work centredness' demanded of officers in local government in fact reinforces the sexual division of labour. Qualified and experienced women are only able to rise to senior level – remaining 'work centred' – if they take on a traditional male pattern of work, prioritising their paid job above other areas of life and relying on a 'wife' (of either sex) at home running the household. Here, the underlying assumption described by women in our study is that without this support at home, motherhood and seniority at work remain incompatible. Their view is also echoed in popular discussions about the 'mummy track': the limited career trajectory and accompanying set of expectations assigned to women employees when they become mothers (Bunting, 2007; Moorhead, 2007; Treanor, 2007; Ward, 2007).

Table 7.1 aims both to capture what these different modifications mean for Hakim's categorisation and to demonstrate their usefulness for theorising organisational cultures and structures. It introduces a new, empirically based category of 'women in contention', using it to refer to those women who faced career options and choices that, if selected, would demand of them significant sacrifices in their family and personal lives. The preferences and past behaviour of these women (as described when we encountered them) showed that in real women's lives there is considerable overlap between the 'women in contention' and 'work-centred' categories (a finding also observed in Sigala, 2005, p 119).

The upper part of Table 7.1 indicates the typical 'characteristics' of women in the categories described, highlighting: their attitudes to paid work and training to progress; the relative importance of economic, social and family policy in their career decisions; and their family circumstances. The second row in the table describes the typical 'work situation' in local government in which GELLM women research participants found themselves, associated with that category. (Hakim's third category of home-centred women has not been included as this group was not encountered in the GELLM sample). As shown earlier in this chapter, it is apparent from the demands placed on women as they move into more senior grades that to continue on this trajectory involves a withdrawal from many family and caring responsibilities.

**Table 8.1 Women's work-lifestyle preferences as they progress to senior levels\***

| | Adaptive (Hakim) | *Women in contention* | Work-centred (Hakim) |
|---|---|---|---|
| C<br>H<br>A<br>R<br>A<br>C<br>T<br>E<br>R<br>I<br>S<br>T<br>I<br>C<br>S | This group is most diverse and includes women who want to combine work and family, plus drifters and unplanned careers.<br><br>Want to work but not totally committed to work career.<br><br><br>Qualifications obtained with the intention of working<br><br>This group is very responsive to government social policy, employment policy, equal opportunities policy…, availability of part-time work and similar work flexibility … and institutional factors generally. | *Diverse group with and without caring responsibilities. Work and family equally important.*<br><br>*Career a vital part of self identity. Committed to work, prepared to sacrifice health and personal time.*<br><br>*Large investment of personal time in qualifications to progress*<br><br>*Responsive to economic opportunity AND social/ employment/ organisational policy* | Childless women are concentrated here. Main priority in life is employment.<br><br>Committed to work.<br><br><br>Large investment in qualifications/training for employment<br><br>Responsive to economic opportunity… Not responsive to social/ employment/family policy. |
| W<br>O<br>R<br>K<br><br>S<br>I<br>T<br>U<br>A<br>T<br>I<br>O<br>N | *Salaries up to £27,000*<br><br>With dependent children: Primary carer.<br><br><br><br><br>Part-time possible; Flexi-time; Hours can be contained | *Salaries £27,000–£34,999*<br><br>*With dependent children: Buying in paid help in the home, heavily reliant on home based husband/ partner (symmetrical roles)*<br><br>*Full-time hours; Suspend progression – 'treading water' if part-time; Long hours; Overtime not reclaimable; Intensifying workload; Pressured work environment and work relationships.* | *Senior Level – £35,000+*<br><br>*With dependent children: Buying in paid help in the home, heavily reliant on home-based husband/ partner (reversed roles)*<br><br>*Full time only; Always on call or on premises; Significant work-life spill-over; Long hours; Overtime not reclaimable; Intensifying workload; Performance management focus; Pressured work environment and relationships.* |

\* Text in italics relates to the GELLM findings; other text has been quoted from Hakim's Table 3, 'Classification of women's work-lifestyle preferences in the 21st century' (Hakim, 2002, p 436).

If we focus on the work situation of those women who were 'in contention' when we studied them, we find that many of these mid-career women were putting their progression on hold until a time when family demands became less time consuming. They were able and willing to make a commitment to their work tasks in terms of the energy, interest, level of creative input, attention to detail, value and ownership they invested (which, for some women, was greater than they had left to give to family members, including dependants). However, they were unwilling to give any more time. Of women aged 45–49 responding to our survey, 40% with children and 61% without children said that they routinely worked between 38 and 47 hours per week. Five per cent of women of this age group, regardless of children, worked 48 hours or more each week.

> 'I see a lot of Heads of Service who are working 12 hours every day.
> I mean, do you want that kind of life? I think you've got to choose.
> And it's so unfair, because some people may want to do that level of
> responsibility, but they can't commit all those hours.' (Local government
> employee, Sandwell)

Hakim's original definition of 'work centrality', which implies meeting all of an employers' demands, however unreasonable or detrimental to health or other family members, does not fit these women, who, in her analysis, would fall instead within her 'adaptive' category.

Within our study, some of the women we encountered did fit Hakim's 'work-centred' category: as we have indicated, to be 'work centred' at the most senior levels in local government is to accept 'extreme' working hours (increasing as the sector continues to restructure). For the senior women we spoke to this has led to their almost complete withdrawal from the timetables of family life and the need to find other family members, friends or paid help to replace them. Those with dependent children acknowledged the primary role of their partner, husband or parents in running their home. Many had distanced themselves geographically too, accepting a long commute to work rather than uprooting the family home. Others had simply waited until their children had left home before progressing with their careers. These women had accepted this time commitment – in one woman's words: 'a life which is not normal'.

They portrayed their round-the-clock hours as an inevitable consequence of the workload they have been given, but this did not stop them continually questioning its negative impact on their health, productivity and family.

> 'I find my work–life balance is appalling – but then on the other hand,
> you know it goes with the territory, and that worries me because you
> can easily just become a workaholic – so that is quite important for
> me to try and sort out, but I never seem to get the time to do that.'
> (Local government employee, Wakefield)

## Policy implications

The absence of women at senior levels in local government is not wholly explained by their lifestyle preferences. A significant minority of women are 'waiting in the wings' at mid-stage career, frustrated that jobs at senior level are not flexible, or part time, or with a workload that can be shared between more people. There are also women (and men) already at senior level who have made the hard choice to leave the day-to-day management of family life to someone else, depriving their families of their potential contribution to rewarding family relationships. In addition, the long hours they commit to work reduce the energy and care they invest in their own health and mental well-being.

The evidence in our study suggests that greater efforts to identify and to support 'women in contention' for senior level jobs, while helpful, will not be enough if women are to join men in equal numbers around the management table in local government. Change is needed too in work organisation and in the design of senior jobs, a development also called for by others and in other chapters in this book (Lewis, 2001; Liff and Ward, 2001). We do not support Hakim's call for separate policies for those who are 'careerists' and 'adaptives'. As shown in Chapter Seven (and also underscored in the Women and Work Commission's Report of 2006), in the economy as a whole, women are not making the best use of their skills, but are 'working below potential' because of expectations about working hours in senior jobs.

In late 2006 the government launched a small (£500,000) fund to provide seed-corn funding to support projects designed to increase the number of senior and quality jobs available on a part-time basis, and exemplar companies running initiatives and practical guides for employers on imaginative ways of team working and job sharing (Crook, 2007; Walton, 2007a, 2007b; Walton and Gaskell, 2007; Women and Work Commission, 2007) that aim to transform gendered and cultural expectations attached to senior roles. These are often quoted in policy and media literature, although this practice of 'intelligent flexibility' is currently only a reality in the minority of organisations (Moynagh and Worsley, 2005, p 180). Some commentators have argued that systematic change will only be achieved when a legal right to work flexibly at all levels is established and significant additional resources are provided to create 'give in the system', allowing alternative models of flexible working to be successful (Crompton et al, 2003; Bunting, 2007; Doherty, 2007).

Finally, government, employers, trade unions and academics must continue to challenge the views of employers and managers, arguing that a sexual division of management roles is no longer morally or economically acceptable. They need to demonstrate that a model of successful work careers (for men or women) that fails to acknowledge the support and nurturing needed by, and demanded of, the family sphere is no longer sustainable in an economy that seeks to achieve full employment in a context of fairness and gender equality.

## Notes

[1] 74% of female respondents had a salary of £18,000 per annum or above (including those working part-time hours earning a percentage FTE). The experiences of women earning below this level have not been discussed in this chapter.

[2] This difference may in part relate to the nature of the London/South East economy in which house prices and childcare costs are higher than in the rest of the country, making full-time work more attractive or imperative, rather than necessarily arising from a lack of flexible working policies.

[3] Defined here (as in the Census) as the public administration, defence and social security sector.

[4] Compulsory competitive tendering (CCT) was introduced by the Conservative government during the 1980s, in an attempt to bring greater efficiency to local government and health services through the use of competition. The White Papers on local government introduced by the Labour government in 1998 and 2001 have extended and refined this approach.

[5] Initiated by Sir Peter Gershon's 2004 review of public sector efficiency (in particular within 'back office', procurement, transaction, service and policy-making functions).

[6] The LGMA initiatives include: comprehensive performance assessment, asset management planning and capital strategies, best value, local public service agreements, local strategic partnerships and community strategies.

[7] Targets are set to stretch the organisation beyond what it would have achieved without making changes to its policy and practices (Boyne, 2001).

[8] In large authorities in 2004/5, the largest proportion of absence days ascribed to specific causes related to stress (20.1%) (Employers Organisation, 2005b, pp 15–16).

[9] Best value performance indicators include BVPI 11a, the percentage of the top 5% of earners that are women. All local authorities in England are obliged to submit information on these indicators to the Audit Commission and they are included in the annual comprehensive performance assessment (CPA) score. This has increased the organisational profile of gender equality work as councils performing well under CPA receive limited 'freedoms and flexibilities', for example fewer inspections. Poorly performing councils can expect to be subject to a range of central government interventions.

[10] Hakim (2002) notes that the classification of 'primary' or 'joint' earner relates to a person's chosen identity. It is not in all cases related to actual levels of income.

# NINE

# Conclusion: policy for a change

*Sue Yeandle*

## The need for change

As shown in earlier chapters of this book, gender equality in local labour markets is a goal not yet attained in the English economy; indeed, evidence gathered in the GELLM research programme suggests it has only very rarely been a priority for agencies responsible for implementing labour market change at local level. Given the gendered nature of participation in the overall labour market, which has long been recognised at national level, and the tendency of most workers, especially women, to work within a relatively short distance from their homes, this is both a remarkable weakness in policy making and a serious barrier to the achievement of wider aspects of gender equality (Yeandle, 2006c).

The principle of gender equality has been enshrined in European economic and employment policy since the late 1950s, and the achievement of fair access to employment for women and men has been an official aim of national public policy since Britain introduced equalities legislation in the 1970s. In the decades since, much progress has been made: in understanding how the labour market operates for women, in documenting differences in male and female engagement with the labour market, and in developing new employment rights, workplace policies and public policy initiatives. As already shown, these have sought to achieve a fairer labour market for women, addressing pay, employment protection, sex discrimination (in education, training, recruitment and promotion), work–life balance and flexible working. More recent policy initiatives have addressed labour market activation, raising employment rates, and developing the childcare system. The fiscal and benefits system has been redesigned too, aiming to 'make work pay' and to shift as many people as possible 'from welfare to work'. There has also been a focus on the economic well-being of different regions, on the specific problems of rural economies, on the regeneration of deprived communities and on tackling 'local pockets of worklessness'. Training and skills policy has been adjusted and reprioritised, and both the trade unions and employers' organisations have adopted a stance that recognises the importance of equal rights and a level playing field for women and men at work.

Yet many groups of women remain seriously disadvantaged in the labour market, and some find it very difficult to access employment or, once in the labour market, to progress in line with their qualifications, skills and experience. Entry into top jobs, especially in management roles, remains hard for women, and with levels of economic inactivity and unemployment still high in deprived neighbourhoods, it is clear that regeneration policies have achieved little for local women. In policy making at both the national and the local level, with government, officials and the various social partners constantly responding to new initiatives and to the rapidly changing global economic environment, it seems no one has stopped to ask whether gender inequality has been the 'blind spot' of public policy making, lying behind the limited success of the many initiatives designed to tackle social exclusion and promote the effective functioning of local labour markets.

Many challenges face national, regional and local policy makers. As outlined in Chapter Two, these include major demographic shifts, calling for higher levels of employment among an extended working age population, as well as the need to respond to the emergence of new markets, to the shifting competitiveness of other economies, to continuous technological change and to the need to operate the economy in ways that are environmentally sustainable. These factors drive organisational developments in the public and private sectors, underpin the new 'skills' agenda, and inform the case for diversity and equality. In an age of greater population diversity – in terms of ethnicity, family and household structures, patterns of age, health, disability and care responsibility – finding new ways of shaping employment opportunities so that jobs mesh better with women's (and men's) increasingly complex lives is of central policy importance. For this to happen, better understanding, at the local level, of gender differences in labour force participation and of how paid and unpaid work fit together in women's and men's lives is needed. To highlight the kind of evidence that is available and could inform these developments, we therefore conclude with a summary of the findings of the GELLM research programme, highlighting their local significance and the importance of specific kinds of evidence for local policy making.

## Evidence from the GELLM research programme

The GELLM *Gender profiles*, the first outputs from the programme, added to the range of gender-disaggregated data available at local level and became important reference documents in most localities (Buckner et al, 2004a–i, 2005a, 2005b, 2006). They were valued both because they were specific to the locality concerned, and because they benchmarked the local situation against regional and national averages. They provided statistical information about both women and men in relation to: the local setting, education and skills, trends and patterns in women's and men's employment, the gender pay gap, unemployment and economic inactivity, diversity and work–life balance.

The profiles showed local agencies that both those who left school at 16 and those staying on in education were making gendered choices that reinforced occupational segregation. They confirmed continued clustering of women in lower-status and lower-paid jobs in all localities. The scale and pace of job change was highly variable from place to place, but in most localities the gendered distribution of job losses and gains had not previously been well understood. In some areas, more female than male full-time manufacturing jobs had been lost in the preceding decade, while rapid growth in part-time jobs had channelled more women into the low-paying retail, hotels and restaurants and social care sectors. In areas that had seen growth in full-time jobs, usually in the business sector and in managerial jobs, local agencies were sometimes surprised to learn that the expansion of these higher-paid positions had benefited men more than women.

Statistical analysis also showed the persistence of low pay, especially in part-time jobs held by women. Local agencies were interested to learn that the gender pay gap was particularly large in managerial and senior level jobs. Considering local data seemed to change perceptions about the pay gap, highlighting the need for local action; some were concerned to discover that the gender pay gap had narrowed only in the lowest-paid sectors, such as retail, hotels and restaurants.

Running counter to some local perceptions, the gender profiles also showed that in many areas high rates of economic inactivity among women were concealing the fact that many women wanted to work. Some had not previously realised how strong the relationship was between employment rates and qualifications among women, and how variable female employment rates were in different places. The large locality differences in the part-time employment rates of lone parents (which emerged later in the statistical work supporting the local research studies), were of particular interest, as women in this group were a target for some local policy interventions. Here the evidence was particularly important in correcting widespread misconceptions about lone parents, especially in relation to their age and family size.

Although most local agencies were attempting to address the disadvantage experienced by people from ethnic minorities, their policies rarely adopted a gendered perspective; the analysis in the gender profiles highlighted the high degree of labour market 'clustering' among women and men in different ethnic groups, both in certain industries and in particular occupations. Finally, few agencies had previously seen local-level analyses of employees' access to flexible working, so it was important for public sector policy makers to see that only 8% of men and 11% of women in England had access to flexi-time, and that there was significant variation between districts. The same was true of data about caring responsibilities and childcare provision.

The multi-method local research studies, which built on the gender profiles, provided an opportunity for investigation of issues of specific local significance. These further highlighted the importance of the local dimension, as show in the six GELLM synthesis reports.

In *Working below potential: women and part-time work* (Grant et al, 2005, 2006g–l; Grant and Price, 2006) we showed that more than half of women in low-paid, part-time jobs were not using their skills, experience or qualifications. Despite strong growth in part-time employment, because there are too few part-time jobs available at an appropriate level, many women cannot find jobs that use their abilities. Managers are often resistant to part-time working in jobs at senior levels, and within workplaces opportunities for advancement for part-time workers are limited. Consequently, women who opt to work part time often become trapped in low-paid work, sometimes losing confidence in their abilities and skills. While part-time employment suits the needs of many employers, enables organisations to operate flexibly and draws additional labour into the labour force, part-time workers are often seen as replaceable and are valued less highly than full-time workers. Their skills frequently go unnoticed by managers, some of whom regard low pay as appropriate for people working part time.

Many qualified and experienced women quit more senior full-time jobs because of the intensity of work and the long hours culture; they need to be reconnected with occupations and careers more fitting to their talents. But because part-time jobs and flexible working patterns are rarely available at senior levels, and distributed unevenly across occupations and industries, there is significant variation between local labour markets in the number and quality of part-time jobs available. Local policy makers need to recognise and tackle this, emphasising the need for more flexible employment in all workplaces and for changes in job design. The study calls for responses at national, regional and local levels in the areas of skills policy, vocational advice and guidance, and work with employers, especially those facing labour or skills shortages. At present, the millions of part-time employees who are locked into jobs below their potential rarely feature in their thinking, planning and activities.

In *Connecting women with the labour market* (Grant et al, 2006a–f), we examined the situation of the 1.4 million women in England who are outside paid work but want a job, finding that the transition into paid employment can be fraught with difficulties, especially for those in deprived neighbourhoods. There was considerable variability in the extent of, and reasons for, women's economic inactivity, and very different unemployment rates in the districts and wards studied. Patterns of disconnection from the labour market were often related to age, ethnicity and family status, yet this was rarely recognised by policy makers, and despite their strong desire to work, local labour market conditions, aspects of their lives, and elements of public policy effectively excluded these women from employment. Women's desire to work was often unacknowledged, with myths and false assumptions about them hampering efforts to support them.

Contemporary developments in public policy emphasise the importance of local strategic plans and partnerships and the need to raise employment rates. Yet centring interventions on benefit claimants overlooks many economically inactive women who are struggling to connect with the labour market, whose needs can only be addressed at local level. Both their desire to work and the way interrupted work histories affect their ability to secure employment need to be acknowledged, and for this a comprehensive set of support services, developed at local level to address the issues affecting local women's lives, is needed. Policy makers need to offer these women work experience and job-focused training, in collaboration with employers, with links to genuine job opportunities. They also need to recognise that many women returning to work want part-time jobs, work during school hours or term time and flexible working hours. Employers – some of whom are struggling to fill local vacancies – need to review the scope for offering more flexible employment. The study also revealed some exploitation of vulnerable women by employers, with pay well below the minimum wage, and a lack of careers advice and practical one-to-one support that listens to women and acknowledges their desire to work.

In *Ethnic minority women and access to the labour market* (Stiell and Tang, 2006a–e; Stiell et al, 2006; Yeandle et al, 2006j), we saw that England's 2.1 million ethnic minority women of working age are very unevenly spread across the country, with important implications for local labour markets. Some groups, in some places, face significant problems of unemployment and of access to better quality jobs, with ethnic minority women often clustered in occupations and industries where employment is insecure. Bangladeshi, Pakistani and Black African women are particularly disadvantaged, but the labour market situation of Indian, Black Caribbean and other minority women is also poor in some localities. In different localities, the populations of ethnic minority women are very different, in terms of their size relative to the total population, ethnic composition, age structure and heritage. In some localities, many ethnic minority women were born outside the UK, or are in poor health, or have complex caring and family responsibilities. Here policy responses tailored to the reality of their lives are urgently needed. But action is also needed to support the growing numbers who have achieved success in the educational system, including many graduates, who tend to be employed below the level for which they are qualified, especially in some localities. Local policy makers need to examine the reasons for this, taking action to eliminate all forms of discrimination.

When ethnic minority women encounter harassment or discrimination, or are otherwise frustrated in their desire to enter or progress within the labour market, the impact on their confidence and self-esteem can be long term and damaging. The study also showed that among those whose first language was not English, many wanted to improve their English, but struggled to access appropriate training. Ethnic minority women often felt that mainstream services did not listen to them properly, and did not recognise their abilities and experience; many wanted better and more accessible information about available services. Engaging in voluntary work had been an important source of support for some, assisting them into education, training and paid employment. Some local voluntary projects offered useful models for the way local mainstream services could be developed to support ethnic minority women.

In *Women's career development in the local authority sector* (Bennett et al, 2006a–e; Bennett and Yeandle, 2006), we focused on qualified women in career-track public sector jobs, finding that the majority of higher-paid women had never used their organisation's flexible employment policies, and that many felt there was an informal rule that working flexibly or from home was not acceptable. Most spoke of increasing work pressures in the sector and of working long hours and unpaid overtime. Those who had reached the top level had often made significant personal sacrifices, including delegating aspects of their family roles, and often had regrets about this. Many younger women were reluctant to move into senior positions where they would be always 'on call'.

Although some organisations had put arrangements in place to tackle these issues, this study also highlighted the urgent need for more flexible and part-time jobs at senior levels. Against a backdrop of well-established commitments to equal opportunities in the sector, and targets relating to women in senior posts in the equality standard and best value processes, it was disappointing that more progress had not been made. Views varied about the potential of the new duty on public sector bodies to promote gender equality (introduced in the 2006 Equality Act) to resolve these issues; it was evident that while this provided an opportunity to change organisational cultures, its impact would depend on effective implementation and commitments at the local level.

In *Addressing women's poverty: local labour market initiatives* (Escott and Buckner, 2006; Escott et al, 2006a–f) we again found that locality is a very important factor for women. Despite recent policy changes, women are still more likely than men to live in poverty, still a persistent feature of some local labour markets. Those without access to affordable and efficient public services, including transport, felt excluded from opportunities available in the wider labour market. In the localities studied, their poverty was reflected in high levels of workless households and high rates of limiting long-term illness and poor health. Local labour markets were functioning poorly, and between 1991 and 2001, against the national trend, women's economic inactivity rates in some wards had increased. Low income was not confined to those who were unemployed or economically inactive, however. In these localities, employed women were concentrated in unskilled and semi-skilled jobs, and often worked close to home, in part-time, low-waged and insecure work.

The picture of 'distance' from the labour market was complex. In some areas, a serious qualifications deficit had arisen, with very low qualification levels running through several generations. But in areas of high deprivation, qualifications did not guarantee employment, and in these areas women with qualifications were also less likely to be in paid employment. In poor households, where women were highly dependent on their own low income or on the low income of a partner, levels of self-esteem and long-term aspiration were also low. While many women aspired to enter paid employment, this was not just an economic decision, and household pressures, including care responsibilities and limited services to support care needs were also important.

While training initiatives had often engaged local women, progression into employment was limited. Services providing support into employment were often fragmented, and the gender dimension was missing from almost all local labour market and economic regeneration strategies. It was evident that local agencies needed to do more to address these inequalities, responding better to women of different ages, ethnicities and with different caring responsibilities. Further work was needed with local employers, too, to address recruitment practices, job flexibility, hours, pay structures and in-house training for women wishing to enter the labour market and to progress within it. This study emphasised the need for longer-term strategic approaches that appreciate the distinctions between men and women, and are based in an understanding of the nature and scale of women's non-participation and their 'distance' from labour market opportunities. These neighbourhoods needed more concentrated support to improve education and skills levels, and investment in services that enable local women to work. In all the areas studied, demand for employment needed to be strengthened by promoting existing jobs in the area, investing in jobs accessible to local residents and integrating the skills and employment agenda with regeneration and equalities policies. Further simplification and greater flexibility in the tax and benefits system, to ease the transition from unemployment into paid work for women, especially those with dependants, was also a central concern for local organisations.

The study of *Local challenges in meeting demand for domiciliary care* (Yeandle et al, 2006c–i, 2007; Yeandle and Shipton, 2006) drew attention to expected increases in the very aged population, highlighting likely local variations but showing widespread rising demand for labour in the social care sector, a strongly feminised segment of the labour market already employing nearly half a million care workers. The study explored the age, sex and ethnic composition of six local domiciliary care workforces, noted that competition for staff came mainly from other parts of the health and social care sector and from retail, hotels and restaurants, and manufacturing employers, and explored how this played out locally. Many providers were struggling to contain the costs associated with high staff turnover; wages were low, employees often incurred training and travel costs, and there was variable success in up-skilling the workforce. This study demonstrated the importance of connecting national and local policy priorities, arguing that heightened awareness of key issues at the local level is needed to inform the emerging debate about how the social care system should be developed, and noting that the emerging 'personalisation' agenda in health and social care has important implications for the social care market. This calls on local agencies to consider not only new skills and training issues, but also to consider where additional, flexible, labour might be found and how new workers can be drawn into the sector.

## Conclusion

Drawing on the linked studies undertaken within the GELLM research programme, this book has engaged with a range of debates, theories and common misperceptions about women's relationship with the labour market, highlighting the dangers of generalising about women's employment situation at the national level, and emphasising the importance of using local-level data that take into account both conditions in the local labour market and the specificity of the local population of women and men in relation to age, ethnicity and levels of qualification and work experience. In emphasising variability, individuality and difference among women, we have aimed to avoid stereotyping them or their needs, and to highlight the importance of reshaping labour market opportunities and organisational practices to achieve a better fit between social, economic, family and individual realities.

We have also highlighted the need to develop detailed policy initiatives based on an appreciation of women's true local situation, encouraging local agencies, including local employers and local public and voluntary sector agencies, to support the aspirations expressed by many women to participate on equal terms in the labour market. This will mean developing support that is tailored to their specific needs and well integrated with local labour market structures and opportunities. We have shown that a wealth of detailed data about women's situation is available at the local level and that by interrogating this evidence it is possible to tease out specific features of local women's economic disadvantage and to identify ways of addressing these. A key observation, relevant to all the localities studied (and therefore very probably more widely as well) is that because gender equality is not yet adequately mainstreamed in the delivery of public policy, critical opportunities to address women's disadvantaged situation in relation to the labour market have repeatedly been missed.

Our study should alert policy makers, in both central and local government, to the impossibility of achieving economic well-being and fairness for all in local economies without recognising the different ways in which the economy, the labour market and the welfare state play out for women and men. Throughout the book we have emphasised that the achievement not only of gender equality, but also of many other key objectives in public policy – in the spheres of employment and productivity, education and skills, economic competitiveness, labour supply and demand, and the well-being of minority communities – can only be achieved if the inequality and disadvantages that exist, and the social and economic challenges ahead, are viewed through a gender lens, taken seriously as a routine consideration in all relevant policy fields, and acted upon with the objective of securing genuine equality of opportunity for all in every local labour market.

# GELLM research programme research methods

This appendix provides a brief outline of the methods used in each main element of the GELLM research programme. Further information about the methods used is also provided in each of the GELLM reports.

## GELLM gender profiles of local labour markets (Buckner et al, 2004 a–i, 2005a, 2005b, 2006)

The 12 GELLM gender profiles related to 12 English local authorities (Birmingham City Council, the London Borough of Camden, East Staffordshire Borough Council, Leicester City Council, Newcastle City Council, Sandwell Metropolitan Borough Council, Somerset County Council, the London Borough of Southwark, Thurrock Council, Trafford Metropolitan Borough Council, Wakefield Metropolitan District Council and West Sussex County Council). They were based on statistical analysis of an extensive range of official data, as follows:

- 2001 Census of Population
- Annual Business Inquiry
- Labour Force Survey (Annual Population Survey)
- New Earnings Survey/Annual Survey of Hours and Earnings
- Data on Educational Attainment (supplied by the Department for Education and Skills)
- Post-16 Destinations re those leaving compulsory education (supplied by Connexions)
- Social Security Benefits data (supplied by the Department for Work and Pensions)
- Childcare statistics (supplied by the Children's Information Service)
- Data on university graduates (supplied by the Higher Education Statistics Agency).

The gender profiles provided detailed gender-disaggregated information on labour market and related issues for each of the participating local authorities. This statistical work was subsequently further developed to provide additional statistical context and analysis, as part of each of the six GELLM local research studies (described below).

## GELLM Local Research Study 1: *Working below potential: women and part-time work* (Grant et al, 2005, 2006g–l)

Participating authorities: Camden, Leicester, Trafford, Thurrock, Wakefield and West Sussex.

The research for this study included:

- negotiating access to 22 workplaces in six localities (see Table A in Grant et al, 2006g);
- a questionnaire survey completed by 333 women part-time workers in these workplaces;
- semi-structured interviews with 89 women in part-time jobs working 'below their potential' in these workplaces;
- interviews with 22 senior managers in these workplaces.

The fieldwork for the study was conducted during 2004 and 2005. The research also involved extensive analysis of statistical data, including the 2001 Census, and focus group interviews with 29 trade union representatives.

The interviews with managers explored: levels of pay and pay structures for part-time workers; factors involved in the determination of part-time pay; the process of pay determination; employers' perspectives on pay rates; the nature of the part-time jobs; the decision-making process involved in the construction of part-time jobs; employers' reasons for the use of part-time employment and the employment of women in these jobs; the significance of the local labour market; and issues associated with the under-utilisation of women's skills and experience.

Managers in participating workplaces distributed a questionnaire to all part-time women workers in the workplace or, in large workplaces, to up to 50 part-time women workers. The questionnaires were used to identify women working below their potential, in terms of qualifications, previous labour market experience and current study and training. Face-to-face interviews (total 89) were conducted with a sample of these women in each workplace, at their workplaces and during working hours. These interviews explored: levels of pay; hours of work; satisfaction with pay and hours; and the motivating factors involved in women working below their potential (eg domestic circumstances, hours of work, expectations and pressures from family and friends, local labour market conditions, transport, and the tax and benefit system). The 29 trade union representatives consulted as part of the study were members of the following unions: AMICUS, AUT, GMB, NATFHE, NUT, Prospect, RCN, PCS, UNISON.

## GELLM local research study 2: *Connecting women with the labour market* (Grant et al, 2006a–f)

Participating authorities: Birmingham, Camden, Sandwell, Thurrock and Wakefield:
   The research for this study included:

*   interviews with 51 representatives from local organisations;
*   10 focus groups involving 101 local women.

The fieldwork for the study was conducted during 2005 and 2006. The research also involved extensive analysis of statistical data, including the 2001 Census. The interviews with key informants explored: the activities and priorities of their organisation; local social and economic conditions; the nature of the local labour market for men and women; the social and economic circumstances of local unemployed and economically inactive women and men; local services; local employment projects; and views about, and experience of, the intermediate labour market (ILM) model.
   The focus groups with women covered the following topics: work history; experience of looking for work; labour market support and advice; reasons for not working; views about not working; aspirations in relation to paid work; views about the ILM model.

## GELLM local research study 3: *Ethnic minority women and access to the labour market* (Stiell and Tang, 2006a–e; Yeandle et al, 2006j)

Participating authorities: Camden, Leicester, Newcastle, Somerset, Southwark.
   This study used a mixed method research design, incorporating:

*   detailed analysis of employment data from the 2001 Census;
*   a review of local information and intelligence using documentary analysis;
*   qualitative research with 93 local ethnic minority women.

The analysis of the 2001 Census drew on the 2001 Census Standard Tables, Commissioned Tables, and Census Microdata (plus 1991 Census data where appropriate), focusing on women in specific ethnic minority groups in selected wards. It explored: population size; age–sex profile; country of birth, household composition; full-time/part-time employment, unemployment, economic inactivity; occupation and industry for women in employment.
   The review of local information and intelligence was undertaken with the cooperation of the participating local authorities, and included information from local statutory, voluntary and community sector organisations that had produced data or reports relating to ethnic minority women and the labour market.

Arts-based workshops were arranged in selected wards with the assistance of the participating local authorities. Local voluntary organisations and local community artists supported the design of the workshop activities. Workshops (three to four in each case) were held over a period of a month, using poetry, music, artwork, photography and games. Participants produced images of their lives and explored their aspirations, skills and capabilities, focusing on labour market issues. They also completed questionnaires and took part in discussions about barriers to employment, job progression and support needs; attitudes and values regarding childcare, caring and employment; existing experience, skills, capacities and qualifications; personal choices and how these are influenced by cultural/family expectations; local barriers to employment such as transport, childcare, education and discrimination.

## GELLM local research study 4: *Career development for women in local authorities* (Bennett et al, 2006a–e; Bennett and Yeandle, 2006)

Participating authorities: Leicester, Sandwell, Southwark and Wakefield.

This study focused on women with educational qualifications and already in jobs with career development potential. It identified women research participants via the grading structure of the selected local authority. The research questions related to women's perceptions of: their opportunities for promotion and advancement within their organisation; their job role and its demands; and their aspirations and attitudes about their career in the sector. The study was conducted in 2005–06 and involved:

- a statistical analysis of local authority employment, using the Labour Force Survey, Census of Population and other relevant sources to describe the wider context of women's employment in the public sector;
- mapping of women's and men's employment within the local authorities concerned, using local authority human resources data and analysing relevant documentation;
- a survey of selected employees, to gather information on age, caring/childcare responsibilities, family situation, and to secure agreement to participate in the focus group discussions (1,871 completed returns, including some from men);
- focus groups (17) with women employees, bringing together women: in middle-ranking/more senior positions, aged approximately 45–59; in the 16–24 and 25–34 age group; aged 35–44 who had caring/childcare responsibilities; and aged 35–44 who had *not* had caring/childcare responsibilities. Each attendee was also invited to return written comments in an open-ended questionnaire;
- face-to-face interviews with 11 senior managers;
- interviews with trade union representatives.

**GELLM local research study 5:** *Addressing women's poverty: local labour market initiatives* **(Escott et al, 2006a–f)**

Participating authorities: Birmingham, East Staffordshire, Newcastle-upon-Tyne, Somerset, Southwark and West Sussex.

The methods used in conducting this study were:

- Analysis of official statistical data to assess the nature and extent of women's poverty and economic disadvantage in the selected geographical areas, using 2001 Census and other relevant sources.
- Documentary analysis, including:
  - a review of relevant academic and other policy literature
  - assessment of existing evaluations for the identified local regeneration initiatives in relation to women's economic circumstances
  - an equalities and gender proofing template was used to facilitate the desk based exercise. The template identified equalities and gender sensitive approaches.
- Interviews with local organisations: semi-structured interviews with 81 representatives from local initiatives in the six districts including local government, regeneration programmes, statutory agencies, employment and training projects, Family Centres, and UNISON. The interview schedule included questions organised under the themes of: social and economic conditions in the locality; women's experiences of living on a low income; locality-based regeneration and employment projects; addressing women's disadvantage in the locality; local services; the local labour market; unemployment and economic inactivity. Staff and other representatives of relevant organisations were interviewed in each of the six localities.
- Focus groups (14) attended by 133 women living in the elected wards. The discussions, held in local community venues, explored: views about the neighbourhood – services, job opportunities, childcare, service improvements and regeneration projects; experiences of work and unemployment – types of job available, levels of income, opportunities and barriers, problems; aspirations for themselves and families; ideas and solutions.

**GELLM local research study 6:** *Local challenges in meeting demand for domiciliary care* **(Yeandle et al, 2006c–h)**

Participating authorities: Birmingham, Newcastle, Sandwell, Somerset, Thurrock and West Sussex.

This study was conducted in 2005-06, and involved:

- a new statistical analysis of the 2001 Census of Population;
- a survey of domiciliary care providers with follow-up telephone interviews;

• interviews with key stakeholders involved in commissioning and delivering domiciliary care services in each of the 6 study areas.

Data from the 2001 Census for England and from the sub-national population projections were used to produce statistical profiles relating to domiciliary care in each locality. These explored: population structure and key labour market indicators; demographic and employment characteristics; demographic/housing/health-related indicators for older people; population and household projections for 2004–28, and provision of unpaid care by people working as care assistants or home carers.

A postal questionnaire was completed by 88 domiciliary care providers (46% response rate) registered with the selected local authorities. They included 17 from the voluntary and community sector, 51 private for-profit organisations, and 17 private not-for-profit organisations. The survey explored providers' employment, training and human resources practices and policies.

Follow-up in-depth interviews were conducted with 41 independent sector providers and with 25 key stakeholders in the selected localities. These interviews explored workforce management, planning and recruitment practices. Interviewees were also asked to supply relevant supporting documentation, which was subjected to documentary analysis.

# Employment and economic activity indicators for the GELLM localities and England

| | Birmingham | | Camden | | East Staffs | | Leicester | | Newcastle | | Sandwell | | Somerset | | Southwark | | Thurrock | | Trafford | | Wakefield | | West Sussex | | ENGLAND | |
|---|---|---|---|---|---|---|---|---|---|---|---|---|---|---|---|---|---|---|---|---|---|---|---|---|---|---|
| Population ('000s) | 977.1 | | 198.0 | | 103.8 | | 279.9 | | 259.5 | | 282.9 | | 498.1 | | 244.9 | | 143.1 | | 210.2 | | 315.2 | | 753.6 | | 49138.8 | |
| Working age population ('000s) | 584.6 | | 140.4 | | 62.8 | | 173.8 | | 163.2 | | 167.8 | | 290.8 | | 165.5 | | 89.9 | | 128.2 | | 193.7 | | 436.6 | | 30211.9 | |
| % working age population | 60 | | 71 | | 60 | | 62 | | 63 | | 59 | | 58 | | 68 | | 63 | | 61 | | 61 | | 58 | | 61 | |
| Economic activity (% working age) | M | W | M | W | M | W | M | W | M | W | M | W | M | W | M | W | M | W | M | W | M | W | M | W | M | W |
| In employment | 63 | 53 | 65 | 56 | 79 | 66 | 65 | 54 | 60 | 55 | 70 | 58 | 79 | 69 | 65 | 57 | 80 | 67 | 77 | 68 | 72 | 64 | 81 | 70 | 74 | 64 |
| Unemployed | 9 | 4 | 7 | 4 | 4 | 3 | 7 | 4 | 8 | 3 | 8 | 4 | 3 | 2 | 8 | 5 | 4 | 3 | 4 | 2 | 5 | 3 | 3 | 2 | 5 | 3 |
| Student | 12 | 13 | 14 | 17 | 5 | 7 | 14 | 15 | 15 | 17 | 6 | 7 | 6 | 7 | 14 | 15 | 4 | 5 | 7 | 8 | 5 | 7 | 6 | 7 | 8 | 9 |
| Retired | 2 | 1 | 1 | 1 | 3 | 2 | 2 | 1 | 2 | 1 | 2 | 1 | 4 | 2 | 1 | 1 | 3 | 1 | 3 | 1 | 3 | 2 | 4 | 2 | 3 | 1 |
| Looking after home or family | 2 | 17 | 1 | 12 | 1 | 15 | 2 | 15 | 1 | 13 | 2 | 17 | 1 | 14 | 1 | 12 | 1 | 16 | 1 | 12 | 1 | 14 | 1 | 14 | 1 | 14 |
| Permanently sick or disabled | 7 | 6 | 7 | 5 | 5 | 4 | 7 | 6 | 10 | 7 | 8 | 7 | 5 | 4 | 6 | 4 | 5 | 4 | 6 | 5 | 10 | 7 | 4 | 3 | 6 | 5 |
| Other | 5 | 6 | 5 | 6 | 2 | 4 | 4 | 5 | 4 | 4 | 4 | 5 | 2 | 3 | 5 | 5 | 2 | 3 | 3 | 3 | 3 | 3 | 2 | 3 | 3 | 4 |
| Employment status (% working age in employment) | | | | | | | | | | | | | | | | | | | | | | | | | | |
| Employee full-time | 79 | 61 | 70 | 70 | 80 | 51 | 79 | 62 | 80 | 59 | 84 | 60 | 74 | 48 | 76 | 71 | 81 | 58 | 78 | 60 | 82 | 53 | 76 | 54 | 78 | 57 |
| Employee part-time | 6 | 34 | 7 | 15 | 4 | 41 | 7 | 34 | 6 | 35 | 5 | 37 | 4 | 42 | 6 | 20 | 3 | 38 | 5 | 34 | 4 | 42 | 4 | 37 | 5 | 36 |
| Self-employed full-time | 13 | 3 | 18 | 9 | 15 | 4 | 12 | 3 | 12 | 3 | 10 | 2 | 19 | 6 | 15 | 5 | 15 | 2 | 15 | 4 | 12 | 3 | 18 | 4 | 15 | 4 |
| Self-employed part-time | 2 | 2 | 5 | 6 | 2 | 3 | 2 | 2 | 2 | 2 | 1 | 2 | 3 | 5 | 3 | 3 | 1 | 2 | 2 | 3 | 2 | 2 | 3 | 5 | 2 | 4 |

| Occupation | Birmingham | | Camden | | East Staffs | | Leicester | | Newcastle | | Sandwell | | Somerset | | Southwark | | Thurrock | | Trafford | | Wakefield | | West Sussex | | ENGLAND | |
|---|---|---|---|---|---|---|---|---|---|---|---|---|---|---|---|---|---|---|---|---|---|---|---|---|---|---|---|
| Managers and senior officials | 14 | 9 | 23 | 17 | 11 | 19 | 12 | 7 | 14 | 9 | 8 | 12 | 17 | 11 | 17 | 13 | 16 | 10 | 21 | 12 | 15 | 9 | 22 | 12 | 19 | 11 |
| Professional | 12 | 11 | 23 | 20 | 8 | 10 | 11 | 9 | 16 | 13 | 6 | 7 | 11 | 9 | 17 | 14 | 7 | 6 | 16 | 12 | 8 | 7 | 12 | 9 | 12 | 10 |
| Associate professionals and technical | 11 | 14 | 23 | 26 | 13 | 10 | 10 | 12 | 12 | 14 | 11 | 9 | 12 | 13 | 18 | 20 | 12 | 11 | 14 | 16 | 12 | 12 | 14 | 14 | 14 | 14 |
| Administrative and secretarial | 6 | 24 | 6 | 17 | 21 | 4 | 6 | 18 | 7 | 20 | 24 | 5 | 4 | 20 | 8 | 21 | 7 | 29 | 6 | 25 | 4 | 21 | 6 | 24 | 5 | 23 |
| Skilled trades | 19 | 2 | 7 | 1 | 3 | 21 | 18 | 2 | 17 | 2 | 3 | 24 | 24 | 4 | 11 | 2 | 21 | 2 | 15 | 2 | 21 | 2 | 19 | 2 | 19 | 2 |
| Personal service occupations | 2 | 13 | 2 | 7 | 13 | 1 | 2 | 12 | 3 | 12 | 12 | 2 | 2 | 15 | 3 | 11 | 2 | 11 | 2 | 11 | 2 | 13 | 2 | 15 | 2 | 13 |
| Sales and customer services | 5 | 11 | 4 | 6 | 12 | 3 | 6 | 12 | 6 | 14 | 13 | 4 | 3 | 13 | 4 | 8 | 4 | 18 | 5 | 12 | 4 | 14 | 4 | 12 | 4 | 12 |
| Process plant and machine operatives | 17 | 4 | 4 | 1 | 4 | 19 | 18 | 12 | 12 | 12 | 7 | 23 | 14 | 3 | 7 | 1 | 18 | 2 | 11 | 2 | 18 | 4 | 10 | 2 | 13 | 3 |
| Elementary occupations | 14 | 13 | 8 | 5 | 16 | 13 | 17 | 16 | 13 | 15 | 16 | 14 | 13 | 13 | 14 | 9 | 14 | 12 | 10 | 8 | 16 | 17 | 11 | 10 | 12 | 12 |
| Industry (selected industries) | | | | | | | | | | | | | | | | | | | | | | | | | | |
| Agriculture, hunting, forestry, fishing | 1 | 0 | 0 | 0 | 1 | 3 | 1 | 0 | 1 | 0 | 0 | 0 | 5 | 2 | 0 | 0 | 1 | 0 | 1 | 0 | 1 | 0 | 3 | 1 | 2 | 1 |
| Energy and water | 1 | 1 | 0 | 0 | 0 | 2 | 1 | 1 | 2 | 1 | 1 | 1 | 2 | 0 | 0 | 0 | 0 | 0 | 1 | 1 | 4 | 1 | 1 | 1 | 1 | 1 |
| Manufacture | 25 | 9 | 6 | 6 | 13 | 31 | 29 | 17 | 15 | 5 | 15 | 35 | 23 | 9 | 7 | 5 | 20 | 7 | 18 | 6 | 23 | 10 | 16 | 7 | 20 | 9 |
| Construction | 10 | 1 | 4 | 1 | 2 | 11 | 8 | 1 | 11 | 1 | 2 | 10 | 13 | 2 | 7 | 1 | 14 | 2 | 10 | 2 | 13 | 2 | 12 | 2 | 11 | 1 |
| Wholesale and retail, restaurants and hotels | 21 | 22 | 17 | 15 | 26 | 19 | 23 | 24 | 20 | 24 | 26 | 21 | 21 | 27 | 17 | 18 | 21 | 32 | 20 | 21 | 24 | 29 | 20 | 22 | 20 | 24 |
| Transport and communication | 9 | 4 | 7 | 4 | 4 | 9 | 9 | 3 | 9 | 4 | 4 | 9 | 7 | 3 | 10 | 4 | 14 | 6 | 10 | 6 | 9 | 4 | 12 | 8 | 9 | 4 |
| Finance and real estate | 16 | 18 | 39 | 32 | 12 | 12 | 12 | 12 | 16 | 15 | 14 | 11 | 12 | 12 | 32 | 26 | 17 | 21 | 23 | 22 | 11 | 14 | 21 | 19 | 18 | 18 |
| Public administration | 4 | 5 | 4 | 4 | 4 | 3 | 4 | 5 | 8 | 8 | 5 | 3 | 7 | 6 | 5 | 7 | 4 | 4 | 4 | 5 | 5 | 6 | 5 | 5 | 6 | 6 |
| Education | 5 | 14 | 5 | 11 | 13 | 3 | 5 | 12 | 6 | 13 | 10 | 3 | 4 | 13 | 5 | 11 | 2 | 10 | 4 | 12 | 3 | 11 | 3 | 11 | 4 | 12 |
| Health and social work | 5 | 21 | 6 | 15 | 19 | 3 | 5 | 19 | 7 | 23 | 19 | 3 | 4 | 20 | 7 | 19 | 2 | 13 | 4 | 20 | 4 | 19 | 4 | 19 | 4 | 19 |

| | Birmingham | | Camden | | East Staffs | | Leicester | | Newcastle | | Sandwell | | Somerset | | Southwark | | Thurrock | | Trafford | | Wakefield | | West Sussex | | ENGLAND | |
|---|---|---|---|---|---|---|---|---|---|---|---|---|---|---|---|---|---|---|---|---|---|---|---|---|---|---|
| Other | 4 | 5 | 13 | 12 | 3 | 6 | 4 | 5 | 4 | 6 | 3 | 5 | 4 | 6 | 9 | 9 | 3 | 5 | 4 | 5 | 3 | 5 | 4 | 6 | 4 | 6 |
| Provision of unpaid care | | | | | | | | | | | | | | | | | | | | | | | | | | |
| People of working age | 11 | 15 | 10 | 8 | 11 | 15 | 11 | 15 | 10 | 15 | 12 | 16 | 10 | 15 | 8 | 11 | 10 | 14 | 10 | 15 | 12 | 17 | 10 | 14 | 10 | 14 |
| People of working age in employment | 11 | 15 | 9 | 7 | 10 | 14 | 11 | 14 | 10 | 15 | 11 | 15 | 10 | 14 | 7 | 10 | 9 | 13 | 10 | 14 | 11 | 16 | 10 | 13 | 10 | 14 |

Source: 2001 Census Standard Tables, Crown Copyright 2003

# GELLM area profiles

These brief area profiles are drawn from each participating local authority's gender profile (where detailed sources are given), except where otherwise indicated. Population figures are from the ONS 2006 mid-year population estimates, and ethnicity figures are from the 2001 Census. Where mentioned, comparisons are with data for England as a whole.

## Birmingham

Birmingham, the second largest city in the UK, has just over 1 million people and a younger population than England as a whole. A third (34%) of residents are from ethnic minority groups, including relatively large Pakistani (11%), Indian (6%) and Black Caribbean (5%) populations. The city has lower than average life expectancy at birth and a high proportion of people with a limiting long-term illness. It includes some of the most deprived areas in the country (Communities and Local Government, n.d.), with 29% of dependent children living in households with no working adult. Men and women in Birmingham are less well qualified than men and women nationally.

Birmingham has a long history of heavy reliance on manufacturing, with recent service sector growth, resulting in fewer jobs in manufacturing, and more employment in banking, finance, insurance, 'other services', distribution, hotels and restaurants. Between 1991 and 2002, the city saw a 39% increase in part-time jobs and a 5% fall in full-time jobs.

Birmingham has relatively low economic activity and employment rates for men, women, young people and lone parents, low part-time employment rates for both sexes, and low levels of self-employment among men. Among those in employment, 74% of men and 83% of women work within the city; a high but declining proportion of them travel to work by bus, although recently travel to work by car (particularly among women) has increased. In 2001, unemployment was relatively high, especially among men; among those then unemployed, 30% of men and 36% of women had not worked for over five years.

Birmingham City Council was a partner in the GELLM research programme between 2003 and 2006, and participated in three GELLM local research studies. The GELLM publications relating to Birmingham are:

- *Gender profile of Birmingham's labour market* (Buckner et al, 2005a)
- *Addressing women's poverty in Birmingham: local labour market initiatives* (Escott et al, 2006a)
- *Connecting women with the labour market in Birmingham* (Grant et al, 2006c)

- *Local challenges in meeting demand for domiciliary care in Birmingham* (Yeandle et al, 2006e).

## Camden

The London Borough of Camden (north London) is socially diverse, with deprived areas adjacent to areas of expensive private housing, and many commuters and students coming into the area each day. It has a relatively high proportion of young adults aged 20–34. Across all ages, 47% of people are from ethnic minority groups, including relatively large White Other (16%), Bangladeshi (6%) and Black African (6%) populations.

General indicators of health and well-being are mixed. Camden has relatively low life expectancy at birth for men (but not for women), and the borough contains some of the most deprived areas in the country (Communities and Local Government, n.d.). Almost a third (31%) of dependent children live in households with no working adult. Camden's men and women are better qualified than men and women nationally, however.

Camden has a high number of jobs in business and professional services and the public sector. There are also a high proportion of businesses employing fewer than 10 people. Between 1991 and 2002, the borough saw a 104% increase in part-time jobs and a 16% rise in full-time jobs.

The borough has low economic activity and employment rates for men, women, young people (reflecting a large student population) and lone parents, and very low part-time employment rates among both sexes. Many residents travel by underground to work, while a significant number travel on foot; of those in employment, 62% of men and 58% of women work outside the borough. In 2001, the unemployment rate was higher for men and women than in England. Among those unemployed, 28% of men and 30% of women had not worked for over five years.

The London Borough of Camden was a partner in the GELLM research programme between 2004 and 2006, participating in three GELLM local research studies. The GELLM publications relating to Camden are:

- *Gender profile of Camden's labour market* (Buckner et al, 2004e)
- *Connecting women with the labour market in Camden* (Grant et al, 2006f)
- *Ethnic minority women and access to the labour market in Camden* (Stiell and Tang, 2006e)
- *Working below potential: women and part-time work in Camden* (Grant et al, 2006l).

## East Staffordshire

East Staffordshire (population just over 100,000) comprises both rural areas and urban centres, with Burton-on-Trent at its centre. The district has a relatively small ethnic minority population (8%), including Pakistani (4%), White Other (0.8%) and White Irish (0.6%) residents.

With decreasing numbers of full-time jobs in manufacturing in the district, the local labour market has undergone a period of significant change, with growing numbers of residents working in distribution, hotels, restaurants, the transport and communications sector and the public sector. Between 1991 and 2002, the district saw a 78% increase in part-time jobs and a 10% increase in full-time jobs.

General indicators of health and well-being in the district are mixed; East Staffordshire has lower than average life expectancy at birth, and a high teenage pregnancy rate – but rates of limiting long-term illness are close to the national average (Communities and Local Government, n.d.), and just 14% of dependent children live in households with no working adult. Men and women in the district are less well qualified than men and women nationally.

By national standards, East Staffordshire has high economic activity and employment rates for men, women and lone parents, as well as high part-time employment rates among women. Most residents in employment work within the district (64% of men and 74% of women); many travel to work by car, although a high proportion of women walk to work. In 2001, unemployment rates were relatively low; among the unemployed, 19% of men and 24% of women had not worked for over five years.

East Staffordshire District Council was a partner in the GELLM research programme between 2003 and 2006, participating in one GELLM local research study. The GELLM publications relating to East Staffordshire are:

- *Gender profile of East Staffordshire's labour market* (Buckner et al, 2004i)
- *Addressing women's poverty in East Staffordshire: local labour market initiatives* (Escott et al, 2006e).

## Leicester

Leicester, the largest city in the East Midlands, has almost 288,000 people and a relatively young population. A high proportion of residents (40%) are from ethnic minority groups, including Indian (26%), Other Asian (2%) and White Other (2%) populations.

General indicators of health and well-being in the city are relatively poor: the city has lower than average life expectancy at birth, a high proportion of people with a limiting long-term illness and some of the most deprived areas in the country (Communities and Local Government, n.d.). A quarter of dependent children live in households with no working adult, and the city's men and women are less well qualified than men and women nationally.

Manufacturing, for long a significant aspect of the local economy, remains critical to the local economy, although manufacturing employment has been declining in recent years, as retail, public administration and other service sector employment has grown in importance. Between 1991 and 2002, the city saw a 29% increase in part-time jobs and a 5% fall in full-time jobs.

Leicester has low economic activity and employment rates for both men and women, and low rates for young people (in part reflecting a large student population) and lone parents; part-time employment rates are low for both sexes. Among those in work, many travel by bus or walk to work, although travel to work by car among women has increased; 71% of men and 81% of women work within the city. In 2001, the unemployment rate for men was relatively high; among the unemployed, 21% of men and 27% of women had not worked for over five years.

Leicester City Council was a partner in the GELLM research programme between 2003 and 2006, participating in three GELLM local research studies. The GELLM publications relating to Leicester are:

- *Gender profile of Leicester's labour market* (Buckner et al, 2004f)
- *Ethnic minority women and access to the labour market in Leicester* (Stiell and Tang, 2006c)
- *Women's career development in Leicester City Council* (Bennett et al, 2006d)
- *Working below potential: women and part-time work in Leicester* (Grant et al, 2006k).

## Newcastle

Newcastle is the largest city in the North East and an important regional centre, with over 270,000 people. It has a relatively young population, including many students. One in 10 residents are from ethnic minority groups, including the city's Pakistani (2%), White Other (2%), and Indian (1%) populations.

General indicators of health and well-being in the city are relatively poor. Newcastle has relatively low life expectancy at birth, a high proportion of people with a limiting long-term illness, especially among men over 25, and a high teenage pregnancy rate. The city has some of the most deprived areas in the country (Communities and Local Government, n.d.), and more than a quarter of dependent children (27%) live in households with no working adult.

Newcastle has low economic activity and employment rates for both men and women, and low rates for young people (reflecting a large student population). The city also has low part-time employment rates among both men and women, low levels of self-employment among men, and a low employment rate among lone parents. Its workforce includes a high but declining proportion of people of both sexes who travel by bus to work; more recently, travel to work by car, particularly among women, has increased; most residents in employment work within the city (63% of men and 76% of women). In 2001, the unemployment rate was higher for men than in England, and long-term unemployment rates were relatively high for both men and women; 32% of unemployed men and 33% of unemployed women had not worked for over five years.

In Newcastle, there has been a trend away from manufacturing, shipping and mining, towards jobs in banking and finance, and in public administration, health and education. Between 1991 and 2002, the city saw a 36% increase in part-time jobs and a 4% rise in full-time jobs.

Newcastle City Council was a partner in the GELLM research programme between 2003 and 2006, participating in three GELLM local research studies. The GELLM publications relating to Newcastle are:

- *Gender profile of Newcastle's labour market* (Buckner et al, 2004c)
- *Addressing women's poverty in Newcastle: local labour market initiatives* (Escott et al, 2006c)
- *Ethnic minority women and access to the labour market in Newcastle* (Stiell and Tang, 2006a)
- *Local challenges in meeting demand for domiciliary care in Newcastle* (Yeandle et al, 2006g).

## Sandwell

The borough of Sandwell includes six small towns, and borders Birmingham, Walsall, Wolverhampton and Dudley. It contains over 287,000 people, and has a relatively high population of children, and of ethnic minority residents (22%), including Indian (9%), Black Caribbean (3%) and Pakistani (3%) populations.

General indicators of health and well-being in the borough are relatively poor. Sandwell has lower than average life expectancy at birth, a high proportion of people with a limiting long-term illness and some of the most deprived areas in the country (Communities and Local Government, n.d.). More than a quarter of dependent children (26%) live in households with no working adult, and Sandwell's men and women are less well qualified than men and women nationally.

Sandwell has a long history of heavy reliance on manufacturing, with recent service sector growth, resulting in fewer jobs in manufacturing, and more employment in banking, finance, insurance and distribution. Between 1991 and 2002, the borough saw a 19% increase in part-time jobs and a 4% fall in full-time jobs.

Sandwell has low economic activity and employment rates for both men and women, but high rates for young people (reflecting its small student population). The borough has low part-time employment rates among men and women, low levels of self-employment among men, and a low employment rate among lone parents. A large but declining proportion of male and female residents travel by bus to work, although recently, travel to work by car, particularly among women, has increased. Just over half of those with jobs work within the borough (54% of men; 58% of women). In 2001, the male unemployment rate was relatively high; among those unemployed, 26% of men and 32% of women had not worked for over five years.

Sandwell Metropolitan Borough Council was a partner in the GELLM research programme between 2003 and 2006, participating in three GELLM local research studies. The GELLM publications relating to Sandwell are:

- *Gender profile of Sandwell's labour market* (Buckner et al, 2004b)
- *Connecting women with the labour market in Sandwell* (Grant et al, 2006b)
- *Local challenges in meeting demand for domiciliary care in Sandwell* (Yeandle et al, 2006d)
- *Women's career development in Sandwell MBC* (Bennett et al, 2006b).

## Somerset

Somerset is a diverse county in the South West of England, with over 518,000 people. It has a relatively old population, with more people over state pension age. Comparatively few residents are from ethnic minority groups (3%), including small White Other (1%), White Irish (0.5%) and Chinese (0.2%) populations.

General indicators of health and well-being in the county are relatively good. Somerset has higher than average life expectancy, average rates of limiting long-term illness, and a low teenage pregnancy rate. Although the county has a number of deprived areas (in Bridgwater) (Communities and Local Government, n.d.), overall it has a low proportion (12%) of dependent children living in households with no working adult. Somerset's men and women are better qualified than men and women nationally.

In recent years Somerset has experienced a decline in manufacturing and agricultural employment and growth in jobs in banking, finance and insurance and distribution, hotels and restaurants. Between 1991 and 2002, the county saw a 62% increase in part-time jobs and a 8% rise in full-time jobs.

Somerset has high economic activity and employment rates for both men and women, including high rates of self-employment, part-time employment and lone parent employment. Its workforce includes a high proportion of women who walk to work, although recently travel to work by car, particularly among women, has increased. Most residents with jobs (74% of men and 80% of women) work within the county. In 2001, the county had relatively low male and female unemployment rates; among those unemployed, 15% of men and 18% of women had not worked for over five years.

Somerset County Council was a partner in the GELLM research programme between 2003 and 2006, participating in three GELLM local research studies. The GELLM publications relating to Somerset are:

- *Gender profile of Somerset's labour market* (Buckner et al, 2004a)
- *Addressing women's poverty in Somerset: local labour market initiatives* (Escott et al, 2006d)
- *Ethnic minority women and access to the labour market in Somerset* (Stiell and Tang, 2006b)

- *Local challenges in meeting demand for domiciliary care in Somerset* (Yeandle et al, 2006i).

## Southwark

The London Borough of Southwark, in central London south of the Thames, has a resident population of over 183,000, and a large number of commuters and students coming into the area each day. Southwark's population is relatively young, and almost half its residents (48%) are from ethnic minority groups, including relatively large Black African (16%), Black Caribbean (8%) and White Other (8%) populations.

General indicators of health and well-being in the borough are relatively poor. Southwark has lower than average life expectancy at birth, a high proportion of people aged 25–34 with a limiting long-term illness, and a high teenage pregnancy rate. The borough has some areas that are amongst the most deprived in the country (Communities and Local Government, n.d.), and almost a third (31%) of dependent children live in households with no working adult. However, Southwark's men and women are better qualified than men and women nationally.

A third of jobs in Southwark are professional jobs in business, banking, finance and insurance services; another third are in the public sector. Between 1991 and 2002, the borough saw a 59% increase in part-time jobs and an 8% rise in full-time jobs.

Southwark has low economic activity and employment rates for men, women and young people (reflecting its large student population); low part-time employment rates among women, low levels of self-employment among men, and a low employment rate among lone parents. Most residents in employment work outside the borough (67% of men and 65% of women), often travelling to work by bus. In 2001, Southwark had relatively high male and female unemployment rates; among those unemployed, 31% of men and 35% of women had not worked for over five years.

The London Borough of Southwark was a partner in the GELLM research programme between 2004 and 2006, participating in three GELLM local research studies. The GELLM publications relating to Southwark are:

- *Gender profile of Southwark's labour market* (Buckner et al, 2005b)
- *Addressing women's poverty in Southwark: local labour market initiatives* (Escott et al, 2006f)
- *Ethnic minority women and access to the labour market in Southwark* (Stiell and Tang, 2006d)
- *Women's career development in the London Borough of Southwark* (Bennett et al, 2006e).

## Thurrock

Thurrock, which lies on the River Thames east of London, has a population of almost 150,000. It has a comparatively young population, with more children, and higher percentages of people aged 25–34. Few residents (7%) are from ethnic minority groups, including small White Other (1.4%), Indian (1.3%) and White Irish (1.1%) populations.

General indicators of health and well-being in the borough are mixed; Thurrock has lower than average life expectancy at birth, a high proportion of older people with a limiting long-term illness, and a high teenage pregnancy rate. Some areas in the borough are among the most deprived in the country (Communities and Local Government, n.d.), but the proportion of dependent children living in households with no working adult is close to the national average (16%). However, Thurrock's men and women are less well qualified than men and women nationally.

In recent years Thurrock has seen a fall in jobs in manufacturing, and in the energy and water industries, but a significant increase in employment in distribution, hotels and restaurants. Between 1991 and 2002, the borough saw a 93% increase in part-time jobs and a 27% rise in full-time jobs.

Thurrock has high economic activity and employment rates for both men and women, and high part-time employment rates for both sexes. It has a high employment rate among male lone parents but not among female lone parents. Just over half of male residents in employment (53%), and 61% of women, work within the borough; the workforce includes a high proportion of people of both sexes who travel to work by train, although recently, travelling to work by car, particularly among women, has increased. In 2001, Thurrock had a relatively high unemployment rate for women; among those unemployed, 21% of men and 22% of women had not worked for over five years.

Thurrock Council was a partner in the GELLM research programme between 2003 and 2006, participating in three GELLM local research studies. The GELLM publications relating to Thurrock are:

- *Gender profile of Thurrock's labour market* (Buckner et al, 2004g)
- *Connecting women with the labour market in Thurrock* (Grant et al, 2006e)
- *Local challenges in meeting demand for domiciliary care in Thurrock* (Yeandle et al, 2006h)
- *Working below potential: women and part-time work in Wakefield* (Grant et al, 2006j).

## Trafford

Trafford lies within Greater Manchester and has a population of over 210,000 people. Its population profile is very similar to the English average, except that it has fewer people aged 16–24. The proportion of residents from ethnic minority groups is the same as for England as a whole (13%), and includes White Irish (3%), White Other (2%) and Indian (2%) populations.

General indicators of health and well-being in the borough are relatively good. Trafford has higher than average life expectancy at birth, a smaller proportion of people with a limiting long-term illness, and a lower teenage pregnancy rate. Although the borough has some areas of deprivation (Communities and Local Government, n.d.), it has a relatively small proportion of dependent children living in households with no working adult (14%). Trafford's men and women are better qualified than men and women nationally, with a high proportion qualified to degree-level or above.

Manufacturing remains an important part of the local economy, but the majority of local jobs are in the service sector; the share of jobs in banking, finance and insurance has increased in recent years. Between 1991 and 2002, the borough saw a 54% increase in part-time jobs and a 23% rise in full-time jobs.

Trafford has high economic activity and employment rates for both men and women. The borough has high full-time employment rates for both sexes, and a high employment rate among lone parents. Its workforce includes many people of both sexes who travel to work by car; recently, among women, the proportion driving to work has increased. Half of male residents in paid jobs work within the borough (50%); the proportion doing so among women is higher (59%). In 2001, unemployment rates for men and women were relatively low; among the unemployed, just 18% of men and 23% of women had not worked for over five years.

Trafford Council was a partner in the GELLM research programme in 2003–04. Data about women and part-time work in Trafford is included in *Working below potential: women and part-time work: synthesis report* (Grant et al, 2006g). The GELLM publication relating to Trafford is:

- *Gender profile of Trafford's labour market* (Buckner et al, 2006).

## Wakefield

The Wakefield District comprises a mix of rural areas, former mining communities and urban centres, with the City of Wakefield at its heart. The population of 321,200 has proportionally fewer young children and people aged 20–24, but more people aged 35–64. Only 3% of residents are from ethnic minority groups, including small Pakistani (1.1%), White Other (0.7%) and White Irish (0.4%) populations.

General indicators of health and well-being in the city are relatively poor. Wakefield has lower than average life expectancy at birth, a high proportion of people with a limiting long-term illness (especially among people aged over 50), and a high teenage pregnancy rate. The city contains some of the most deprived areas in the country (Communities and Local Government, n.d.), and has a high proportion of dependent children living in households with no working adult

(19%). The district's men and women are less well qualified than men and women nationally.

With the decline of the mining industry and falling numbers of full-time jobs in manufacturing, the district has undergone a period of significant labour market change. Growing numbers of people in Wakefield are now finding jobs in service industries such as distribution, hotels, restaurants, the transport and communications sector and the public sector. Between 1991 and 2002, the city saw a 33% increase in part-time jobs and a 3% rise in full-time jobs.

Wakefield has high rates of economic activity and employment for younger men and women, but low rates for people aged 50 to state pension age, and high part-time employment rates among women. By contrast there are low levels of self-employment among men, and a low employment rate among lone parents. The workforce includes a high but declining proportion of women who travel by bus to work; however, more recently, more women have been driving to work. Most residents in employment work within the district (64% of men and 77% of women). In 2001, Wakefield had a relatively high unemployment rate for both sexes, although among the unemployed, only 18% of men and 23% of women had not worked for over five years.

Wakefield Metropolitan District Council was a partner in the GELLM research programme between 2003 and 2006, participating in three GELLM local research studies. The GELLM publications relating to Wakefield are:

- *Gender profile of Wakefield's labour market* (Buckner et al, 2004d)
- *Connecting women with the labour market in Wakefield* (Grant et al, 2006d)
- *Women's career development in Wakefield MDC* (Bennett et al, 2006c)
- *Working below potential: women and part-time work in Wakefield* (Grant et al, 2006h).

## West Sussex

The county of West Sussex lies on the coast of central southern England and includes seven districts: Adur, Arun, Chichester, Crawley, Horsham, Mid Sussex, and Worthing. The population (770,800 people) is relatively old, with more people aged over 50. A small number (6%) are from ethnic minority groups, including small White Other (2%), White Irish (0.9%) and Indian (0.8%) populations.

General indicators of health and well-being in the county are relatively good. West Sussex has higher than average life expectancy at birth, a low proportion of people with a limiting long-term illness, and a low teenage pregnancy rate. The county is relatively affluent, ranked 133 out of 149 counties where 149 is the least deprived (Communities and Local Government, n.d.), and only 11% of dependent children live in households with no working adult. West Sussex's men and women are better qualified than men and women nationally.

West Sussex is predominantly a service sector economy; financial and other business activities, distribution, hotels and catering, and public administration are particularly important. Both agriculture and tourism provide significant employment in some parts of the county, sectors often associated with seasonal and low-paid work. Between 1991 and 2002, the county saw a 46% increase in part-time jobs and a 31% rise in full-time jobs.

West Sussex has high economic activity and employment rates for both men and women, including high part-time employment rates (both sexes), high levels of self-employment among men, and a high employment rate among lone parents. Its workforce includes a high proportion of people of both sexes who drive to work. Most residents in employment work within the county, especially women (56% of men and 67% of women). In 2001, the county had relatively low unemployment rates for men and women; among those unemployed, 12% of men and 18% of women had not worked for over five years.

West Sussex County Council was a partner in the GELLM research programme between 2003 and 2006, participating in three GELLM local research studies. The GELLM publications relating to West Sussex are:

- *Gender profile of West Sussex's labour market* (Buckner et al, 2004h)
- *Addressing women's poverty in West Sussex: local labour market initiatives* (Escott et al, 2006b)
- *Local challenges in meeting demand for domiciliary care in West Sussex* (Yeandle et al, 2006f)
- *Working below potential: women and part-time work in West Sussex* (Grant et al, 2006i).

# References

Acker, J. (1998) 'The future of "gender and organisations": connections and boundaries', *Gender, Work and Organization*, vol 5, no 4, pp 195–206.

Adams, L. and Carter, K. (2007) *Black and Asian women in the workplace: the employer perspective*, Manchester: Equal Opportunities Commission.

Alcock, P., Beatty, C., Fothergill, S. and Yeandle, S. (eds) (2003) *Work to welfare: how men become detached from the labour market*, Cambridge: Cambridge University Press.

Alexander, S. (1976) 'Women's work in 19th century London' in J. Mitchell and A. Oakley (eds) *The Rights and Wrongs of Women*, Harmondsworth: Penguin Books.

Anderson, T., Forth, J., Metcalf, H. and Kirby, S. (2001) *The gender pay gap: final report to DfEE*, London: National Institute for Economic and Social Research.

Arnot, M., David, M. and Weiner, G. (1999) *Closing the gender gap: postwar education and social change*, Cambridge: Polity Press.

Audit Commission (2007) 2006/2007 Best Value Performance Indicator Data for English Councils, www.audit-commission.gov.uk.

Baines, E. (1970) 'The woollen manufacture of England, with special reference to the Leeds Clothing District', in K.G. Ponting (ed) *Baines' account of the woollen manufacture of England*, Newton Abbott: David and Charles.

Beatty, C., Fothergill, S., Gore, T. and Powell, R. (2007) *Barrow's incapacity claimants*, Sheffield: Centre for Regional Economic and Social Research, Sheffield Hallam University.

Beatty, T. and Fothergill, S. (1999) *Incapacity benefit and unemployment*, Sheffield: Centre for Regional Economic and Social Research, Sheffield Hallam University.

Becker, G.S. (1985), 'Human capital, effort and the sexual division of labor', *Journal of Labor Economics*, vol 3, S33–S58.

Becker, G.S. (1993) *Human capital: a theoretical and empirical analysis, with special reference to education* (3rd edn) Chicago: University of Chicago Press.

Beechey, V. and Perkins, T. (1987) *A matter of hours: women, part-time work and the labour market*, Cambridge: Polity Press.

Bennett, C. (2000) 'Mainstreaming in organisations: strategies for delivering women's equality in UK local government', PhD thesis, Sheffield: Sheffield Hallam University.

Bennett, C. (2008) 'Owning and implementing labour market research: a partnership of academics, trade unions, equality advocates and local government officers in the UK', *Equal Opportunities International*, vol 27, no 2, pp 181–98.

Bennett, C. and Booth, C. (2002) 'From equal opportunities to recognising diversity: gender mainstreaming in Structural Funds and UK regeneration', *European Journal of Women's Studies*, vol 9, no 4, pp 430–46.

Bennett, C. and Yeandle, S. (2006) 'Organisational culture, management systems and employment practices in three local authorities: does gender still matter?', Paper presented to the International Labour Process Conference, Birkbeck College, University of London, April.

Bennett, C., Tang, N. and Yeandle, S. (2006a) *Women's career development in the local authority sector: synthesis report*, GELLM Series 5 Part 1, Sheffield: Centre for Social Inclusion, Sheffield Hallam University.

Bennett, C., Tang, N. and Yeandle, S. (2006b) *Women's career development in Sandwell MBC*, GELLM Series 5 Part 2, Sheffield: Centre for Social Inclusion, Sheffield Hallam University.

Bennett, C., Tang, N. and Yeandle, S. (2006c) *Women's career development in Wakefield MDC*, GELLM Series 5 Part 3, Sheffield: Centre for Social Inclusion, Sheffield Hallam University.

Bennett, C., Tang, N. and Yeandle, S. (2006d) *Women's career development in Leicester City Council*, GELLM Series 5 Part 4, Sheffield: Centre for Social Inclusion, Sheffield Hallam University.

Bennett, C., Tang, N. and Yeandle, S. (2006e) *Women's career development in the London Borough of Southwark*, GELLM Series 5 Part 5, Sheffield: Centre for Social Inclusion, Sheffield Hallam University.

Bennett, F. and Hirsch, D. (2001) 'The Employment Tax Credit and issues for the future of in-work support', *Findings*, Ref: N31, York: Joseph Rowntree Foundation.

Bennett, F. and Millar, J. (2005) 'Making Work Pay?' *Benefits*, vol 13, no 42, issue 1, pp 28–34.

Berthoud, R. (2007) *Work-rich and work-poor: three decades of change*, York: Joseph Rowntree Foundation.

Berthoud, R. and Blekesaune, M. (2007) *Persistent employment disadvantage*, DWP research report no 416, Leeds: Department for Work and Pensions.

Bhavnani, R. with PTI (2006) *Ahead of the game: the changing aspirations of young ethnic minority women*, Manchester: Equal Opportunities Commission.

Birmingham City Council (2006) *Employment figures for Birmingham*, Birmingham: BEIC report, www.birminghameconomy.gov.uk.

Blackwell, L. (2001) 'Occupational sex segregation and part-time work in modern Britain', *Gender Work and Organization*, vol 8, no 2, pp 146–63.

Blackwell, L. and Guinea-Martin, D. (2005) 'Occupational segregation by sex and ethnicity in England and Wales, 1991 to 2001', *Labour Market Trends*, vol 113, pp 501–11.

Blossfeld, H. and Hakim, C. (eds) (1997) *Between equalization and marginalization: women working part-time in Europe and the United States of America*, Oxford: Oxford University Press.

Bond, S., Hyman, J., Summers, J. and Wise, S. (2002) *Family-friendly working: putting policy into practice*, Bristol: The Policy Press.

Booth, C. and Yeandle, S. (1999) 'European Union Equality Policy: its significance for regional regeneration and development', *Regional Review*, vol 9, no 2, pp 3–5.

Booth, C., Batty, E., Gilroy, R., Dargan, L., Thomas, H., Harris, N. and Imrie, R. (2004) *Planning and diversity: research into policies and procedures*, London: ODPM.

Boston, S. (1980) *Women workers and the trade unions*, London: Davis-Poynter.

Botcherby, S. (2006) *Pakistani, Bangladeshi and Black Caribbean women and employment survey: aspirations, experiences and choices*, Manchester: Equal Opportunities Commission.

Boyne, G.A. (2001) 'Planning, Performance and Public Services', *Public Administration*, vol 79, pp 73–88.

Bradley, H. (1989) *Men's work, women's work: a sociological history of the sexual division of labour in employment*, Minneapolis: University of Minnesota Press.

Bradley, H., Healy, G., and Mukherjee, N. (2002) *A double disadvantage? Minority ethnic women in trade unions*, London: UNISON.

Bradley, H., Healy, G., Forson, C. and Kaul, P. (2007) *Workplace cultures: what does and does not work*, Manchester: Equal Opportunities Commission.

Bradshaw, J., Finch, N., Kemp, P., Mayhew, E. and Williams, J. (2003) *Gender and poverty in Britain*, Manchester: Equal Opportunities Commission.

Brah, A. and Shaw, S. (1992) *Working choices, South Asian young women and the labour market*, Research Paper no 91, Department of Employment.

Braybon, G. (1981) *Women workers in the First World War: the British experience*, London: Croom Helm.

Brewer, M. and Shephard, A. (2004) *Has Labour made work pay?* York: Joseph Rowntree Foundation.

Brewer, M., Goodman, A., Muriel, A. and Sibieta, L. (2007) 'Poverty and inequality in the UK', Briefing Note no 73, London: Institute of Fiscal Studies.

Brook, K. (2004) 'Labour market data for local areas by ethnicity', *Labour Market Trends*, vol 112, pp 405–16.

Brown, C. (1984) *Black and White Britain*, London: Policy Studies Institute.

Brownhill, S. and Darke, J. (1998) *Rich mix: inclusive strategies for urban regeneration*, York: Policy Press/Joseph Rowntree Foundation.

Bruegel, I. (2000) 'Making gender statistics empowering', *Radical Statistics*, vol 74, available online, www.radstats.org.uk

Bryson, A., Ford, R. and White, M. (1997) *Lone mothers, employment and well-being*, York: Joseph Rowntree Foundation.

Buckner, L. and Yeandle, S. (2005) *We care, do you?* London: Carers UK.

Buckner, L. and Yeandle, S. (2006) *Who Cares Wins, statistical analysis: Working carers – evidence from the 2001 Census*, London: Carers UK.

Buckner, L., Tang, N. and Yeandle, S. (2004a) *Gender profile of Somerset's labour market*, GELLM Series 1 Part 1, Sheffield: Centre for Social Inclusion, Sheffield Hallam University.

Buckner, L., Tang, N. and Yeandle, S. (2004b) *Gender profile of Sandwell's labour market,* GELLM Series 1 Part 2, Sheffield: Centre for Social Inclusion, Sheffield Hallam University.

Buckner, L., Tang, N. and Yeandle, S. (2004c) *Gender profile of Newcastle's labour market,* GELLM Series 1 Part 3, Sheffield: Centre for Social Inclusion, Sheffield Hallam University.

Buckner, L., Tang, N. and Yeandle, S. (2004d) *Gender profile of Wakefield's labour market,* GELLM Series 1 Part 4, Sheffield: Centre for Social Inclusion, Sheffield Hallam University.

Buckner, L., Tang, N. and Yeandle, S. (2004e) *Gender profile of Camden's labour market,* GELLM Series 1 Part 5, Sheffield: Centre for Social Inclusion, Sheffield Hallam University.

Buckner, L., Tang, N. and Yeandle, S. (2004f) *Gender profile of Leicester's labour market,* GELLM Series 1 Part 6, Sheffield: Centre for Social Inclusion, Sheffield Hallam University.

Buckner, L., Tang, N. and Yeandle, S. (2004g) *Gender profile of Thurrock's labour market,* GELLM Series 1 Part 7, Sheffield: Centre for Social Inclusion, Sheffield Hallam University.

Buckner, L., Tang, N. and Yeandle, S. (2004h) *Gender profile of West Sussex's labour market,* GELLM Series 1 Part 8, Sheffield: Centre for Social Inclusion, Sheffield Hallam University.

Buckner, L., Tang, N. and Yeandle, S. (2004i) *Gender profile of East Staffordshire's labour market,* GELLM Series 1 Part 9, Sheffield: Centre for Social Inclusion, Sheffield Hallam University.

Buckner, L., Tang, N. and Yeandle, S. (2005a) *Gender profile of Birmingham's labour market,* GELLM Series 1 Part 10, Sheffield: Centre for Social Inclusion, Sheffield Hallam University.

Buckner, L., Poole, G. and Yeandle, S. (2005b) *Gender profile of Southwark's labour market,* GELLM Series 1 Part 11, Sheffield: Centre for Social Inclusion, Sheffield Hallam University.

Buckner, L., Tang, N. and Yeandle, S. (2006) *Gender profile of Trafford's labour market,* GELLM Series 1 Part 12, Sheffield: Centre for Social Inclusion, Sheffield Hallam University.

Buckner, L., Yeandle, S. and Botcherby, S. (2007) *Ethnic minority women and local labour markets,* Manchester: Equal Opportunities Commission.

Bunting, M. (2007a) 'Baby, this just isn't working for me', *Guardian,* 1 March.

Bunting, M. (2007b) *Willing slaves: how the overwork culture is ruling our lives,* London: HarperCollins.

Burchardt, T. (2003) *Being and becoming: social exclusion and the onset of disability,* CASE Report 21, London: ESRC Centre for Analysis of Social Exclusion, London School of Economics.

Burchell, B.J., Dale, A. and Joshi, H. (1997) 'Part-time work among British women' in H. Blossfeld and C. Hakim (eds) *Between equalization and marginalization: women working part-time in Europe and the United States of America*, Oxford: Oxford University Press.

Burke, R. and Vinnicombe, S. (2005) 'Advancing women's careers', *Career Development International*, vol 10, no 3, pp 165–7.

Cabinet Office (2005) *Improving the prospects of people living in areas of multiple deprivation in England*, London: Prime Minister's Strategy Unit and ODPM/Cabinet Office.

Carvel, J. (2006) 'Workaholic managers sacrifice 19m days of holiday each year', *Guardian*, 15 June.

Charles, N. and James, E. (2003) 'The gender dimensions of job insecurity in a local labour market', *Work, Employment and Society*, vol 17, no 3, pp 531–52.

Clark, S.C. (2000) 'Work/family border theory: a new theory of work–life balance', *Human Relations*, vol 53, no 6, pp 747–70.

Cochrane, A. (1999) 'Just another failed experiment? The legacy of the Urban Development Corporations', in Imrie, R. and Thomas, H. (eds) *British urban planning policy: an evaluation of the urban development corporations*, London: Sage.

Cockburn, C., (1991) *In the way of women: men's resistance to sex equality in organizations*, London: Macmillan.

Coleman, D. and Rowthorn, R. (2004) 'The economic effects of immigration into the United Kingdom', *Population and Development Review*, vol 10, no 4, pp 579–624.

Communities and Local Government (n.d.) *Indices of Deprivation 2004*, http://www.communities.gov.uk.

Connexions (2004) *Post-16 destinations statistics*, London: DfES.

Connolly, S. and Gregory, M. (2007) *Moving down: women's part-time work and occupational change in Britain 1991–2001*, Department of Economics Discussion Paper Series no 359, Oxford: University of Oxford.

Cooper, C.L. and Sutherland, V. (2006) 'Stress and the changing nature of work' in Clements-Croome, D. (ed), *Creating the productive workplace* (2nd edn), Abingdon: Taylor and Francis.

Cousins, C. and Tang, N. (2004) 'Working time and work and family conflict in the Netherlands, Sweden and the UK', *Work, Employment and Society*, vol 18, no 3, pp 531–49.

Coward, R. (1993) *Our treacherous hearts: why women let men get their way*, London: Faber & Faber.

Coyle, A. (1984) *Redundant women*, London: The Women's Press.

CPAG (2005) *Poverty: the facts*, London: Child Poverty Action Group.

Crompton, R. (1996) *Women and work in modern Britain*, Oxford: Oxford University Press.

Crompton, R. (ed) (1999) *Restructuring gender relations and employment: the decline of the male breadwinner*, Oxford: Oxford University Press.

Crompton, R. (2002), 'Employment, flexible working and the family', *British Journal of Sociology*, vol 53, no 4, pp 537–58.

Crompton, R. (2006) *Employment and the family: the reconfiguration of work and family life in contemporary societies*, Cambridge: Cambridge University Press.

Crompton, R., Dennett, J. and Wigfield, A. (2003) *Organisations, careers and caring*, Bristol: The Policy Press.

Crompton, R. and Harris, F. (1998) 'Explaining women's employment patterns: "orientations to work" revisited', *British Journal of Sociology*, vol 49, no 1, pp 118–36.

Crompton, R. and Sanderson, K. (1990) *Gendered jobs and social change*, London: Unwin Hyman.

Crook, J. (2007) 'Nothing special about achieving gender equality', *Guardian*, 13 August.

Curran, M. (1988) 'Gender and recruitment: people and places in the labour market', *Work, Employment and Society*, vol 2, no 3, pp 335–51.

Daguerre, A. and Taylor-Gooby, P. (2003) 'Adaption to labour market change in France and the UK; convergent or parallel tracks?', *Social Policy and Administration*, vol 37, no 6, pp 625–38.

Dale, A., Shaheen, N., Kalra, V. and Fieldhouse, E. (2002) *The labour market prospects for Pakistani and Bangladeshi women*, Working Paper no 11, ESRC Future of Work Series, Leeds: University of Leeds.

Dale, A., Jackson, N. and Hill, N (2005a) *Women in non-traditional training and employment*, EOC Working Paper Series, no 25, Manchester: Equal Opportunities Commission.

Dale, A., Lindley, J. and Dex, S. (2005b) *A life-course perspective on ethnic differences in women's economic activity in Britain*, Working Paper 2005-08, Manchester: Cathie Marsh Centre for Census and Survey Research.

Daniel, W. W. (1968) *Racial discrimination in England*, Harmondsworth: Penguin Books.

Darton, D. and Hurrell, K. (2005) *People working part-time below their potential*, Manchester: Equal Opportunities Commission.

Davidoff, L. (1986) *Our work, our lives, our words/women's history and women's work*, London: Palgrave Macmillan.

DCLG/DWP (2007) *Working neighbourhoods fund*, London: Department for Communities and Local Government.

Deacon, A. (2002) *Perspectives on welfare: ideas, ideologies and policy debates*, Buckingham: Open University Press.

Dean, H. and Shah, A. (2002) 'Insecure families and low-paying labour markets: comments on the British experience', *Journal of Social Policy*, vol 31, no 1, pp 61–80.

Deem, R (1978) *Women and schooling*, London: Routledge and Kegan Paul.

Deem, R. (1980) *Schooling for women's work*, London: Routledge and Kegan Paul.

Delamont, S. (1989) *Knowledgeable women: structuralism and the reproduction of elites*, London: Routledge.

DfES (2007a) *Gender and education: the evidence on pupils in England*, London: Department for Education and Skills.

DfES (2007b) *National curriculum assessments, GCSE and equivalent attainment and post-16 attainment by pupil characteristics, in England 2005/06*, www.dfes.gov.uk.

Diamond, J. and Liddle, J. (2005) *The management of regeneration*, London: Routledge.

Dickerson, A., Homenidou, K. and Wilson, R. (2006) *Working futures 2004–20014: sectoral report*, Wath-upon-Dearne: Sector Skills Development Agency.

DOE (1977) *Policy for the inner cities*, London: HMSO.

Doherty, L. (2008) 'Gender equality at work: who pays the price?', Inaugural professorial lecture, Sheffield Hallam University, Sheffield, 7 February 2008.

DSS (1998) *New ambitions for our country: a new contract for welfare*, Cm 3805, London: Stationery Office.

DWP (2004) *Households below average income 1994/5–2002/3*, London: Department for Work and Pensions.

DWP (2006) *A new deal for welfare: empowering people to work*, Cm 6730, London: Department for Work and Pensions.

DWP (2007) *Opportunity for all: indicators update 2007*, London: Department for Work and Pensions, Family, Poverty and Work Division.

DWP (2008) *Transforming Britain's labour market: ten years of New Deal*, London: Department for Work and Pensions.

EC (2005) *Confronting demographic change: a new solidarity between the generations* (COM 2004 95 final), Luxembourg: Office for Official Publications of the European Communities.

EC (2007) *Towards common principles of flexicurity: more and better jobs through flexibility and security*, Luxembourg: Office for Official Publications of the European Communities.

Ellison, N. and Pierson, C. (eds) (2003) *Developments in British social policy 2*, Basingstoke: Palgrave Macmillan.

Employers Organisation (2005a) *The local government workforce England and Wales 2005*, http://www.idea.gov.uk.

Employers Organisation (2005b) *Sickness absence in local government 2004/2005*, http://www.lge.gov.uk.

EOC (2001) *Just pay: report of the Equal Pay Task Force*, Manchester: Equal Opportunities Commission.

EOC (2003) *Women and men in Britain,* Manchester: Equal Opportunities Commission.

EOC (2004) *Response to Trade and Industry Committee Inquiry into UK employment regulation*, Manchester: Equal Opportunities Commission.

EOC (2005a) *Britain's hidden brain drain – final report: the EOC's investigation into flexible and part-time working*, Manchester: Equal Opportunities Commission.

EOC (2005b) *Free to choose: tackling gender barriers to better jobs. Summary report on EOC's investigation on workplace segregation of men and women*, Manchester: Equal Opportunities Commission.

EOC (2005d) *Free to choose: tackling gender barriers to better jobs. England final report – EOC's investigation into workplace segregation and apprenticeships*, Manchester: Equal Opportunities Commission.

EOC (2005e) *Part-time is no crime – so why the penalty? Interim report of the EOC's investigation into flexible and part-time working, and questions for consultation*, Manchester: Equal Opportunities Commission.

EOC (2006) *Moving on up? Bangladeshi, Pakistani and Black Caribbean women and work. Early findings from the EOC's investigation in England, Interim report*, Manchester: Equal Opportunities Commission.

EOC (2007) *Moving on up? The way forward. Report into the EOC's investigation into Bangladeshi, Pakistani and Black Caribbean women at work. Final report*, Manchester: Equal Opportunities Commission.

Escott, K. (2007) *From getting by to getting on: women's employment and local regeneration programmes*, Liverpool: Renew North West in partnership with Oxfam.

Escott, K. and Buckner, L. (2005) 'Women and labour markets; building gender analysis into the regional competitiveness agenda', paper presented to the Regional Studies Association Conference, London, 24 November.

Escott, K. and Buckner, L. (2006) *Addressing women's poverty: local labour market initiatives: synthesis report*, GELLM Series 6 Part 1, Sheffield: Centre for Social Inclusion, Sheffield Hallam University.

Escott, K. and Punn, S. (2006) 'Tackling gender inequality: linking research to policy making and mainstreaming', *Local Economy*, vol 21, no 2, pp 219–25.

Escott, K., Price, C. and Buckner, L. (2006a) *Addressing women's poverty in Birmingham: local labour market initiatives*, GELLM Series 6 Part 2, Sheffield: Centre for Social Inclusion, Sheffield Hallam University.

Escott, K., Price, C. and Buckner, L. (2006b) *Addressing women's poverty in West Sussex: local labour market initiatives*, GELLM Series 6 Part 3, Sheffield: Centre for Social Inclusion, Sheffield Hallam University.

Escott, K., Price, C. and Buckner, L. (2006c) *Addressing women's poverty in Newcastle: local labour market initiatives*, GELLM Series 6 Part 4, Sheffield: Centre for Social Inclusion, Sheffield Hallam University.

Escott, K., Price, C. and Buckner, L. (2006d) *Addressing women's poverty in Somerset: local labour market initiatives*, GELLM Series 6 Part 5, Sheffield: Centre for Social Inclusion, Sheffield Hallam University.

Escott, K., Price, C. and Buckner, L. (2006e) *Addressing women's poverty in East Staffordshire: local labour market initiatives*, GELLM Series 6 Part 6, Sheffield: Centre for Social Inclusion, Sheffield Hallam University.

Escott, K., Price, C. and Buckner, L. (2006f) *Addressing women's poverty in Southwark: local labour market initiatives*, GELLM Series 6 Part 7, Sheffield: Centre for Social Inclusion, Sheffield Hallam University.

Esping-Andersen, G. (1993) 'Mobility regimes and class formation' in Esping-Andersen, G. (ed) *Changing classes: stratification, mobility and post-industrial societies*, London: Sage.

ESRC (2007a) *Population in the UK,* UK Fact Sheets, ESRC, www.esrc.ac.uk.

ESRC (2007b) *Ethnic minorities in the UK,* UK Fact Sheets, ESRC, www.esrc.ac.uk.

EU (2004) *Facing the challenge: the Lisbon strategy for growth and employment.* Report from the High Level Group chaired by Wim Kok, November, Luxembourg: Office for Official Publications of the European Communities.

Fagan, C. (2001) 'Time, money and the gender order: work orientations and working-time preferences in Britain', *Gender, Work and Organization*, vol 8, no 3, pp 239–66.

Fagan. C. and O'Reilly, J. (1998) 'Conceptualising part-time work: the value of an integrated comparative perspective', in O'Reilly, J. and Fagan, C. (eds) *Part-time prospects; an international comparison of part-time work in Europe, North America and the Pacific Rim*, London: Routledge.

Faggio, G. and Nickell, S. (2003) 'The rise in inactivity among adult men', in Dickens, R., Gregg, P. and Wadsworth, J. (eds) *The labour market under New Labour*, Basingstoke: Palgrave.

Felstead, A., Quinn, M. and Sung, J. (2002) *Baseline labour market information for the East Midlands*, report submitted to the East Midlands FRESA Forum, Leicester: Centre for Labour Market Studies.

Finch, N. (n.d) *Labour supply in the UK*, York: Social Policy Research Unit, University of York.

Finn, D. (2003) 'Employment policy', in Ellison, N. and Pierson, C. (eds) *Developments in British social policy*, Basingstoke: Palgrave Macmillan.

Formby, E., Tang, N. and Yeandle, S. (2004) *Supporting work–life balance using non-standard hours childcare*, Sheffield, Centre for Social Inclusion, Sheffield Hallam University.

Francesconi, M. and Gosling, A. (2005) *Career paths of part-time workers*, EOC Working Paper Series no 19, Manchester: Equal Opportunities Commission.

Fried, M. (1998) *Taking time: parental leave policy and corporate culture*, Philadelphia: Temple University Press.

Fuller, G. (2007) 'Equal pay for council workers: whose bill is it anyway', *Personnel Today*, no 27, March, available at www.personneltoday.com/articles/article.aspx?liarticleid=39877&printerfriendly=true

Gallie, D., Paugam, S. and Jacobs, S. (2003) 'Unemployment, poverty and social isolation', *European Societies,* vol 5, no 1, pp 1–32.

Gatrell, C.J. (2004), *Hard labour: the sociology of parenthood*, Maidenhead: Open University Press.

Gilbert, A., Phimister, E. and Theodossiou, I. (2003) 'Low pay and income in urban and rural areas: evidence from the British Household Panel Survey', *Urban Studies*, vol 40, no 7, pp 1207–22.

Gillan, A. (2005) 'Work until you drop: how the long-hours culture is killing us', *Guardian,* 20 August.

Ginn, J., Arber, S., Brannen, J., Dale, A., Dex, S., Elias, P., Moss, P., Pahl, J., Roberts, C. and Rubery, J. (1996) 'Feminist fallacies: a reply to Hakim on women's employment', *British Journal of Sociology*, vol 7, no 1, pp 167–74.

Goos, M. and Manning, A. (2003) 'McJobs and MacJobs: the growing polarisation of jobs in the UK' in Dickens, R. Gregg, P. and Wadsworth, J. (eds) *The labour market under New Labour*, Basingstoke: Palgrave Macmillan.

Gordon, I. and Turok, I. (2005) 'How urban labour markets matter' in Buck, N., Gordon, I., Harding, A. and Turok, I. (eds) *Changing cities: rethinking urban competitiveness, cohesion and governance*, Basingstoke: Palgrave Macmillan.

GOYH (2004) *Single programming document: Objective 1 South Yorkshire*, Part 4, Wath-upon-Dearne, GOYH, www.goyh.gov.uk.

Grant, L. (2000) 'Crossing the Atlantic: US welfare reform and the degradation of poor women', in Dean, H., Woods R. and Sykes, R. (eds) *Social policy review 12*, London: Social Policy Association.

Grant, L. and Buckner, L. (2006) *Connecting women with the labour market: synthesis report,* GELLM Series 3 Part 1, Sheffield: Centre for Social Inclusion, Sheffield Hallam University.

Grant, L. and Escott, K. (2004) 'Low paid, part-time work: the under-utilisation of women's potential', Paper presented to the Work, Employment and Society conference, UMIST, Manchester, 1–3 September.

Grant, L. and Price, C. (2006) *Working below potential: how trade union representatives view women and part-time work*, GELLM Series 2 Part 7, Sheffield: Centre for Social Inclusion, Sheffield Hallam University.

Grant, L. and Yeandle, S. (2005) 'Part-time employment and women's welfare: results from a new analysis of why women take part-time jobs', Paper presented to the Social Policy Association Annual Conference, University of Bath, 27–9 June.

Grant, L and Yeandle, S. (2007) 'Part-time employment and gender equality: towards welfare friendly labour markets?', Paper presented at European Sociological Association Conference, Glasgow, 3–6 September.

Grant, L., Yeandle, S. and Buckner, L. (2005) *Working below potential: women and part-time work,* Working Paper Series no 40, Manchester: Equal Opportunities Commission.

Grant, L., Buckner, L., Poole, G. and Price, C. (2006a) 'Women outside paid employment: getting to grips with local labour markets', *Local Economy,* vol 21, no 2, pp 200–10.

Grant. L., Price, C. and Buckner, L. (2006b) *Connecting women with the labour market in Sandwell*, GELLM Series 3 Part 2, Sheffield: Centre for Social Inclusion, Sheffield Hallam University.

Grant. L., Price, C. and Buckner, L. (2006c) *Connecting women with the labour market in Birmingham*, GELLM Series 3 Part 3, Sheffield: Centre for Social Inclusion, Sheffield Hallam University.

Grant. L., Price, C. and Buckner, L. (2006d) *Connecting women with the labour market in Wakefield*, GELLM Series 3 Part 4, Sheffield: Centre for Social Inclusion, Sheffield Hallam University.

Grant. L., Price, C. and Buckner, L. (2006e) *Connecting women with the labour market in Thurrock*, GELLM Series 3 Part 5, Sheffield: Centre for Social Inclusion, Sheffield Hallam University.

Grant. L., Price, C. and Buckner, L. (2006f) *Connecting women with the labour market in Camden*, GELLM Series 3 Part 6, Sheffield: Centre for Social Inclusion, Sheffield Hallam University.

Grant, L., Yeandle, S. and Buckner, L. (2006g) *Working below potential: women and part-time work: synthesis report*, GELLM Series 2 Part 1, Sheffield: Centre for Social Inclusion, Sheffield Hallam University.

Grant, L., Yeandle, S. and Buckner, L. (2006h) *Working below potential: women and part-time work in Wakefield*, GELLM Series 2 Part 2, Sheffield: Centre for Social Inclusion, Sheffield Hallam University.

Grant, L., Yeandle, S. and Buckner, L. (2006i) *Working below potential: women and part-time work in West Sussex*, GELLM Series 2 Part 3, Sheffield: Centre for Social Inclusion, Sheffield Hallam University.

Grant, L., Yeandle, S. and Buckner, L. (2006j) *Working below potential: women and part-time work in Thurrock*, GELLM Series 2 Part 4, Sheffield: Centre for Social Inclusion, Sheffield Hallam University.

Grant, L., Yeandle, S. and Buckner, L. (2006k) *Working below potential: women and part-time work in Leicester*, GELLM Series 2 Part 5, Sheffield: Centre for Social Inclusion, Sheffield Hallam University.

Grant, L., Yeandle, S. and Buckner, L. (2006l) *Working below potential: women and part-time work in Camden*, GELLM Series 2 Part 6, Sheffield: Centre for Social Inclusion, Sheffield Hallam University.

Grant, L., Escott, K. and Buckner, L. (2007) 'Women's disconnection from dynamic labour markets in England', Paper presented to the International Labour Process Conference, Amsterdam, Netherlands, 2–4 April.

Greed, C. (2005) 'Overcoming the factors inhibiting the mainstreaming of gender into spatial planning policy in the UK', *Urban Studies*, vol 42, no 4, pp 719–49.

Green, A. and Owen, D. (2006) *The geography of poor skills and access to work*, York: Joseph Rowntree Foundation.

Griffin, C. (1985) *Typical girls? Young women from school to the job market*, London: Routledge and Kegan Paul.

Grimshaw, D. and Rubery, J. (2001) *The gender pay gap: a research review*, Manchester: Equal Opportunities Commission.

Grimshaw, D. and Rubery, J. (2007) *Undervaluing women's work*, EOC Working Paper Series no 53, Manchester: Equal Opportunities Commission.

Grimshaw, D., Beynon, H., Rubery, J. and Ward, K. (2002) 'The restructuring of career paths in large service sector organisations: "delayering", upskilling and polarisation', *Sociological Review*, vol 50, no 1, pp 89–116.

Guest, D.E. (2002) 'Perspectives on the study of work–life balance', *Social Science Information*, vol 41, no 2, pp 255–79.

Hakim, C. (1979) *Occupational segregation*, Research Paper no 9, London: Department of Employment.

Hakim, C. (1991) 'Grateful slaves and self-made women: fact and fantasy in women's work orientations', *European Sociological Review*, vol 7, no 2, pp 101–21.

Hakim, C. (1995) 'Five feminist myths about women's employment', *British Journal of Sociology*, vol 6, no 3, pp 428–55.

Hakim, C. (1996) 'The sexual division of labour and women's heterogeneity', *British Journal of Sociology*, vol 47, no 1, pp 178–88.

Hakim, C. (2000) *Work–lifestyle choices in the 21ˢᵗ century: preference theory*, Oxford: Oxford University Press.

Hakim, C. (2002) 'Lifestyle preferences as determinants of women's differential labour market careers', *Work and Occupations*, vol 29, no 4, pp 428–59.

Hakim, C. (2005) 'Sex differences in work–life balance goals', in Houston, D.M. (ed) *Work–life balance in the 21st century*, Houndmills: Palgrave Macmillian.

Halford, S. and Savage, M. (1995) 'Restructuring organisations, changing people', *Work, Employment and Society*, vol 9, no 1, pp 97–122.

Halford, S., Savage, M. and Witz, A. (1997) *Gender, careers and organisations, current developments in banking, nursing and local government*, Houndsmills: Macmillan.

Hall, K., Bance, J. and Denton, N. (2004) *Diversity and differences: minority ethnic mothers and childcare*, Surrey: Directions Research.

Halsey, A.H., Heath, A. and Ridge, J.M. (1980) *Origins and destinations*, Oxford: Clarendon Press.

Hamilton, K. and Jenkins, L. (2000) 'A gender audit for public transport: a new policy tool in the tackling of social exclusion', *Urban Studies*, vol 37, no 10, pp 1793–800.

Hamilton, K., Jenkins, L., Hodgson, F. and Turner, J. (2005) *Promoting gender equality in transport*, Manchester: Equal Opportunities Commission.

Hanson, S. and Pratt, G. (1995) *Gender, work and space*, London: Routledge.

Harkness, S. (1999) 'The 24 hour economy: changes in working times', in Gregg, P. and Wadsworth, J. (eds) *The state of working Britain*, Manchester: Manchester University Press.

Harkness, S. (2002) *Low pay, times of work and gender*, EOC Research Discussion and Working Paper Series, Manchester: Equal Opportunities Commission.

Hatton, T.J. and Tani, M. (2005) 'Immigration and inter-regional mobility in the UK, 1982–2000', *Economic Journal*, vol 115, no 507, pp F342–58.

Hayward, B., Fong, B. and Thornton, A. (2007) *The third work–life balance employer survey*, Employment Relations Research Series no 86, London: Department for Business, Enterprise and Regulatory Reform.

Heiler, K. (1998) 'The "petty pilfering of minutes" or what has happened to the length of the working day in Australia?', *International Journal of Manpower*, vol 19, no 4, pp 266–80.

Helms, G. and Cumbers, A. (2006) 'Regulating the new urban poor: local labour market control in an old industrial city', *Space and Polity*, vol 10, no 1, pp 67–86.

Herrington, A.E. (2004) 'The impact of non-standard working practices on the accountancy and architecture professions', PhD Thesis, Sheffield: Sheffield Hallam University.

Hill, D. (2000) *Urban policy and politics in Britain*, Hampshire: Macmillan Press Ltd.

Hirsch, D. with Millar, J. (2004) *Labour's welfare reform: progress to date*, JRF Foundation, Ref 44, York: Joseph Rowntree Foundation.

HM Treasury (2003) *A full employment strategy for Europe*, London: HM Treasury.

HM Treasury (2004a) *Child poverty review*, London: HM Treasury.

HM Treasury (2004b) *Choice for parents, the best start for children: a 10 year strategy for childcare*, London: HM Treasury.

HM Treasury (2004c) *Opportunity for all: the strength to take long-term decisions for Britain*, Cm 6408, London: HM Treasury.

HM Treasury (2007) *Sub-national review of economic development and regeneration*, London: HM Treasury, Department for Business Enterprise and Regulatory Reform and Department for Communities and Local Government.

HM Treasury/DWP (2001) *The changing welfare state: employment opportunity for all*, London: HM Treasury.

Hochschild, A. R. (1997) *The time bind: when work becomes home and home becomes work*, New York, Metropolitan Books.

Holdsworth, C. and Dale, A. (1997) 'Ethnic differences in women's employment', *Work, Employment and Society*, vol 11, no 3, pp 435–55.

Hoskyns, C. (1986) 'Women's equality and the European Community', in Feminist Review, *Waged Work: A Reader*, London: Virago.

Houston, D.M. (ed) (2005) *Work–life balance in the 21st century*, Houndmills: Palgrave Macmillan.

Houston, D.M. and Marks, G. (2005) 'Working, caring and sharing: work-life dilemmas in early motherhood', in Houston, D.M. (ed) *Work–life balance in the 21st century*, Houndmills: Palgrave Macmillan.

Hufton, O. (1995) *The prospect before her: a history of women in Western Europe*, London: HarperCollins.

Hurrell, K. (2005) *Facts about women and men in Great Britain 2005*, Manchester: Equal Opportunities Commission.

IDeA (2007) *The equality standard*, revised 2007, http://www.idea-knowledge.gov.uk.

Jacobs, J.A. and Gerson, K. (2004) *The time divide: work, family and gender inequality*, Cambridge, MA: Harvard University Press.

Jagger, N. (2005) *Mapping the wider care workforce*, Brighton: Institute for Employment Studies.

Jahoda, M., Lazarsfeld, P.F. and Zeisel, H. (1972) *Marienthal: the sociology of an unemployed community* (first published 1933), London: Tavistock.

Jenkins, S. (2004) 'Restructuring flexibility: case studies of part-time female workers in six workplaces', *Gender, Work and Organization*, vol 11, no 3, pp 306–33.

Jones, P. and Dickerson, A. (2007) *Poor returns: winners and losers in the job market*, EOC Working Paper Series No 52, Manchester: Equal Opportunities Commission.

Junor, A. (1998) 'Permanent part-time work: new family-friendly standard or high intensity cheap skills', *Labour and Industry*, vol 8, no 3, pp 77–93.

Kelvin, P. and Jarrett, J. (1985) *Unemployment: its social and psychological effects*, Cambridge: Cambridge University Press.

Kemp, P.A. (2005) 'Social security and welfare reform under New Labour', in Powell, M., Bauld, L. and Clarke, K. (eds) *Social policy review*, Bristol: Policy Press.

Kemp, P., Bradshaw, J., Dornan, P., Finch, N. and Mayhew, E. (2004) *Routes out of poverty*, York: Joseph Rowntree Foundation.

Kersley, B., Alpin, B., Forth, J., Bryson, A., Bewley, H., Dix, G., and Oxenbridge, S. (2005) *Inside the workplace: first findings from the 2004 Workplace Employment Relations Survey (WERS 2004)*, ESRC/ACAS/PSI, London: Department of Trade and Industry.

Kingsmill, D. (2001) *The Kingsmill review of women's pay and employment*, London: DTI.

Kodz, J., Kersley, B. and Strebler, M. (1998) *Breaking the long hours culture*, Brighton: Institute for Employment Studies.

Law, R. (1999) 'Beyond "women and transport": towards new geographies of gender and daily mobility', *Progress in Human Geography*, vol 23, no 4 pp 567–88.

Leitch, S. (2006) *Prosperity for all in the global economy: world class skills*, Leitch Review of Skills, London: HM Treasury.

Lewis, J. (1992) *Women in Britain since 1945: women, family, work and the state in the post-war years*, Oxford: Basil Blackwell.

Lewis, J. (2001) 'The decline of the male breadwinner model: implications for work and care', *Social Politics,* vol 8, pp 152–69.

Lewis, J. and Giullari, S. (2005) 'The adult worker model family, gender equality and care: the search for new policy principles and the possibilities and problems of a capabilities approach', *Economy and Society*, vol 34, issue 1, pp 76–104.

Lewis, S. (2001) 'Restructuring workplace cultures: the ultimate work-family challenge?', *Women in Management Review*, vol 6, no 1, pp 21–9.

Lewis, S. and Lewis, J. (eds) (1996) *The work–family challenge*, London: Sage.

LGAR (2005) *Local government employment survey 2005: employee jobs in local authorities as at June 2005 England & Wales*, http://lgar.local.gov.uk.

LGAR (2007a) *Local government employment digest*, no 367, October, http://lgar.local.gov.uk.

LGAR (2007b) *State of local government*, http://lgar.local.gov.uk.

Liff, S. and Ward, K. (2001) 'Distorted views through the glass ceiling: the construction of women's understandings of promotion and senior management positions', *Gender, Work and Organization*, vol 8, no 1, January, pp 19–36.

Lindley, J., Dale, A. and Dex, S. (2004) 'Ethnic differences in women's demographic, family characteristics and economic activity profiles, 1992–2002', *Labour Market Trends*, vol 112, no 4, pp 153–65.

Lister, R. (1989) 'Social security' in McCarthy, M. (ed) *The new politics of welfare: an agenda for the 1990s?* Basingstoke: Macmillan.

Lister, R. (2006), 'Children (but not women) first: New Labour, child welfare and gender', *Critical Social Policy*, vol 26, pp 315–35.

Local Government Employers (2007) *Salaries and Numbers Survey 2006*, presented by Joint Negotiating Committees for Chief Executives and Chief Officers of Local Authorities, February 2007, London: LGE, http://www.lge.gov.uk.

Low Pay Commission (2003) *Building on success: the national minimum wage*, Fourth Report of the Low Pay Commission, Crown copyright online publication, http://www.lowpay.gov.uk.

Lupton, R. (2003) *Poverty street: the dynamics of neighbourhood decline and renewal*, Bristol: Policy Press.

Machin, S. and McNally, S. (2006) *Gender and student achievement in English schools*, London: Centre for the Economics of Education, London School of Economics.

Madden, A. (2004) 'Gendered subject choices' in Claire, H. (ed) *Gender in education 3–19: a fresh approach*, London: Association of Teachers and Lecturers.

Manning, A. (2003) *Monopsony in motion: imperfect competition in labor markets*, Princeton: Princeton University Press.

Manning, A. and Petrongolo, B. (2004) *The part-time pay penalty*, Report for the Women and Equality Unit, London: Department of Trade and Industry.

Manning, A. and Swaffield, J. (2005) *The gender gap in early-career wage growth*, Centre for Economic Performance Discussion Paper, London: London School of Economics.

Martin, J. and Roberts, C. (1984) *Women and employment: a lifetime perspective* London: HMSO.

Martin, R. and Wallace, J. (1984) *Working women in recession: employment, redundancy and unemployment* Oxford: Oxford University Press.

Martin, S. and Bovaird, T. (2005) *Service improvement: a progress summary from the meta-evaluation of the Local Government Modernisation Agenda*, Local Regional Government Research Programme, London: ODPM.

Massey, D. (1993) 'Power-geometry and progressive sense of place' in Bird, J., Curtis, B., Putnam, T. and Robertson, G. (eds) *Mapping the futures: local cultures, global change*, London: Routledge.

Massey, D. (1997) 'Industrial restructuring as class restructuring: production decentralisation and local uniqueness' in McDowell, L. and Sharp, J. (eds) *Space, gender, knowledge: feminist readings*, London: Arnold.

May, M., Brunsdon, E. and Craig, G. (eds) *Social policy review 8*, London: Social Policy Association.

McCarthy, M. (ed) (1990) *The new politics of welfare: an agenda for the 1990s?* Basingstoke: Macmillan.

McDowell, L. and Sharp, J.P. (1997) *Space, gender and knowledge*, London: Arnold.

McKnight, A. (2005) 'Employment: tackling poverty through "work for those who can", in Hills, J. and Stewart, K. (eds) *A more equal society? New Labour, poverty, inequality and exclusion*, Bristol: Policy Press.

McRae, S. (2003) 'Constraints and choices in mothers' employment careers: a consideration of Hakim's preference theory', *British Journal of Sociology*, vol 54, no 3, pp 317–38.

Millar, J. (2000) *Keeping track of welfare reform: the New Deal Programme*, York: York Publishing Services/Joseph Rowntree Foundation.

Millar, J. and Ridge, T. (2001) *Families, poverty, work and care*, Research Paper no 153, Leeds: DWP.

Miller, L., Neathey, F., Pollard, E. and Hill, D. (2004) *Occupational segregation, gender gaps and skill gaps*, Working Paper Series no 15, Manchester: Equal Opportunities Commission.

Minoff, E. (2006) *The UK commitment: ending child poverty by 2020*. Washington, DC: Center for Law and Social Policy.

Modood, T., Berthoud, R., Lakey, J., Nazroo, J., Smith, J., Virdee, S. and Beishan, S. (1997) *Ethnic minorities in Britain - diversity and disadvantages*, London: Policy Studies Institute.

Moorhead, J. (2007) 'Time is not on my side', *Guardian*, 1 March.

Morell J., Boyland, M., Munns, G. and Astbury, L. (2001) *Gender equality in payment practices*, EOC Research Discussion Series, Manchester: Equal Opportunities Commission.

Moynagh, M. and Worsley, R. (2005) *Working in the twenty-first century*, Leeds: The Tomorrow Project, ESRC.

Murray, C. (1984) *Losing ground*, New York: Basic Books.

Neathey, F., Dench, S. and Thomson, L. (2003), *Monitoring progress towards pay equality*, EOC Discussion Series, Manchester: Equal Opportunities Commission.

Neathey, F., Willison, R., Ackroyd, K., Regan, J. and Hill, D. (2005) *Equal pay reviews in practice*, EOC Working Paper Series no 33, Manchester: Equal Opportunities Commission.

Noon, M. and Hoque, E. (2001) 'Ethnic minorities and equal treatment: the impact of gender, equal opportunities policies and trade unions', *National Institute Economic Review* no 176, pp 105–15.

NRU (2003) *New Deal for Communities: national evaluation annual report*, Research Report, Wetherby: Office of the Deputy Prime Minister.

NRU (2006) *Local enterprise growth initiative*, London: Department for Communities and Local Government.

ODPM (2003) *Sustainable communities: Building for the future*, London: ODPM.

ODPM (2004) *Sustainable communities plan*, London: ODPM.

ODPM (2005) *Smarter neighbourhoods: Better neighbourhoods*, London: ODPM/ Neighbourhood Renewal Unit.

ONS (1993) *1991* 'Great Britain sample of anonymised records', Individual File (computer file]) distributed by the Cathie Marsh Centre for Census and Survey Research, University of Manchester.

ONS (1997) 'Population estimates Table 6', *Population Trends,* vol 90, pp 55–6.

ONS (2006a) *Annual Population Survey 2005–2006*, distributed by the Economic and Social Data Service.

ONS (2006b) *Focus on gender*, London: National Statistics, October.

ONS (2006c) *2001* 'United Kingdom sample of anonymised records', Individual licensed file (computer file) distributed by the Cathie Marsh Centre for Census and Survey Research, University of Manchester.

ONS (2006d) 2001 'United Kingdom sample of anonymised records, controlled access microdata'. The support of the Office for National Statistics (and General Register Office for Scotland and Northern Ireland Statistical Research Agency where appropriate), CCSR and ESRC/JISC Census of Population Programme is gratefully acknowledged. The authors alone are responsible for the interpretation of the data.)

ONS (2006e) '2001 United Kingdom small area microdata', Licensed file (computer file) distributed by the Cathie Marsh Centre for Census and Survey Research, University of Manchester.

ONS (2007) *Social trends 37*, London: National Statistics.

Oppenheim, C. and Lister, R. (1996) 'Ten years after the 1986 Social Security Act' in M. May, E. Brunsdon and G. Craig (eds) *Social Policy Review 8*, London: Social Policy Association.

O'Reilly, J. and Fagan, C. (1998) (eds) *Part-time prospects: an international comparison of part-time work in Europe, North America and the Pacific Rim,* London: Routledge.

Oxfam (2005) *Into the lion's den: a practical guide to including women in regeneration,* Oxford: Oxfam UK Poverty Programme.

Oxfam/RTPI (2007) *A place for everyone? Gender equality and urban planning,* ReGender Briefing Paper, Oxford: Oxfam.

Page, R.M. (2007) 'Without a song in their heart: New Labour, the welfare state and the retreat from Democratic Socialism', *Journal of Social Policy*, vol 36, no 1, pp 19–37.

Pahl, J.M. (1989) *Money and marriage*, Basingstoke: Macmillan Education.

Palmer, G., MacInnes, T. and Kenway, P. (2006) *Monitoring poverty and social exclusion 2006*, York: Joseph Rowntree Foundation.

Parikh, A., Ederveen, S. and Nahuis, R. (2007) 'Labour mobility and regional disparities: the role of female labour participation', *Journal of Population Economics,* vol 20, no 4, p 895.

Parkinson, M., Palin, M., Champion, T., Simmie, J., Turok, I., Crookston, M., Llewlyn-Davies, Y., Katz, B., Park, A., Beurube, A., Coones, M., Dorling, D., Glass, N., Hutchins, M., Kearns, A., Martin, R. and Wood, P. (2006) *State of English cities*, London: ODPM.

Payne, S. and Pantazis, C. (1997) 'Poverty and gender', in Gordon, D. and Pantazis, C. (eds) *Breadline Britain in the 1990s*, Aldershot: Ashgate.

Peck, J. (1996) *Work-place: the social regulation of labor markets*, Guildford: New York.

Peck, J. and Theodore, N. (2000) 'Work first: workfare and the regulation of contingent labour markets', *Cambridge Journal of Economics*, vol 24, pp 119–38.

Phillips, B. and Taylor, A. (1980) 'Sex and skill: notes towards a feminist economics', *Feminist Review*, vol 6, pp 78–88.

Pillinger, J. (1992) *Feminising the Market: women's pay and employment in the European Community*, London: Macmillan Press.

Pinchbeck, I. (1981) *Women workers and the Industrial Revolution, 1750–1850*, London: Virago.

Platt, L. (2006) *Pay gaps: the position of ethnic minority women and men*, Manchester: Equal Opportunities Commission.

Platt, L. (2007) *Poverty and ethnicity in the UK*, York: Joseph Rowntree Foundation.

Proctor, I. and Padfield, M. (1999) 'Work orientations and women's work: a critique of Hakim's theory of the heterogeneity of women', *Gender, Work and Organization*, vol 6, no 3, pp 152–62.

Public Sector Review (2008) 'Misconceptions of working in the public sector', http://www.publicsectorreview.com.

Purcell, K. (2002) *Qualifications and careers*, EOC Working paper series no 1, Manchester: Equal Opportunities Commission.

Purcell, K. and Elias, P. (2004) *Higher education and gendered career development*, ESRU/IER Research Paper no 4, Coventry: University of Warwick.

Purcell, K., Elias, P., Davies, R. and Wilton, N. (2005) *The class of '99: a study of the early labour market experience of recent graduates*, DfES Research Report no 691, Annesley, Nottingham: DfES Publications.

Raco, M. (2007) *Building sustainable communities*, Bristol: Policy Press.

Rake, K. (2001) *Women's incomes over the lifetime*, London: Stationery Office.

Rainbird, H. (2000) 'Skilling the unskilled: access to work-based learning and the lifelong learning agenda', *Journal of Education and Work*, vol 13, no 2, pp 183–97.

Ranson, S. and Rutledge, H. (2005) *Including families in the learning communities: family centres and the expansion of learning*, York: Joseph Rowntree Foundation.

Rees, T. (1992) *Women and the labour market*, London: Routledge.

Reid, L. L. (2002) 'Occupational segregation, human capital, and motherhood: black women's higher exit rates from full-time employment', *Gender and Society*, vol 16, no 5, pp 728–47.

Ritchie, H., Casebourne, J. and Rick, J. (2005) *Understanding workless people and communities: a literature review*, Research Report no 255, London: DWP.

Robson, K. and Berthoud, R. (2003) *Early motherhood and disadvantage: a comparison between ethnic groups*, ISER Working Paper no 2003-29, Colchester: University of Essex.

Rosenblatt, G. and Rake, K. (2003) *Gender and poverty*, London: Fawcett Society supported by Oxfam and Ajahama Charitable Trust.

Rowlingson, K. and Berthoud, R. (1996) *Disability, benefits and employment*, DSS Research Report no 54, London: Department of Social Security.

Saner, E. (2007) 'The hidden brain drain', *Guardian*, 4 June.

SEU (1998) *Bringing Britain together: a national strategy for neighbourhood renewal*, Cm 4045, London: Stationery Office.

SEU (2001) *New commitment to neighbourhood renewal: a national strategy action plan*, London: Cabinet Office.

SEU (2004) *Jobs and enterprise in deprived areas*, London: ODPM.

Shafer, S., Winterbotham, M. and McAndrew, F. (2005) *Equal Pay Reviews Survey 2004*, EOC Working Paper Series no 32, Manchester: Equal Opportunities Commission.

Shaw, C. (2006) '2004-based national population projections for the UK and constituent countries', *Population Trends*, vol 123, pp 9–20.

Sheridan, A. (2004) 'Chronic presenteeism: the multiple dimensions to men's absence from part-time work', *Gender, Work and Organization*, vol 11, no 2, pp 207–25.

Shields, M.A. and Wheatley Price, S. (2002) 'The English language fluency and occupational success of ethnic minority immigrant men living in English metropolitan areas', *Journal of Population Economics*, vol 15, pp 137–60.

Shields, M.A. and Wheatley Price, S. (2003) *The labour market outcomes and psychological well-being of ethnic minority migrants in Britain*, Home Office Online Report 07/03, www.homeoffice.gov.uk/rds/pdfs2/rdsolr0703.pdf.

Sigala, M. (2005) 'Part-time employment among women with preschool children: organisational cultures, personal careers and sense of entitlement', in Houston, D.M. (ed) *Work–life balance in the 21st century*, Houndsmills: Palgrave Macmillan.

Simpson, L., Purdam, K., Tajar, A., Fieldhouse, E., Gavalas, V., Tranmer, M., Pritchard, J. and Dorling, D. (2006) *Ethnic minority populations and the labour market: an analysis of the 1991 and 2001 Census*, DWP Research Report no 333, London: DWP.

Simpson, R. (1998) 'Presenteeism, power and organisational change: long hours as a career barrier and the impact on the working lives of women managers', *British Journal of Management*, vol 9, S1, pp 37–50.

Skills for Business (n.d.) 'The Leitch Review summary: a roadmap directing UK towards world class skills by 2020', www.skillsforbusiness.biz.

Sly, F., Thair, T., and Risdon, A. (1999) 'Disability and the labour market: results from the winter 1998/99 LFS', *Labour Market Trends*, vol 107, no 9, pp 455–66.

Smith, D. J. (1974) *Racial disadvantage in employment*, London: Political and Economic Planning.

Spender, D. (ed) (1987) *The education papers: women's quest for equality in Britain 1850–1912*, New York: Routledge and Kegan Paul.

Squires, J. (2003) 'Reviewing the UK equality agenda in the context of constitutional change' in A. Dobrowolsky and V. Hart (eds) *Women Making Constitutions: New Politics and Comparative Perspectives,* Basingstoke: Palgrave.

Sriskandarajah, D., Cooley, L. and Kornblatt, T. (2007) *Britain's immigrants: an economic profile,* London: IPPR.

Stiell, B. and Tang, N. (2006a) *Ethnic minority women and access to the labour market in Newcastle,* GELLM Series 4 Part 2, Sheffield: Centre for Social Inclusion, Sheffield Hallam University.

Stiell, B. and Tang, N. (2006b) *Ethnic minority women and access to the labour market in Somerset,* GELLM Series 4 Part 3, Sheffield: Centre for Social Inclusion, Sheffield Hallam University.

Stiell, B. and Tang, N. (2006c) *Ethnic minority women and access to the labour market in Leicester,* GELLM Series 4 Part 4, Sheffield: Centre for Social Inclusion, Sheffield Hallam University.

Stiell, B. and Tang, N. (2006d) *Ethnic minority women and access to the labour market in Southwark,* GELLM Series 4 Part 5, Sheffield: Centre for Social Inclusion, Sheffield Hallam University.

Stiell, B. and Tang, N. (2006e) *Ethnic minority women and access to the labour market in Camden,* GELLM Series 4 Part 6, Sheffield: Centre for Social Inclusion, Sheffield Hallam University.

Stiell, B., Tang, N., Bennett, C. and Price, C. (2006) 'Building policy/research relationships: using innovative methodologies to engage ethnic minority women', *Local Economy*, vol 21, no 2, pp 211–18.

Stockton-on-Tees Borough Council (2007) 'Report on workforce profile comparison 2006–2007', March, www.egenda.stockton.gov.uk.

Tam, M. (1997) *Part-time employment: a bridge or a trap?*, Aldershot: Avebury.

Taylor-Gooby, P., Larsen, T. and Kananen, J. (2004) 'Market means and welfare ends: the welfare state experiment', *Journal of Social Policy*, vol 33, no 4, pp 573–92.

Theodore, N. and Peck, J. (2000) 'Searching for best practice in welfare to work: the means, the method and the message', *Policy and Politics*, vol 29, pp 81–98.

Thewlis, M., Miller, L. and Neathey, F. (2004) *Advancing women in the workplace: statistical analysis,* Working Paper Series no 12, Manchester: Equal Opportunities Commission.

Tilly, C. (1996) *Half a job: bad and good part-time jobs in a changing labour market,* Philadelphia, PA: Temple University Press.

Tomlinson, J. (2006) 'Part-time occupational mobility in the service industries: regulation, work commitment and occupational closure', *Sociological Review,* vol 54, no 1, pp 66–86.

Toynbee, P. (2003) *Hard work: life in low pay Britain,* London: Bloomsbury.

Travers, T., Tunstall, R. and Whitehead, C. with Pruvot, S. (2007) *Population mobility and service provision – a report for London councils,* London: London School of Economics.

Treanor, J (2007) 'Women quit before hitting glass ceiling', *Guardian*, 8 March.

TUC (2006a) 'Managers top 2006 long hours league table', www.tuc.org.uk.

TUC (2006b) *Working time in the public sector,* London: TUC.

Turner, A. (2005) *A new pensions settlement for the twenty-first century: the second report of the Pensions Commission,* London: Stationery Office.

Turok, I. and Edge, N. (1999) *The jobs gap in Britain's cities,* Bristol: Policy Press/ Joseph Rowntree Foundation.

Urban Task Force (1999) *Towards an urban renaissance,* London: E and FN Spon.

Van Ham, M. and Buchel, F. (2006) 'Unwilling or unable? Spatial and socio-economic restrictions on females' labour market access', *Regional Studies,* vol 40, no 3, pp 345–57.

Walby, S (1986) *Patriarchy at work: patriarchal and capitalist relations in employment,* Cambridge: Policy Press.

Walby, S (1988) *Gender segregation at work,* Milton Keynes: Open University Press.

Walby, S. (1997) *Gender transformations,* Routledge: London.

Walby, S. (2002) 'Gender and the new economy: regulation or deregulation?', Paper presented to ESRC seminar 'Work, life and time in the new economy', LSE, October.

Walker, A. (1990) 'The strategy of inequality: poverty and income distribution in Britain 1979–89' in Taylor, I. (ed) *The social effects of free market policies,* Brighton: Harvester Wheatsheaf.

Walker, A. and Walker, C. (1987) *The growing divide: a social audit 1979–1987,* London: Child Poverty Action Group.

Walker, R. and Wiseman, M. (2003) 'Making welfare work: UK activation policies under New Labour', *International Social Security Review,* vol 56, pp 3–29.

Walsh, K. (1999) 'Myths and counter-myths: an analysis of part-time female employees and their orientations to work and working hours', *Work, Employment and Society*, vol 13, no 2, pp 179–203.

Walton, P. (2007a) *Hours to suit: working flexibly at senior and managerial levels,* London: Working Families.

Walton, P. (2007b) *Hours to suit part II: working flexibly at senior and managerial levels in the public and voluntary sectors,* London: Working Families.

Walton, P. and Gaskell, L. (2007) *Flexi exec,* London: Working Families.

Ward, L. (2007) 'Mothers bear brunt of discrimination at work', *Guardian,* 1 March.

Warren, T. (2001) 'Divergent female part-time employment in Britain and Denmark and the implications for gender equity', *Sociological Review,* vol 49, no 4, pp 548–67.

Warren, T. and Walters, P. (1998) 'Appraising a dichotomy: a review of 'part-time/full-time' in the study of women's employment in Britain', *Gender, Work and Organization*, vol 5, no 2, pp 102–18.

WBG (2005) *Women's and children's poverty: making the links*, London: Women's Budget Group.

Webster, D. (2006) 'Welfare Reform: Facing up to the Geography of Worklessness', *Local Economy*, vol 21, no 2, pp 107–16.

White, M., Hill, S., McGovern, P., Mills, C. and Smeaton, D. (2003) '"High-performance" management practices, working hours and work-life balance', *British Journal of Industrial Relations*, vol 41, no 2, pp 175–96.

White, M., Hill, S., Mills, C. and Smeaton, D. (2004) *Managing to change? British workplaces and the future of work*, Houndmills: Palgrave Macmillan.

Wigfield, A. (2001) *Post-Fordism, gender and work*, London: Ashgate.

Wilson, R., Homenidou, K. and Dickerson, A. (2006) 'Working futures 2004–2014', National report, IER, University of Warwick.

Women and Equality Unit (2003) *Individual incomes of men and women 1996/7 to 2001/2*, London: DTI.

Women and Work Commission (2006) *Shaping a fairer future*, London: Department for Trade and Industry.

Women and Work Commission (2007) *Towards a fairer future: implementing the Women and Work Commission recommendations*, London: Department for Communities and Local Government.

Worrall, L. and Cooper, C. (2000) *The quality of life 2000 survey of managers' changing experiences*, Manchester: Institute of Management and UMIST.

Yeandle, S. (1996) 'Women and work', in Booth, C., Darke, J. and Yeandle, S. (eds) *Changing places: women's lives in the city*, London: Paul Chapman.

Yeandle, S. (2003) 'The international context' in Alcock, P., Beatty, C., Fothergill, S., Macmillan, R. and Yeandle, S., *Work to welfare: how men become detached from the labour market*, Cambridge: Cambridge University Press.

Yeandle, S. (2005) 'Unlocking the potential contribution of all', Paper presented to the Equality and Diversity Forum Seminar: Equality, Social Exclusion and Class, London, 11 October.

Yeandle, S. (2006a) 'Supporting women's engagement with their local labour markets: introduction', *Local Economy*, vol 21, no 2, pp 197–9.

Yeandle, S. (2006b) 'Local labour markets and the gender pay gap; new evidence from the GELLM programme on factors constraining progress towards pay equality in England', Paper presented to the European Sociological Association Interim Conference, Lisbon, 6–8 September.

Yeandle, S. (2006c) *GELLM director's final report 1 September 2003–3 August 2006*, Sheffield: Centre for Social Inclusion, Sheffield Hallam University.

Yeandle, S. (2007) 'Challenges in delivering domiciliary care: issues for employers, carers and the state', Paper presented to the ESRC Seminar Series Gender, Employment and the Labour Market, EWERC, University of Manchester, 28 February.

Yeandle, S. and Buckner, L. (2007) *Carers, employment and services: time for a new social contract?* Carers Employment and Services Report Series no 6, London: Carers UK.

Yeandle, S. and Macmillan, R. (2003) 'The role of health in labour market detachment', in Alcock, P., Beatty, C., Fothergill, S., Macmillan, R. and Yeandle, S. (eds) *Work to welfare: how men become detached from the labour market*, Cambridge: Cambridge University Press.

Yeandle, S. and Shipton, L. (2006) 'The changing face of domiciliary care: job design, job content and employers' experiences', Paper presented to the Social Policy Association Annual Conference, University of Birmingham, July.

Yeandle, S., Buckner, L., Gore, T. and Powell, R. (n.d.) *Gender profile of South Yorkshire's Labour Market 2000,* Rotherham: Objective 1 Programme Directorate.

Yeandle, S., Booth, C. and Bennett, C. (1998) *Criteria for success of a mainstreaming approach to gender equality*, Sheffield, CRESR Research Report, Sheffield Hallam University.

Yeandle, S., Crompton, R., Wigfield, A. and Dennett, J. (2002) *Employed carers and family-friendly employment policies*, Bristol: Policy Press.

Yeandle, S., Escott, K., Grant, L., and Batty, E. (2003) *Women and men talking about poverty*, Working Paper Series no 7, Manchester: Equal Opportunities Commission.

Yeandle, S., Bennett, C., Buckner, L., Shipton, L., and Soukas, A. (2006a) *Who cares wins: the social and business benefits of supporting working carers,* London: Carers UK.

Yeandle, S., Phillips, J., Scheibl, F., Wigfield, A. and Wise, A. (2006b) *Line managers and family-friendly employment: roles and perspectives,* Bristol: Policy Press.

Yeandle, S., Shipton, L. and Buckner, L. (2006c) *Local challenges in meeting demand for domiciliary care: synthesis report*, GELLM Series 7 Part 1, Sheffield: Centre for Social Inclusion, Sheffield Hallam University.

Yeandle, S., Shipton, L. and Buckner, L. (2006d) *Local challenges in meeting demand for domiciliary care in Sandwell*, GELLM Series 7 Part 2, Sheffield: Centre for Social Inclusion, Sheffield Hallam University.

Yeandle, S., Shipton, L. and Buckner, L. (2006e) *Local challenges in meeting demand for domiciliary care in Birmingham*, GELLM Series 7 Part 3, Sheffield: Centre for Social Inclusion, Sheffield Hallam University.

Yeandle, S., Shipton, L. and Buckner, L. (2006f) *Local challenges in meeting demand for domiciliary care in West Sussex*, GELLM Series 7 Part 4, Sheffield: Centre for Social Inclusion, Sheffield Hallam University.

Yeandle, S., Shipton, L. and Buckner, L. (2006g) *Local challenges in meeting demand for domiciliary care in Newcastle*, GELLM Series 7 Part 5, Sheffield: Centre for Social Inclusion, Sheffield Hallam University.

Yeandle, S., Shipton, L. and Buckner, L. (2006h) *Local challenges in meeting demand for domiciliary care in Thurrock*, GELLM Series 7 Part 6, Sheffield: Centre for Social Inclusion, Sheffield Hallam University.

Yeandle, S., Shipton, L. and Buckner, L. (2006i) *Local challenges in meeting demand for domiciliary care in Somerset*, GELLM Series 7 Part 7, Sheffield: Centre for Social Inclusion, Sheffield Hallam University.

Yeandle, S., Stiell B. and Buckner, L. (2006j) *Ethnic minority women and access to the labour market: synthesis report*, GELLM Series 4 Part 1, Sheffield: Centre for Social Inclusion, Sheffield Hallam University.

Yeandle, S., Bennett, C., Buckner, L., Fry, G. and Price, C (2007) *Carers employment and services report series*, London: Carers UK.

YWCA (2001) *Young, urban and female*, Oxford: YWCA.

Younger, M. and Warrington, M. with Gray, J., Rudduck, J., McLellan, R., Bearne, E., Kershner, R. and Bricheno, P. (2005) *Raising boys' achievement*, Research Report RR636, London: Department for Education and Skills.

# Index

Page references for notes are followed by n.